HENRY MILLER
AND JAMES LAUGHLIN

Henry Miller
AND
James Laughlin

/ · /

SELECTED LETTERS

EDITED BY GEORGE WICKES

Constable · London

First published in Great Britain 1996
by Constable and Company Limited
3 The Lanchesters, 162 Fulham Palace Road
London W6 9ER
Published in the United States of America
by W.W.Norton & Company Inc., New York
Copyright © 1996 James Laughlin
Copyright © 1996 Estate of Henry Miller
ISBN 0 09 475770 4
Printed in Great Britain by
St Edmundsbury Press Ltd
Bury St Edmunds, Suffolk

A CIP catalogue record for this book
is available from the British Library

Whatever disorder, illogic, irrelevancies, etc. one may find in my works—and they exist, viewed objectively—they nevertheless belong and form an integral part of my books, because they are always facets of me. And my aim, from the beginning, has been to give myself—totally. No evasions, no compromises, no falsifications. Distortions and exaggerations, yes! But for aesthetic reasons, to make the truth more truthful. To put it another way, I put down what comes to me in the way it is given. I don't question how it is given or by whom. I obey, I yield. I know "it" knows better than I. I am the receiving station. This is my "purity," if you like. And my credo, as writer. Or—"my water-mark."

—HM to Bob MacGregor, December 12, 1955

CONTENTS

INTRODUCTION
ix

NOTES ON THE TEXT
xxv

ACKNOWLEDGMENTS
xxix

LETTERS
1

BIBLIOGRAPHY: WRITINGS BY HENRY MILLER PUBLISHED
BY NEW DIRECTIONS
275

INDEX
277

INTRODUCTION

The correspondence between James Laughlin and
Henry Miller began toward the end of 1934 or early
in 1935. Laughlin, a twenty-year-old student, had
taken a year's leave from Harvard with the idea of
becoming a writer and was studying poetry with
Ezra Pound in Rapallo. Miller at the age of forty-
two had just published his first book, *Tropic of Cancer*, in Paris and sent a copy to Pound. Here is how
Laughlin tells the story:

Every day part of the very pleasant curriculum of the
Ezuversity was that I would have lunch with him and
Dorothy and whatever visitors were coming along
through. We'd have lunch in the dining room of what he
called the Albuggero Rapallo. It was right on the front
there and it was very interesting because the Gaudier
head—the hieratic head—was in the corner. The apartment was on the fifth floor of the building and they'd
never dared to try to take it up in the elevator. So Ezra
sat there, his majestic hieratic head in the corner of the
dining room, and the waiters would bring in tourists to
look at it and everybody enjoyed it very much. So we
had lunch there every day and he talked about everything
that came into his head or he'd pick out some letters from
his tremendous correspondence to discuss.

One day he had with him a book and he threw it across the table to me: "Waal, Jas, here's a dirty book that's really good. You'd better read that if your morals can stand it." So I read it and I thought it was wonderful. So I got Henry's address from Ezra and I wrote to him and that was how that correspondence started.[1]

The opening letters in the correspondence have not survived, and only one letter remains from 1935—the first to appear in this selection. Almost all the letters from the early years are Miller's. Laughlin's were probably left behind with other papers when Miller left Paris in 1939. Later Laughlin would have made carbon copies, but in those early years he seldom did so.

Laughlin cannot recall exactly when they first met, but it could have been as early as June 1935, when Miller returned to Paris after a sojourn in New York, or any time in the latter 1930s when Laughlin made several trips to Europe. During that period Miller was living at 18 Villa Seurat, and he recalls Laughlin's visit there in a letter written in April 1944: "I remember you waking up early that morning in the Villa Seurat, seeing my program of Notes on the wall (about Lawrence) and saying in your usual way—all crap or something to that effect."

When Laughlin founded New Directions in 1936, he was determined to publish Miller in America. That year he published two pieces from Miller's new book, *Black Spring,* in the first *New Directions in Prose and Poetry,* and the following year he published another section of *Black Spring* in the second annual anthology. In 1936 he also managed to publish an excerpt from Miller's *Aller Retour New York* in the Harvard *Advocate*—somewhat bowdlerized but still sufficiently provocative to be banned in Boston. Actually, though the name of Henry Miller was enough to create scandal by itself, political ambition was the motive behind the ban, and, as Laughlin explains, the prosecution was mollified by Harvard advocacy.

There was a very enterprising young district attorney in Cambridge and he saw the opportunity of getting himself some newspaper exposure by having the cops pick up the stock of the *Advocate* with "Glittering Pie" in it. Oh, there were wonderful headlines in the papers: "Decadence at Harvard" and all sorts of stuff like that. I don't think he really wanted to prosecute; he just wanted to get publicity for a while. We got him two tickets to the Harvard-Yale game on the 50-yard line from somebody we knew, and he was very happy with those, so the case just faded away and was never presented.[2]

In 1939, Laughlin published three excerpts from Miller's latest shocker, *Tropic of Capricorn,* in the *New Directions* annual for that year and also brought out the first book by Henry Miller to appear in this country. This was the relatively inoffensive *Cosmological Eye,* a collection of essays and narratives drawn mostly from a volume published in Paris the previous year. Laughlin created a striking jacket cover by having a photograph of his own eye superimposed on a photograph of a cloud. The cover seems to have caught the eye of Ingmar Bergman, for the book with its Surrealist jacket plainly visible appeared in Bergman's film *Three Strange Loves.*

In 1940, after spending almost ten years in Paris, Miller was forced by the threat of war to leave Europe. He landed in New York in January and spent much of that year there off and on. By this time Laughlin had graduated from Harvard and moved the New Directions office to New York, so the two were able to meet several times to discuss further publications. Miller proposed and Laughlin accepted the table of contents for a second miscellany, published the following year as *The Wisdom of the Heart.* However, Miller objected vehemently to the contract for that book, which he felt gave the publisher an unfair advantage over the author.

As a result negotiations broke down between them and had to be arbitrated by Miller's literary agents, Russell & Volkening, even though they found their client "incapable of understanding any normal business relationship" and suggested that Laughlin tell him to "get his damn books published for himself." These words were reported to Laughlin by John Slocum, a young member of the firm, who while representing the writer also sympathized with the publisher, whom he had known at Harvard: Slocum had been president of the *Advocate* the year it published Miller's "Glittering Pie" and was well aware of Laughlin's interest in Miller and familiar with New Directions from its inception. His view was therefore more moderate than that of others at Russell & Volkening: "Knowing that you want to publish him, I wouldn't suggest such a strong course, but I think you have been more than fair to him, but have made one fatal mistake; you haven't made it clear to him how much more he is getting from you than he would get from other publishers."[3]

Relations between author and publisher were strained for several years, during which Miller corresponded mainly with others at New Directions and perfunctorily at that. He objected to the way Laughlin had edited *The Cosmological Eye* and *The Wisdom of the Heart:* to the contents he had added to the first, to his failure to cite the original publication of the individual pieces in both collections, to the books' very titles. "Somehow, curse you," he wrote, "you've succeeded in imposing on my work two titles of your own." (Instead of *The Wisdom of the Heart,* Miller wanted the second miscellany to be entitled *The Enormous Womb*.) Though he continued to feel aggrieved, the correspondence shows that they met at least twice for dinner during 1941, when both were in Los Angeles, and Laughlin remembers a party in Hollywood where the author of *Tropic of Cancer* was being fêted as a celebrity.

While differences over the contract for *The Wisdom of the Heart* were being resolved, Laughlin read the manuscript of Miller's next book and declined to publish it. Although it might appear that he did so because of their differences, the more plausible explanation is that he found *The Colossus of Maroussi* disappointingly tame and inappropriate for his avant-garde press. He was not alone in being unenthusiastic about Miller's account of his sojourn in Greece. Some ten publishers turned the manuscript down before it was accepted by the Colt Press in San Francisco. Eventually Laughlin thought better of the book and after protracted negotiations with Jane Grabhorn of the Colt Press obtained its release and brought it out under the New Directions imprint in 1946.

Several other small presses in California took up Henry Miller in the 1940s, bringing out minor works in brochures and pamphlets. Among the amateur publishers were Bern Porter, a Berkeley physicist, and George Leite, a cab driver in Oakland. Porter was the most active, producing a half dozen Miller items, including a collection of open letters to the public entitled *The Plight of the Creative Artist in the United States of America* (1944). In one of the open letters, first published in *The New Republic,* Miller criticized Laughlin bitterly: "A great many people think him to be my champion and benefactor. Nothing could be further from the truth." But a postcard to Laughlin shows that they were reconciled almost immediately after, and Miller added a

footnote to the *New Republic* letter when it was
reprinted in the Bern Porter pamphlet:

Just as this letter was going to press James Laughlin
paid me a visit. In a few moments our differences were
settled and we parted good friends. I am sorry not to be
able to retract everything I said about him in this letter,
insofar as it concerns the past, but I do feel confident in
saying that we shall get along well in the future. I should
like to add that when Mr. Laughlin read this letter in *The
New Republic* he had the grace and courage to suggest that
I might use it in a collection of miscellaneous pieces
which he is bringing out. Naturally I have no desire to
perpetuate an ancient wound. Hence these few words,
healing words.[4]

Thereafter Miller would have other complaints
about his publisher but none so serious, and the new
collection of miscellaneous pieces shows that their
disagreements had not kept them from working
together. That collection, the third of its kind, was
to appear in 1944 as *Sunday After the War*.

In the open letter published in *The New Republic,*
Miller complained that Laughlin had failed to publish his banned books of the 1930s. There is quite a
bit of correspondence on the subject of those books,
reflecting Laughlin's desire to publish them but also
his fears that he might then lose the financial support
of his family, on which New Directions depended.
Throughout the 1940s he cherished the hope of
bringing out *Black Spring,* the least objectionable of
the banned books, in a de luxe edition with illustrations by such artists as Chagall, Miró, Ernst, or
Léger, the idea being that an expensive edition sold
by subscription could get by the censors while a
cheap edition within reach of corruptible youth
would not. Miller himself was of two minds, wanting to see his best work published in America but
worried about prosecution, fearful not only of land-

ing in jail for obscenity but of being sued for libel
by his first wife and others he had written about in
Black Spring. He did not object, however, to
"pirated" editions of the banned books, for which
he could disclaim responsibility. Several of these
appeared in the 1940s.

References to Huntington Cairns often occur in
the correspondence, for "the censor," as Miller
called him, served as legal adviser to the federal
authorities who proscribed his books; yet despite his
official role Cairns took a personal interest in Miller
and liked his writings. But the ban was not to be
challenged until 1961, when Barney Rosset of Grove
Press published *Tropic of Cancer*. Miller hesitated a
long time before allowing himself to be talked into
publication. Throughout his transactions with Rosset he kept in touch with Laughlin, anxious to have
his opinion and concerned that Laughlin's rights be
respected. Rosset also deferred to New Directions'
prior claims, but Laughlin had no desire to engage
in the kind of litigation that was bound to ensue.
"As you know," he wrote to Miller on May 8, 1961,
"I hate anything to do with courts, lawyers, etc.,
but Barney really seems to thrive on it. More power
to him."

Obscenity was not the only charge made against
Miller, and Laughlin is no doubt right in concluding
that Miller's anarchism troubled the censors even
more. Then, too, his anti-Americanism won him no
friends. This element appears most prominently in
the book he wrote about his travels around the
country after his return from Europe, a book whose
title proclaims his attitude toward his native land:
The Air-Conditioned Nightmare. He received an
advance for this work from a major New York publisher, Doubleday Doran, and an advance for magazine rights from that pillar of respectability, the

Atlantic Monthly. Then, as if to thumb his nose at such patronage, he wrote savage criticism of the country that neither was willing to publish. An excerpt appeared in England, in Cyril Connolly's *Horizon,* and caught Laughlin's eye, possibly because of its comment on Pittsburgh, the home town he had never loved. The letter he wrote to Miller has not survived, but his praise of the excerpt during the period when they were on the outs may have softened Miller's resentment. Ultimately it led to the publication by New Directions of *The Air-Conditioned Nightmare* and the book Miller regarded as its sequel, *Remember to Remember.*

After traveling around the country Miller settled in California, first in Los Angeles for three years, then in Big Sur, where he found a small community of kindred spirits living in splendid isolation perched far above the rugged Pacific coastline. Conditions were primitive at Big Sur, but Miller took to roughing it as though he had been an outdoorsman and not a city dweller all his life. Laughlin by this time had established his ski lodge in the mountains of Utah and was spending considerable stretches of time there, conducting his New Directions business by mail. From Utah he frequently went on to San Francisco to visit Kenneth Rexroth and occasionally traveled down the coast to visit Miller as well. He remembers camping out with Rexroth at Anderson Creek in one of the old shacks that had been built to house the convicts who worked on the coast highway. Laughlin went there first in 1944, shortly after Miller had moved to Big Sur, and was so taken with the area that he wanted to have a cabin there himself.

Miller remained in Big Sur for sixteen years, making the place synonymous with his bohemian way of life. In *Big Sur and the Oranges of Hieronymus Bosch,* he celebrated his fellow writers, artists, and mystics, including among the latter Laughlin's cousin Jean Wharton.

Money was always a problem for Henry Miller. His writings had never brought in much—during the early 1940s his paintings earned more—and for years he had lived by his wits, hatching up one scheme after another but more often borrowing money from his many friends. Money was a problem when it came in, too, for he was generous and improvident and seemed determined to get rid of it as fast as he could. Like others at Big Sur, he depended on Jake the mailman to bring food and other supplies as well as mail from the outside world. During the month he would run up a bill with the intention of paying it off on the first of the following month, only to find himself short of funds when that date came around. Finally he hit upon the scheme of having New Directions provide him with a monthly stipend based on his annual earnings. The amount was not large, but it was at least predictable.

When the war in Europe ended, Miller suddenly found himself rich. But his newfound wealth was tied up in francs earned by the Obelisk Press in Paris from the sales of his banned books, mostly to American troops. The problem was to get around currency restrictions that kept those francs from being converted into dollars. By the time a solution was found, the franc had been devalued, Miller's windfall was considerably reduced, and he was soon back to begging or borrowing again. In the postwar years, however, his income from foreign sources gradually increased as French, German, Italian, and other publishers brought out his work in translation, to be followed later by the Japanese, until his foreign earnings far exceeded his relatively small income from American sales. None of his New

Directions books was ever a big seller, and he was always more highly esteemed abroad than at home.

In the postwar era the correspondence is increasingly concerned with foreign publication, with Miller raising all sorts of questions about foreign rights and agents, increasingly confused and eager to rid himself of the details. Dissatisfied with his American and British agents, he wanted to find the right person to represent him at home and abroad: "I want an enthusiast, like myself," he wrote on June 12, 1946. Above all, he explained in another letter, dated June 21, 1946, "I certainly don't need an American agent and I begin to wonder now what I need a foreign one for. I merely wanted to escape a lot of drudge work. . . . I'd like to withdraw from all practical matters and just write." Laughlin was only too willing to help; on June 18, 1946, he wrote: "Please rest assured of my desire to help in any way possible to get you published in every language of the globe." Eventually Miller entrusted all his foreign publications to his very able literary agent in Paris, Michael Hoffman, and so did New Directions. Hoffman became a loyal friend to all concerned.

Miller was right to describe himself as an enthusiast. He was forever taking up the cause of writers he admired and urging them on Laughlin, usually without result. *The Books in My Life* is full of his enthusiasms, many of them for writers who never caught fire in this country, like Jean Giono and Blaise Cendrars. Laughlin did publish Miller's autobiographical ruminations on Rimbaud, first in two issues of the annual anthology and later as a book, *The Time of the Assassins*. But Miller's greatest coup, as far as New Directions was concerned, came when he recommended Hermann Hesse's *Siddartha*. There are quite a few letters back and forth about this book, Miller repeatedly expressing his enthusiasm as he rereads it four or five times, Laughlin cautiously interested but concerned about finding a translation that captures the spirit of the original. Miller, whose German was equal to the task, declined to do the job himself, feeling he had no gift for translation. However, he offered to write a preface and ended up playing a major role in choosing and editing the translation. *Siddartha* enjoyed a modest success until the 1960s, when it became one of the sacred scriptures of the young and New Directions' greatest best seller, ultimately selling over 1,300,000 copies in paperback alone.

For a period of about five years beginning in 1952 Laughlin spent most of his time and energy working with the Ford Foundation as president of Intercultural Publications, editing *Perspectives USA,* a magazine he launched with the idea of making new developments in American intellectual and creative life accessible to countries that had been cut off during the war. The magazine, published in England, France, Germany, and Italy, appeared in four languages, with the British edition intended for distribution to other European countries. Later the process was reversed, bringing the culture of other countries to American readers in a series of "Perspectives" on individual countries published as supplements to the *Atlantic Monthly*.

Needless to say, this activity left little time for New Directions, so Laughlin had to find someone else to manage the day-to-day affairs of his publishing house. The new editor-in-chief was Robert M. MacGregor, whose particular interest was the theatre, where he had made a name for himself by translating Stanislavsky and founding Theatre Arts Books, an enterprise he continued while running New Directions. His experience in the theatre world proved particularly useful when Miller wrote his one and only play, *Just Wild about Harry,* in 1961. MacGregor's affinity with Zen Buddhism and his friendship with Yukio Mishima (a New Directions author) also served Miller well when he wrote his "Reflections on the Death of Mishima." And his familiarity with Japan struck a responsive chord in Miller, who had long dreamed of traveling to "the Orient."

Miller was never to go there, but during the period of their correspondence MacGregor traveled to Japan, and Laughlin made several trips to Asian countries while editing his "Perspectives" on those countries. He was particularly taken with India, where he spent the longest period. In the process he developed an interest in Eastern philosophy and religion that made him sympathetic with Miller's "mysticism" and brought him closer to another of his authors, Thomas Merton. Surprisingly, New Directions served as an intermediary between these two writers, who found they had more in common than anyone would have suspected. Laughlin urged Miller to visit Merton in his monastery, as he often did himself, and smuggled Miller's forbidden books to Merton.

MacGregor proved to be invaluable to New Directions and continued to play a major role after Laughlin returned. He was an extremely dedicated editor, frequently bringing work home with him, going to great lengths to help his authors, and writing letters at all hours. Miller, who did not always appreciate MacGregor's efforts, could on occasion do so:

Bob, when I read your letters, which are so explicit and overly generous, I pity you. You are doing three men's work, it seems to me. So am I. That's why I can say it, and mean it. Take care of yourself. *You* make the trips abroad hereafter—and let Jay handle the c/s.

(April 25, 1957)

MacGregor wrote back: "Don't pity me. I get lots of satisfaction out of my work." (April 30, 1957) No doubt the volume of work had increased over the years as New Directions grew from a small subsidized enterprise to something far more substantial, so that even after Laughlin's return there was more than enough to keep both men busy. On one occasion MacGregor wrote to Miller: "Although we are only a few feet from each other here, we are both so busy, that sometimes we don't know what the other is up to." (August 8, 1960)

Laughlin deeply appreciated MacGregor's qualities, not only his ability as an editor but his friendship and loyalty: "He was an extraordinarily able man, and spent a lot of time covering up for my lapses. So devoted and always protecting me. . . . He was a great publisher and could have been a top executive editor in a big house had he not preferred to stay at ND because of our arrangement that he could spend as much time as he needed on his excellent Theatre Arts Books program."[5]

From 1952 until his death in 1974, MacGregor carried on most of the correspondence with Miller. As a result he had to bear the brunt of Miller's bitter complaints about his poor earnings and New Directions' failure to promote or distribute his books properly—the usual stuff of authors' correspondence with their publishers. As a rule MacGregor showed great patience and forbearance, but once or twice he felt compelled to point out that Miller's books simply did not sell very well. The fact is that New Directions never published the books that made Miller famous, not to say notorious, and earned him large sums of money. Compared to the *Tropics* and other works in the same vein, the books published by New Directions seemed quite unexciting, and Miller's royalties suffered accordingly. But New Directions deserved credit for publishing a large body of his work and keeping it in print. No other publisher would have supported him thus year in and year out over a period of forty years.

Miller lived on for some five and a half years after MacGregor but produced no new work for New Directions during that period. In fact, the writings that appeared in his last few years are mainly odds and ends, most of them dating back to earlier periods, published by amateurs or by university presses. New Directions brought out only one book by Miller in the 1970s, a facsimile of the notebook he kept in 1940–41 while making the trip recorded in *The Air-Conditioned Nightmare*. Understandably his correspondence dwindled toward the end, though he remained more or less in touch with Laughlin and maintained a friendly correspondence with Griselda Ohannessian, who replaced MacGregor as Miller's principal link with New Directions.

Of her, Laughlin was written: "Griselda is, in her way, as good as Bob, a remarkable administrator and editor." He also found her adept at dealing with Miller after MacGregor's death. "Then Griselda took over with Henry. He was getting cranky by then and she handled him with teasing, which he seemed to enjoy; I don't think I wrote to him much in the later years. I don't recall any big bust-up but I found his complaints hard to deal with and things just tapered off. And Capra took over his little books so there wasn't too much business to write about."[6]

As a rule most correspondence between author

and publisher has to do with business. But in the case of New Directions and especially of James Laughlin, the relationship was usually far more than that. As his reminiscences about Ezra Pound, William Carlos Williams, Kenneth Rexroth, and Thomas Merton amply demonstrate, Laughlin had a closer personal relationship with his authors than almost any other publisher, often visiting them and playing a part in their lives. And though he was not as close to Miller as he was to a number of others, the personal note turns up frequently in this correspondence. His final assessment is of Miller the man rather than the writer:

Henry had a wonderful zany sweetness and kindness about him that I don't think comes out in his books, even the ones we did. He reminded me of a kindly grocery store man in a Florida town I knew when I was a boy. And this fellow talked the same way Henry did with those constant "uhs," as if the master of words didn't know what to say next. He had great kindness, helping people if he could. We found that we had to send him his royalties monthly because if we sent them to him in a chunk he would give it all away in a week, and then write for more. I thought the movie they made about him was awful. It didn't catch the real Henry at all.[7]

Even when he comments as a publisher on his author's books, Laughlin strikes a personal note: "I admired and respected him, and loved his writing, but I didn't coddle him."[8]

Notes

1. GW interview of JL, June 16–18, 1992.
2. *Ibid*.
3. Letter from John Slocum to JL, June 8, 1940.
4. HM, *The Plight of the Creative Artist in the United States of America* (Bern Porter, 1944), p. 18.

5. Letter from JL to GW, July 10, 1992.

6. *Ibid*. The Capra Press in Santa Barbara was the main publisher of Miller's new work during the last years of his life.

7. Letter from JL to GW, June 13, 1991. The movie in question is *Henry and June*.

8. *Ibid*.

NOTES ON THE TEXT

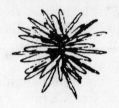

The correspondence between Henry Miller and
New Directions runs to more than 1,600 items,
ranging from postcards to single-spaced letters up to
four or more pages long. Included are letters to and
from two of Miller's wives, Lepska and Eve, and
others at New Directions besides James Laughlin,
notably Robert MacGregor, who was Miller's chief
correspondent for the period 1952–74, and Griselda
Ohannessian thereafter. The first surviving letter,
from Miller, dates from November 2, 1935, and the
last, also from Miller, is dated October 17, 1979.

Not all of the correspondence has survived,
though most of Miller's letters were preserved and
are to be found in the New Directions Archive at
Laughlin's home in Norfolk, Connecticut. Carbon
copies of the New Directions side of the correspondence are there too, including most of these written
from the 1950s on.

Most of the originals from New Directions for
the period from 1950 through 1960 were deposited
in the Library of the University of California at Los
Angeles and are to be found in the Henry Miller
Collection there. That collection also includes a
handful of letters, mostly from Laughlin, dating

from 1961 to 1967, and a few carbon copies of Miller's letters to New Directions.

Until the 1950s the Miller letters far outnumber those surviving from New Directions, but after MacGregor takes up the correspondence there are almost as many from him as from Miller, and his are often very long, while Miller's are more likely to be short messages and requests, many of them transmitted on postcards.

Most of the letters from Laughlin and MacGregor were dictated, so irregularities of punctuation and spelling, for instance, can be attributed to secretaries rather than the correspondents themselves, who often did not proofread at all or did so in haste and without concern for detail. (At the top of one long letter MacGregor scrawled: "Dear Henry—I haven't time the time to read this. Hope you have. Bob.") For that reason such irregularities have been silently corrected.

Miller on the other hand wrote his own letters (very legibly by hand or accurately on the type-writer) and was quite punctilious about the rules, so it seemed desirable to preserve certain features of his writing, such as his spelling of "enuf" and "thru" and his old-fashioned tendency to write "every body," "some one," "note book," and "post card" as two words.

The editorial practice established by Hugh Witemeyer in the first volume published in this series—*William Carlos Williams and James Laughlin: Selected Letters*—has been followed as a general rule, though letters in the present volume have been more often excerpted rather than quoted in full. Ellipses are indicated in the body of the letters, but no attempt has been made to account for the many postscripts and marginalia which are a common feature of Miller's letters and occasionally appear in those of other correspondents. When used as punctuation by the writers themselves, ellipsis marks are placed in angled brackets. Occasionally a handwritten addition to a typed letter has been indicated by angled brackets when it seems particularly significant.

In addition to the abbreviations employed by previous editors in this series—ALS for autograph letter signed, TLS for typed letter signed, TL for typed letter unsigned, PCS for signed postcard—CC is used here to indicate a carbon copy. Other abbreviations are HM for Henry Miller, JL for James Laughlin, RM for Robert MacGregor, GW for George Wickes, ND for New Directions, and *ND* for the annual publication *New Directions in Prose and Poetry*.

Most of the letters are dated, and even when they are not, dates can almost always be determined or approximated. The place of origin is given when it is provided or placed in brackets when it can be inferred. Virtually all of MacGregor's letters were written from New York, whether dictated to New Directions secretaries or typed at his apartment. Laughlin's letters were usually written on New Directions stationery, which gives his Norfolk address as well as that of the New York office, so the letterhead is no indication of his whereabouts; for that matter he could well be writing or dictating from another location altogether. There were periods when he regularly spent weekdays in New York and weekends in Norfolk, but he also spent considerable periods at his ski resort in Utah, and he was often on the move. Miller wrote from a number of different locations, but once settled in a place (Paris in the 1930s, Big Sur from 1944 to 1961, Pacific Palisades thereafter) he usually stayed put, though he made several prolonged trips to Europe in the fifties and sixties.

The writers' signatures are copied as written, or in the case of carbon copies and unsigned letters (of which there are quite a number) as typed at the end of the letters.

ACKNOWLEDGMENTS

My greatest debt is to James Laughlin, who not only commissioned this project but helped me every step of the way, providing copies of the manuscripts in his possession, offering a wide range of background material, answering questions, and thoughtfully lending support and encouragement. He and his wife Gertrude Huston received me most hospitably in Norfolk, giving me the run of the archives and library as well as the pleasure of joining them in their daily round, including a trip through the woods every afternoon for a swim in Tobey Pond.

I am grateful to the University of Oregon for a sabbatical leave, during which I completed most of the editorial work, and to the Camargo Foundation, where half of it was done under idyllic circumstances.

Henry Miller's letters are published with the permission of his children, Barbara, Valentine, and Tony Miller.

The Library of the University of California at Los Angeles supplied copies of the letters from James Laughlin and New Directions in its Henry Miller Collection. Anne Caiger, Manuscripts Librarian, facilitated my use of manuscripts in that collection.

At New Directions, Peter Glassgold, Griselda Ohannessian, and Peggy Fox were willing as always to answer all kinds of questions, and Declan Spring conducted a thorough search of the New York office, ferreting out many wayward bits of correspondence buried in the files.

I am indebted to Henry Miller's biographers for much information about his life and times: to Jay Martin for *Always Merry and Bright* (Capra Press, 1978), to Mary Dearborn for *The Happiest Man Alive* (Simon & Schuster, 1991), and to Robert Ferguson for *Henry Miller: A Life* (W. W. Norton, 1991). Conveniently for me, the latter two made their appearance just as I was about to embark on this enterprise.

Also timely was the publication of *Henry Miller: A Bibliography of Primary Sources* (1993), compiled and published by Lawrence J. Shifreen and Roger Jackson. The latter, who did the bulk of the work, kindly reviewed my text, correcting several errors and supplying additional details from his vast store of learning about Miller's works.

Another bibliographer, John A. Harrison, Director of Libraries at the University of Arkansas, is currently compiling a bibliography of New Directions publications, from which he provided material for my Bibliography of writings by Henry Miller published by New Directions.

Many other librarians offered encouragement that was all the more appreciated when they had no relevant materials in their collections. One in particular, Stephen Crook, Librarian of the Berg Collection of the New York Public Library, went out of his way to be helpful.

I also owe thanks to Bette Bauer for checking a multitude of nagging details in the text; to David Cooper for more information about Thomas Merton than I could have anticipated; to Barney Rosset for documentation about his publication of *Tropic of Cancer;* to my editors at W. W. Norton, Jennifer DiToro, Cecil Lyon, and Ann Adelman; and not least to Molly Westling for aiding and abetting in a thousand ways my work on an author who is hardly her favorite.

HENRY MILLER
AND JAMES LAUGHLIN

LETTERS

1. TL-2   Nov. 2nd. [1935]
                                             [Paris]

DEAR LAUGHLIN:

Just a hasty note in reply to your last. Yes, I got
the three copies all right and answered it immediately, but having mislaid your Cambridge address, I
sent the letter to your home address. It won't matter
greatly to me one way or the other about printing
the whole thing—only, as I said in my letter, the
bastards ought to have had the decency to mention
that it was an instalment, etc. etc.

Meanwhile I've dispatched to you the *Aller Retour*
and the Ibiza letter. About "Jabberwhorl Cronstadt"—don't allow it to go to print without con-
sulting me first, I beg you. You see, my publisher is
also acting as my agent, and he will be sore if I
ignore him. He is doing his damndest to get some
stories of mine accepted in England. In America he
is working through a friend of his, an agent named
Marion Saunders—on East 35th St.

I wrote Alfred Kreymborg the other day suggesting that if he and Paul Rosenfeld were not going

1

to use that part of *Black Spring* called "Into the Night Life," which was submitted to them by Madeleine Boyd for publication in their coming Anthology of American writers, that he should forward this manuscript to you. That is one of the manuscripts, the principal one, which I gave Doc Williams who has since written to me that they were thrown away(!!)

Had a card from Walter Lowenfels saying that his agent Barthold Fles was negotiating with Scribner's about *Black Spring*. They're crazy, of course, and I've already informed him that it's going to be brought out here, but he persists in trying nevertheless—because an American edition could be brought out simultaneously with the French. . . .

The last word is this: Fred, Michael Fraenkel and myself came to a decision last night, after much previous discussion, to collaborate on a book to be called *Hamlet*. It's to be exactly one thousand pages long, not one page less or one page more. It may end in the middle of a sentence. And we're going to get it out from Belgium, via Carrefour Press.

I'll be writing you again shortly. If you can dig up any subscriptions for *Aller Retour* I'll appreciate it. I need them. In a few days I'll send you a copy of Connolly's review of *Tropic* and *Aller Retour* in the *New Statesman*.

What's the name of that magazine in Ohio you submitted "Cronstadt" to?

And have you ever run into Hiler? I think you should. He's waiting for you.

Sincerely,
HENRY

/ · /

the Ibiza letter: HM's pamphlet, *What Are You Going to Do About Alf?*, soliciting funds to support his fellow writer Alfred Perlès, printed at his own expense by HM, who pocketed the few contributions.

"Jabberwhorl Cronstadt": Part of *Black Spring,* published together with "Into the Night Life" in the first *ND* (1936).

Madeleine Boyd: New York literary agent who was representing HM at this time.

Doc Williams: HM had met William Carlos Williams during his sojourn in New York earlier in 1935.

Walter Lowenfels: (1897–1976), American poet and friend of HM in Paris who had recently returned to the U.S. Lowenfels is caricatured and parodied in "Jabberwhorl Cronstadt."

Fred: Alfred Perlès (1897–1990), "Viennese French writer," HM's close friend and boon companion in Paris. He appears as the character named Carl in *Tropic of Cancer* and *Black Spring. Aller Retour New York,* which had just been published in Paris, was written in the form of a letter to Perlès.

Michael Fraenkel: (1896–1957), American writer, co-author and publisher of the *Hamlet* correspondence under his own imprint (Carrefour Press). HM wrote the first of the *Hamlet* letters on the same day as this letter to JL. Fraenkel appears in *Tropic of Cancer* as Boris.

Connolly: Cyril Connolly (1903–1974), English critic and editor.

Hiler: Hilaire Hiler (1898–1966), American artist, friend of HM in Paris, recently returned to the U.S. He, HM, and William Saroyan collaborated on a series of essays on modern art, *Why Abstract?,* published by ND in 1945. HM wrote a piece on "Hiler and His Murals" in *The Air-Conditioned Nightmare,* also published by ND in 1945.

2. TL-2

Sept. 7, 1936.
[Paris]

DEAR LAUGHLIN:

You'll probably think I've gone off my nut suddenly shooting all this correspondence into you. Fact is I *am* a little off my nut. For a space now I'm terribly, desperately gay. I feel hopeful for about a year to come. Due to the turn of international affairs, primarily, *and* the fact that I'm getting so deeply involved in *Capricorn* that I'm fast losing my grip on the sordid reality. In this coming year 1936–37 I want to get a number of things published: *The Letters to Emil,* the *Hamlet* book with Fraenkel, a volume of short stories, the "Scenario," and possibly the Lawrence book. The least ray of hope increases my pace enormously. I am really a demon for work, when I work. *"Un travailleur acharné!"*

Yesterday I wrote a long letter to Saroyan; we have been corresponding a bit—I like him, he warms me up, and we have a hell of a lot in common⟨. . .⟩I feel closer to him than to any other American writer. Well Saroyan keeps urging me to get after Bennett Cerf, of Random House. . . . Cerf now has *Black Spring* and should have read it. He read *Tropic* and wrote Kahane that it was hopeless to consider, but that he was enormously impressed, *by parts of it.* (Always the parts! these farts. They never will go the whole hog.)

Now, when I was writing you about the *Letters to Emil* perhaps I forgot to mention that Mencken had also recommended, in case Knopf fell down, trying Huebsch, of the Viking Press, and Lincoln Schuster, of Simon and Schuster. Saying that I could use his name. I am thinking, in my temporary enthusiasm and effervescence, that it would be a good idea to get them all interested at once and let them vie with one another in going for it. I am thinking, Laughlin, me boy, that you're the guy I must count on over there. I was thinking about it all night. Shit, you're a *Gentile,* which counts tremendously, in the first place, and you're dogged (I can see that from your mug), and you don't give a shit, and well, a lot of things combined. I keep suggesting things to do, as if you were my plenipotentiary, and I hope you don't mind. I'm at the boiling point now—for action. One year to go before the crash comes. After that Europe is going to be wiped off the map. That's what I feel in my boots. So, let's go! . . .

Yours,
HENRY.

/ • /

Letters to Emil: HM's letters to his friend Emil Schnellock, documenting his emergence as a writer, were finally published by ND in 1989.

"Scenario": "inspired by a phantasy called *The House of Incest* written by Anaïs Nin." First published as a pamphlet by the Obelisk Press in 1937, then reprinted in *Max and the White Phagocytes* (Obelisk, 1938) and by ND in *The Cosmological Eye* (1939).

the Lawrence book: HM struggled with his study of D. H. Lawrence for years but was never satisfied that he had completed it. *The World of Lawrence* was finally published by the Capra Press in 1980.

Saroyan: HM had met the writer William Saroyan (1908–1981) during his visit to New York the previous year. Stories by Saroyan appeared in *ND 2* and *3*.

Kahane: Jack Kahane (1887–1939), British publisher in Paris specializing in erotica. His Obelisk Press first published HM's works of the 1930s, ranging from the *Tropics* and *Black Spring* to pamphlets like *What Are You Going to Do About Alf?*

Mencken: The American essayist and editor H. L. Mencken (1880–1956) was one of many writers to whom HM had sent his *Tropic of Cancer* when it first appeared.

3. TL-2   Samedi. [October, 1936]
                           [Paris]

DEAR LAUGHLIN:

. . . The only reason I mentioned that I had still some copies of *Aller Retour* was in hopes of getting a little dough with which to buy some copies of *Black Spring* for all the friends who demand them. I have a list of 35 good old friends who are clamoring for copies. I owe practically every one of them money, if not money, more than money, for favors received, for this and that, bed and board, what not. My whole life has been borrowed through, and begged and stolen, if you get what I mean. Since the day I left Western Union, 1924, I think it was, I never did an honest day's work—with the exception of the few months on the *Tribune* here. You can imagine how much I am indebted to all and sundry. I pass many a night awake, dreaming of what I would do if I won the lottery—that is, how I would distribute the first ten thousand dollars worth of the dough. I have a daughter who is supposed to be about 18 now—haven't seen her since she was six or seven. Don't know where she is or what she does in life. Have aged parents who write me heart-rending letters about their poverty—and besides that, a sister who is a half-wit, incapable of earning a living. It's a beautiful tale. That's why sometimes I get crack-brained ideas. Alors, think it over and let me know if you have any suggestion to make. I'm not holding you down to anything. I'm just thinking on it. If you're all tied up don't let it worry you—just tell me you can't be bothered. And above all, no dough! I'm not trying to appeal to your sympathy. I have enough to get by on day by day, and if that were all, everything would be hunky-dory. Compared to the working classes I'm living like a pasha. My appetites are too big for my means, that's all. And every day counts. I'm going into the red more and more.

If you ever run across Fles, the agent, ask him to show you the long story (about 45 pages) called "Max." You'll like it.

Henry

/ • /

the Tribune: In 1931 HM had worked briefly as a proofreader for the
Paris edition of the *Chicago Tribune*.

4. ALS-4

Nov. 10, 1936
Paris

DEAR LAUGHLIN—

. . . I just finished a 50-page burlesque on
"*Money*—and how it gets that way," which I have
dedicated to Ezra. You'll like it, I think—it's just a
broad farce without a bit of sense in it. Kahane says
he will bring it out in pamphlet form *cheap*. Which
is excellent. And there can be no objection to this on
grounds of obscenity. . . .

Had a letter from Martha Foley ordering a copy
of *Black Spring*. I think she'll be asking for a story
soon. By the way, didn't you receive the copy of
B.S. I sent you thru Matisse? He wrote me the other
day saying he had mailed it to you from N.Y. *Do let
me know*. . . .

Keep me *au courant*. I am in fine fettle these days.
If only the war doesn't break too soon!

HENRY

/ • /

Ezra: HM dedicated his travesty of economic theory to Ezra Pound
because Pound had acknowledged receipt of *Tropic of Cancer* by asking
him to consider: "What is money? who makes it / how does it get that
way?///"

Martha Foley: Editor of *Story* Magazine.

Matisse: Pierre Matisse, French art dealer in New York, son of the
painter Henri Matisse.

5. ALS-2

5/4/37
[Paris]

DEAR LAUGHLIN—

If you still have those excerpts from *Capricorn* which I sent you some time back, and if you are not making immediate use of them, I would like to get them back.

Durrell in Corfu is starting a campaign to get the ban lifted on *Tropic.* You will probably hear about it soon. I am still aces high with the censor. I think we'll have his "connivance"—*entre nous.*

The first volume of *Capricorn* will be brought out in January 1938—definitely. A couple of months later *Max and the White Phagocytes* (a collection of stories and essays, which I finished recently). And also in '38 a new illustrated edition of *Aller Retour N.Y. . . . .*

Durrell's *Black Book,* which I have just read in manuscript, convinces me of his genius. It is extraordinary—but also unpublishable in England or America. Keep in touch with him. He is a coming man!!

And by the way, I notice you accepted Anaïs Nin's ragpicker story. Did she ever show you the one on the *Abortion?* That's the one you ought to take. It's powerful. Whereas the ragpicker thing is her weakest. Really.

I have just written an excellent article of some 30 pages on her diary—called "Un Etre Etoilique." Sent a copy to Marion Saunders. You should have a look at it some time.

Stock have just signed up with me to print *Aller Retour* and *Black Spring*—in one volume (sic!). A crazy idea, but they seem to have their own private reasons for doing so. Anyway, progress!

As ever,
HENRY

/ • /

Capricorn: "Three chapters from 'Tropic of Capricorn' " appeared in
ND 4 in 1939, the year the book itself was published in Paris.

Durrell: Lawrence Durrell (1912–1990), English writer living in
Greece, whose fan letter precipitated a voluminous correspondence and
lifelong friendship with HM. A selection from that correspondence
was published by E. P. Dutton in 1963 and a fuller version, *The Durrell-Miller Letters, 1935–1980,* by ND in 1988.

the censor: Huntington Cairns, legal adviser to the U.S. Treasury
Department, consulted on questions of censorship.

Anaïs Nin: (1903–1977), American writer living in France, literary con-
fidante, patroness, and lover of HM.

"Un Etre Etoilique": HM's essay on Anaïs Nin and her diary, published
as a pamphlet by Obelisk Press in 1937, was reprinted in *Max and the
White Phagocytes* and *The Cosmological Eye.*

6. TL-1

Sept. 17, 1937
Paris

DEAR LAUGHLIN:

We sent you a copy of the new *Booster* the other
day. . . . We want to know if you will lend us, the
Booster editors, a hundred dollars, for which we will
pay whatever rate of interest you may demand, and
work the debt off month by month. We need just
that amount to bring out *The Booster* each month.
We started without a cent, by borrowing money to
pay the printer. The ads pay all expenses, but we
don't collect until the ad is printed—and the printer
wants to be paid in advance. A hundred dollars

seems like nothing, but as you know over here it is a lot and getting bigger and bigger every day. Think it over *and wire* if it is O.K. . . .

By the way, can we cooperate in any practical, material way, with your *New Directions* here? If we are not sunk immediately, for financial reasons, we will do something yet with *The Booster,* you'll see. Kahane, my publisher, wants to take it over, publish and finance it, but we are still a bit leery of him. I am also bringing out the first volume, on my own, of Anaïs Nin's 53-volume diary—a hundred francs the copy. Shoot!

HENRY.

/ · /

The Booster: Two months earlier HM had written to Lawrence Durrell: "My friend Fred Perlès is just being given a sort of white elephant in the way of a lousy magazine, owned by the American Country Club, and called *The Booster.*" From a house organ reflecting its members' social activities, Perlès, HM, and Durrell transformed it into a zany literary magazine boosting themselves and their friends.

7. ALS-2   5/31/38
                                             Paris

DEAR LAUGHLIN—

I don't think I'll be sending you any script after all. What I'd like to see published you either can't or won't take—so what's the use? I've thought about it all quite seriously, but I don't see that anything's to be done since we hold such diametrically opposite views. You're thinking now about your public, your buyers, your family etcetera etcetera. And I think only of what I want done. Deadlock.

I've got a chance now, what with *Delta, Phoenix* and *Volontés* (to say nothing of the separate brochures and the Villa Seurat Series) to do most everything I please. Why should I compromise? To please America? Or to please *you?* I don't see it. I'm playing my hand for all it's worth. Winner takes all—that's always been my motto.

This is not directed against you, but against a change of policy. I'm playing a long-winded game. I have the patience of Job. Which I suppose means this finally—that I have full confidence in myself.

And if you think all this is because I'm living on the fat of the land, you're greatly mistaken. Tomorrow I must hustle about to try and raise a thousand francs which is hanging over from my *1936* tax bill. They give me 3 days to cough up or seize the belongings.

And a word about the "family." My old man, 72 yrs. of age now, has just been thru an operation which will finish him. Begs me to try to send him $3.00 a week—and I can't do it! Does that make it clear?

As ever,
HENRY MILLER

P.S. Or should I add that my friends advise me to do something about my daughter—now going on 18 or 19. Her mother is in terrible straits—and a bit goofy to boot.

/ · /

Delta, Phoenix and Volontés: Three literary magazines which readily accepted HM's stories and essays at this time. *Delta* was the new name given to *The Booster* at the insistence of the American Country Club. *The Phoenix,* a quarterly edited in Woodstock, N.Y., by James Peter Cooney, published a long story and two substantial essays by HM in its first three issues. *Volontés* published HM's writings every month, translated by the editor, Roger Pelorson. Along with other writers, HM also contributed cash every month to keep *Volontés* going.

Villa Seurat Series: Edited by HM and published by the Obelisk Press, included *Max and the White Phagocytes* by HM, *The Black Book* by Lawrence Durrell, and *The Winter of Artifice* by Anaïs Nin.

8. TL-2   June 8, 1938
                                             Paris

DEAR LAUGHLIN,

. . . I don't wish to try to bludgeon you into taking things which apparently you have no love for. But I would like to correct you, if possible, in your interpretation of what I am after sometimes, when you say it's "mystic" or this or that. If anybody is on the earth, it is me! But I have a big wingspan. I can fly. I have polarity. What I am after essentially is "reality," which is beyond religiousness, beyond mysticism. *Capricorn* will be as different from *Black Spring* as the latter was from *Cancer*. Because of my searching, or, if you like, my development. The difference between literature for consumption and literature as art lies in this constant effort to express what has been derived from experience (of all sorts) and is real. It isn't a question of honesty, even, or sincerity: it's beyond that. It is in the very nexus of creation. Well, that's that⟨. . .⟩make what you can of it. You unfortunately give me the impression, from your talk and from your letters—and from your ill-advised criticism and preaching (which of course I can't swallow), that you imagine me to get off the track now and then. The track for you is what you would like to see me do. But I am bent on the discovery of my self, not on fulfilling somebody's preconceived program, don't you see? If anybody has himself under control, is pursuing his own destiny like an arrow, it is me. The whole trouble with criticism in general is an innate conservatism, a desire willy-nilly to refer the author back to either tradition, or the author's own frame of reference. But there are individuals who are like quicksilver, and they elude the critics. It is not perversity that makes them elusive or contradictory—it is their own inner drive, their urge. I wish you could get that straight. . . .

Finally—you shouldn't feel hurt or wounded if I lace into you. Shit, it isn't only the 20 years difference between us, but a world of things I've been through, thought out, discarded, rearranged. You'll never have my problems—luckily for you. And above all, don't delude yourself by saying that *I* can do certain things because I am a genius and that you can't because you're an average American. That is self-delusion. When I speak of strategy, I mean something different from *adaptation.* The great problem in life is how to keep your integrity without rendering your efforts null and void. . . .

HENRY

9. TLS-1   October 19, 1938
                                      Paris

DEAR LAUGHLIN,

I only received your $200 yesterday at the American Express here in Paris. You misread the address of my second cable, which was from *Marseilles!* The first was from Bordeaux, but I left there the Saturday after peace was arranged, under the impression that nobody had responded to my cables. Money from several sources has been following about all through the Midi, and always just failing to reach me. Anyway, thanks a great deal, and let's hope nothing will balk you from publishing the works soon. I can't imagine quite how you intend to get away with it, but no doubt you have plans. Probably you are thinking to bring them out in limited editions for subscribers only, at first. Anyway, good luck to you! . . .

The *Max* book is just out and copy will be sent you. The *Money* brochure too, but I'm not sending that to you, as you are not interested. *Capricorn,* volume one ("On the Ovarian Trolley"), Kahane promises to bring out in January or February next year. . . .

I had hoped, when I accepted your offer, to put aside a good part of that money for a return ticket in case of need, but found I had so many debts that I paid it all out within two hours of its arrival. Kahane, according to our agreement, got a third of it. Anyway, it was good to smell for a few hours. I am flat broke to-day, but my credit has improved.

Must tell you too that Cairns, the censor, cabled me $50.00 also, which I received too late, and which I returned to him yesterday. He is really a good guy, and I respect him. We have just sent a new issue, a big one, and a most daring one, of *Delta,* due before Xmas. It is called "Special Peace and Dismemberment Number," and is dedicated to our two good Czechoslovak friends, Milada Souckova and Dzenek Rykr of Prague.

Have had no letter from you in all this time—no doubt it went astray. There is no Hotel Beauvau at Bordeaux, that was Marseilles. So write me again, will you, and give me all the dope. In any case, I am very glad that it should be *you* who takes me on as

American publisher. I promised Knopf the Lawrence book, and will keep my promise—but that doesn't mean necessarily that they will accept it—I rather think they won't.

Cordially yours,
HENRY.

/ · /

Bordeaux: HM had gone to Bordeaux in a panic during the Munich crisis with the idea that he could escape across the Atlantic from there, and had cabled JL, Huntington Cairns, and others for funds.

The Max book: Max and the White Phagocytes, published by the Obelisk Press.

Knopf: Blanche Knopf showed interest in several of HM's works at this time but never in fact published him.

10. CC-2   October 31, 1938

DEAR HENRY,

I'm sorry that the money went to Bordeaux instead of to Marseilles. I guess we took the cable over the telephone and in that way it got mixed up. Sorry.

Yes, the consensus of expert advice seems to be a limited edition at about five dollars for subscribers, sent by express, with the stores taking orders only. That I think would be pretty safe. Then perhaps later we could have a cheap edition when people have gotten used to the book.

Our royalty rate is 10% of the net take until costs of production and distribution are paid off and then 50% of the take thereafter. I don't think you will find better treatment than that anywhere. That is the arrangement with Pound, Williams, etc. If it is a five dollar book the net take will be three dollars and you will get thirty cents a copy. The $200.00 is, of course, an advance against royalties, and I won't be able to give any more advances till I see how the thing goes.

I have set the publicity campaign in motion already with announcements and will build toward fall 1939 publication of *Cancer*. It will take that long to get things oiled properly so that everything will go smoothly. Do you have any changes you want to make from the Paris text?

I'm looking forward to the new books. Send along the *Money* too, as I want all of you for my collection. . . .

As you know, I have never taken much stock in the Lawrence book. Nevertheless, I would like to have the next option after Knopf. Best results are obtained by doing all the books from one house. It makes the publisher more willing to spend money on advertising if he thinks he'll be getting it back on a series of books.

I am very much impressed with Durrell's book. It's good. I think I must try to get him for *New Directions* next year. I don't know about publishing him as he is English. I mean I feel it my duty to America to publish you here but about an Englishman I don't care so much. However, it would be fine to have excerpts from the *BB* in the next *ND*.

What about copyrights? I take it that Kahane has never taken out anything. I don't know what he could have taken out. I'll find out from Cairns whether we can get a copyright on it here without getting into trouble. I don't believe that the central government operates any censorship on books printed inside the country. Cairns works I think for the Treasury Department which handles incoming stuff. I think our trouble would come from local officials to whom a complaint was brought by a vice society or a religious body. The Catholic church is raising a hell of a stink about such things these days. Sumner, however, is momentarily quiescent. Morris Ernst, of course, who I know would love to have me hire him to fight through a trade edition, but he is damn expensive and I'm not sure that it would work again. The obscenity in *Ulysses* was much better integrated than it is with you. With you it sticks out like hell. Well, we'll see what happens.

So much for the moment.

/ • /

50% of the take: presumably a secretary's misunderstanding of dictation; JL would have said 15%.

Durrell's book: The Black Book, written under the influence of *Tropic of Cancer* and published by the Obelisk Press in HM's Villa Seurat Series. An excerpt appeared in *ND 4.*

Sumner: John S. Sumner, secretary of the New York Society for the Prevention of Vice. His name was a byword for censorship.

Morris Ernst: New York lawyer who argued the landmark case for James Joyce's *Ulysses* against charges of obscenity, making it legal to publish the book in the U.S.

11. ALS-4   Nov. 16th 1938
                                             Paris

DEAR LAUGHLIN—

. . . The terms you give are marvellous! How can you do it? You are the Jesus Christ of the publishing world! Kahane gets a cut of a third on my rake-off, you know. He is doing things now, at long last. "Continenta" opens a big world-wide campaign about my work in a few weeks. So don't weaken! I never expected you to come across with publication, in view of your family etc—I am still dazed! And even if you are thwarted at the last minute, there will be excellent results all around. . . .

HENRY

P.S. I don't expect more money from you until it's due me. You did splendidly by me. Thanks again. I am incurably insolvent. I realize at last that I am a gambler, like Dostoevski. Only the stakes are life-and-death!

12. ALS-2   Dec. 3rd [1938]
                                     Paris

DEAR LAUGHLIN—

Would you let me know just as quickly as possible whether you or any friend of yours or rare book-seller would care to buy the few copies I have on hand of the first editions of *Tropic of Cancer* and *Black Spring*. I have 28 of *Tropic* and 12 of *Blk. Spring*. There are no others existing anywhere— except what were purchased by individuals. I have combed the bookshops here for them—offering a premium on them—but there are no more. The ones I have are in first-rate condition, absolutely untouched.

I have held on to them a long while, in the hope of cleaning up later—but as I need money badly now for my trip to America, I want to unload. However, no matter what happens, I won't let them go for a song. I offer them now in a lump—but if I don't get a good offer I will gradually give them away to friends.

Have no idea what they are worth to-day. I know this only, that people report to me that in London the first edition of *Cancer* brings 5 pounds—and the 3rd edition two pounds.

Nor do I know what to suggest about shipping them to one in America. If you have a good bank, it might be possible to send them in small packages to you or anybody else care of a bank—or better still, if you have a friend on board of directors, to address them direct to him. Have done this for friends with London banks.

Point is, if any offer is made, to cable me—and if I accept, then money should be cabled me, *I* to pay cable charges. Because I intend to leave before Xmas, money or no money. Don't advertise fact that I am coming over, please, as I want to duck people, even my friends. Am going to explore America alone in my own fashion—writing the book (America, the air-conditioned nightmare) as I go along. Will have about $20.00 a week to live on and pay travelling expenses with while over there. Now I am scouting about for fare.

HENRY.

P.S. Would also like to sell original typescript of *Tropic of Cancer* to some one some day. Differs considerably from book—and much larger—also contains original real names of characters. But for this I want from 500 to 1,000 dollars—no less. Would sell bound note-books too, which are valuable documents for future.

13. ALS-4   April 23, 1939
                                               Paris

DEAR LAUGHLIN,

I've been informed from various sources that you
don't intend to bring out *Tropic* until the late Fall—
on account of the publicity created by the article you
had inserted in *Time*. Is that what you mean by
delay? Or do you mean an "indefinite" delay?

Just let me say this, in answer to your letter of the
10th, registering a strange note of despondency—
that, if for any reason, you would like to back out
of your agreement with me, you have only to say
so, I won't hinder you. I say this because I always
suspect that your *real* difficulty is with your family.
Your pride may not permit you to admit that that is
the reason. But you don't need to conceal anything
from me. If you would like to dissolve the arrangement I shan't reproach you.

My own logic tells me that, if you have suffered
losses with some of your other publications, you
should recover them with the publication of *Tropic*.
I can also envisage your going to jail for it, and possibly being put out of business. The fact that Cairns
is liberal-minded and friendly towards me has nothing to do with its probable reception by the public
and the critics. *You are up against taboos—the "mores."*

Capricorn may cause trouble for all of us here,
because of the Puritanical wave coming in with the
war fever. Kahane hasn't released it yet, tho' it is
published.

The *Max* book has been received most favorably
everywhere, though creating no stir like *Tropic,* naturally. But certain people are surprised that I could
write in the manner of the essays. . . .

I don't know when I shall be able to send you a

copy of *Capricorn*. (I won't send them to America
parcel post this time—only in sealed envelopes—and
that costs about a dollar for mailing.) But Cairns
took back with him an uncorrected proof copy of
the book, which perhaps you could borrow or look
at there in Washington. . . .

As for things improving—don't look forward to
it. Things will constantly get worse. We are in for a
world-wide dissolution which may require the rest
of the century to work out. Adjust yourself to "bad
times." Figure always on the worst, and you can't
go wrong.

I am thinking to publish on my own eventually
and put no price on the books. I will accept whatever one wishes to offer me, as alms, or as apprecia-
tion of services rendered. The reading public is
diminishing rapidly, and it is just. I hope the great
majority sink back into illiteracy—it would be better
for the artist.

Yours,
HENRY.

/ • /

article you had inserted in Time: On November 21, 1938, *Time* magazine
had published an article on JL, announcing that ND would publish
Tropic of Cancer.

14. CC-1   May 7, 1939

DEAR HENRY:

No, I have not lost heart. I am only waiting for
some cash to turn up. I would not think of publishing *Tropic* without five thousand dollars handy—to

promote it as it deserves, and to pay a good lawyer to defend it in case of prosecution. Foolish to try to get out a book like that on a shoestring. But I certainly intend to do it and I hope you won't be too impatient.

In the meantime I am thinking of doing the *Max* in the fall. This could be done on a small scale without doing it injustice. And there would not be much likelihood of censorship trouble with that. What do you think of that idea? Let me know. Is there anything new that ought to be added to that group of things? And I think there ought also to be something for *New Directions 1939*.

Please send me a copy of *Capricorn* by first class mail and I shall remit. I am most anxious to see what it is like. . . .

I think you're right about the collapse of "civilization."

Grüssen

/ · /

Max: JL took all but one essay from *Max and the White Phagocytes,* adding three sections from *Black Spring* and two other pieces to make up *The Cosmological Eye* (ND, 1939).

New Directions 1939: HM contributed three excerpts from *Tropic of Capricorn* to *ND 4*.

15. TLS-3   May 16, 1939
                                                   Paris

DEAR LAUGHLIN—

Answering your letter of May 7th at once, as I am leaving here for good on a long voyage the 30th or 31st of this month. . . .

I am going with Durrell to Corfu—first stop. Write him there—c/o the Ionian Bank, Ltd. Corfu, Greece. I shall probably hit America late Summer or Fall, as I will clean up the Mediterranean world first and then to England *and* Ireland! (Erin go bragh!) I love Ireland! I have friends there too—everywhere in fact. On the other hand, I may only come to America after India. I have warm invitations from a dozen or more leading writers there—could stay a year on their hospitality, if I chose. But I rather think I will reserve India for my China-Tibet venture. Anyway, feel absolutely free, footloose, gay and insouciant—about everything. I am taking a Sabbatical year—*on nothing.* Just a valise and a cane from New Caledonia, as a talisman.

Don't pay me for *Capricorn*—it's coming to you! Whenever you are flush sit down and write out an American Express check in my name for whatever you can spare—that's the safest and most agreeable way to get money. I owe to date over $25,000.00. But I firmly believe the day will come when I pay off *all* my debts—and I'll do it by cable and with 10% interest! . . .

HENRY.

16. CC-1   June 5, 1939

DEAR HENRY:

Your trip sounds great. I hope it is really a fact and not just a dream. Don't fall overboard. Don't get sunstroke. The world needs you a bit yet.

I hope that a *Capricorn* gets through. I want to publish a little of it in *New Directions* in order to have an American copyright. This will prevent later pirating. I wish I had had the sense to do that with *Cancer*. We are OK on *Black Spring* in that respect. We could fight a pirating of that with our copyrights on the sections.

Look, can you let me know how to get a look at some of those pieces you mentioned in your letter to Pearce? I would like to look over everything that is available and make up a book that would be the best possible assortment—show all the sides of your genius. . . .

I'm optimistic this week. I've got my Harvard diploma, and a guy in our mill in Pittsburgh has invented a photo-electric eye for Bessemer converters that may revolutionize the steel industry and bring in millions. Also maybe not. But it's nice to think about—like your journey to Tibet.

Up whiskers!

/ • /

Pearce: Charles A. Pearce, an editor at Harcourt Brace to whom HM had written proposing a book of essays and suggesting he discuss the idea with JL. Later a partner in Duell, Sloane & Pearce, which first published HM's *The Smile at the Foot of the Ladder* (1948).

17. ALS-2 Sept. 8th 1939
Aboard S.S. *Sophia*

DEAR LAUGHLIN—

Just returning to Corfu from Athens where I spent a week or so with the Durrells. I'm writing you particularly to ask you to send copies of *New Directions*—all you can spare of back issues—to the following two Greek authors. The first named (Katsimbalis) is editor of a review, the best review in Athens. He knows English literature well and is interested in learning about contemporary American writers. If you could write him & tell him the names of the leading ten Americans with a few titles, he would appreciate it. He has translated a number of modern Greek poets into English—and translated Eliot's *Waste Land,* I believe, into Greek—modern *demotic* Greek. Besides, he is a marvellous chap—a man of about 45—a character, a volcano. He knows everything and with Cendrars should be put down as the best story teller I ever met. He is now planning to bring out an English number of his review—which is ten years old—and will translate fragments of Durrell's and my work, as well as others.

The other man (Seferiades) is the leading Greek poet today—a good friend of Katsimbalis—and, in my opinion, a fine poet. He is about 37 yrs. old. Also a good fellow. And thoroughly conversant with English. Tell him of the American poets today. I could only think of Robinson Jeffers and Robert Frost. . . .

I understand the war has broken out. We were talking of everything else these last few days. . . .

I left my most precious notebooks etc. with Kahane in Paris. Wonder will I ever see them again. Wonder will I ever see Paris again.

Got your announcement about books—O.K. But if you use a fragment of *Capricorn* in the Anthology, no *cuts* please! And if you ever send money, make it in form of an American Express check—nothing else is of any value.

Salut!
HENRY.

/ • /

Katsimbalis: George Katsimbalis, the "colossus" of HM's book about Greece, *The Colossus of Maroussi.*

Cendrars: HM later devoted a chapter to Blaise Cendrars (1887–1961) in *The Books in My Life* (ND, 1952). "Cendrars was the first French writer to look me up, during my stay in Paris, and the last man I saw on leaving Paris."

Seferiades: Giorgos Stylianou Seferiades (1900–1971), who wrote under the pen name George Seferis, Nobel Prize winner 1963.

18. ALS-6   October 18th 1939
                                              Athens, Greece

DEAR LAUGHLIN—

A few days ago I wrote a letter to Cairns asking if he would appeal to a number of people whose names I gave him for funds to cover my passage back to America. I didn't include your name on the list as I did not feel sure you would respond. The situation is very much like that of last September, only worse. What help I might have counted on from good friends in France and England is ruled out now because of the war restrictions on sending money out of the country—the warring countries. On top of it all Kahane died suddenly, just when my royalties were due. His affairs are rather in a mess, I am informed. I don't know if the business will be continued or not. He had begun paying me a regular sum monthly—I received it twice only when he up and died. . . .

I have a friend leaving for New York shortly from whom I can expect a small sum regularly, should I wish to stay on. I would much prefer to stay on, of course. It needs only about $60.00 a month to live here modestly. I might do it for less, once I knew I would receive the money regularly from America. I would then go to a small island—there are loads of them. I'd rather stay alone on some small island and go on with my work than come to America and look for a job of some kind. The thought of that terrorizes me. . . .

HENRY.

19. ALS-6   Dec. 7th 1939
                                                Athens

DEAR LAUGHLIN—

Received your letter of Nov. 22nd a few hours after I had mailed you the card. Seferiades and Katsimbalis received their copies of *N.D. '38* and the other day Durrell received 2 copies of *N.D. '39*. I haven't seen anything. I was pleased that you selected the (3) fragments you did from *Capricorn*—excellent! And your prefatory note on Durrell was the best from your pen I have yet seen. I haven't read the text thoroughly to see if excisions had been made. I don't quite know, from your letter, whether you are talking of printers' deviltry in connection with *Capricorn* excerpts in the *Max* book. I hope not the latter! It seems to me that if you must get guarantees from your printer I'll have to get guarantees from *you*. It's no good your shifting the onus on to the printer. I must hold *you* responsible—you're the publisher and you're the man I'm dealing with. Also, I don't think the question of money sacrificed should be mentioned. When you agree to do a thing you either do it or don't do it—the reasons you give for breaking your word are superfluous. I wouldn't bowdlerize a man's work at any price. You know

it's one thing I'm sensitive about. The day I decide
to surrender to the critics, or to public opinion, or
to the *printers* (!) I'll do it of my own accord. I could
have been published in America long ago had I
wanted to compromise. Also I could always have an
advance of a few hundred dollars if I wanted to do a
book to order. I'm surprised that you should offer
to seduce me, or traduce me with such a proposition. From now on I'll never ask you for a penny.
You fall back on your role of business man. O.K.
But one can be a business man and a human being,
a friend, at the same time. The two are not incom-
patible. You give me to believe that I am still
unknown and so unsaleable—in America. (500
advance orders is really a flop!) But this is your
affair—as entrepreneur. It's up to you to create a
demand, to make me known, no? I think you made
a mistake to swerve from your original plan, which
was to begin at the beginning—with *Tropic of Cancer*. You wanted to play safe and so you must suffer
the consequences. On the other hand, let me say that
I think it suicidal on your part to attempt to force
the stronger works on the public, in face of the bans.
Why couldn't they be brought out in de luxe editions, quite privately and secretly? The censor has
done his part—he's been most liberal—and shown
himself a real friend to boot. I wouldn't fight him—
at least until he gives the signal. He would be only
too pleased to see us win, but you can't expect him
to hamstring himself in the open. It's a problem, I
confess. Things must be done with extreme tact—
and foresight. No use putting your head down and
charging like a bull. You'll have to find a hole in
the armor-plate somewhere—that's my frank belief.
Meanwhile, no more compromises! I am going to
hold you to that. I give you notice now that if in
future anything of mine is printed with emendations

or excisions I shall consider it a breach of faith on
your part—a breach of contract. I won't make a
fuss, because I don't believe in that, but I won't have
anything more to do with you. Mind you, I know
you are acting in good faith and with full desire to
aid me. I know you mean well—I never doubted
that. But if you play the wrong game you hurt me
and I can't let you do that—not with eyes open, at
any rate.

You mention something about "bad reviews" of
Cancer and *Capricorn*. Where? When? I haven't seen
them. Entre nous, there is no such thing as a "bad"
review, if you mean by that an attack. Every thing
can be converted to good. The critics often win
adherents for a book by slamming it unmercifully—
that's part of their ignorance—and sometimes it's
just devilish cunning on their part. They save their
face with the review and they give the bag away to
the discerning reader. . . .

I may be back in America in January. My address
is c/o Gotham Book Mart. I am going to sneak in
quietly. I don't want to meet a lot of people—and
especially not my old friends. I hope to get out of
N.Y. quickly—for the South and West. Wish I
could take a trip with you in your car when you go
selling. It would be interesting.

I intend to make a whirlwind tour of the States,
writing fast and furiously as I go along—the book I
announced: *America, the Air-Conditioned Nightmare*.
Better not bruit it about—they might make it
unpleasant for me in some places if they knew what
I was up to. I have a lot of new friends in America I
will look up—especially in out of the way places. I
want to pass through anonymously, not as H.M.
the writer. I want to see it from the ground up.
(Faulkner is one man I'd like to meet—and
Steinbeck. Do you know either, personally?). . . .

Remember, be human, that's all that matters. The rest is *"en marge."*

H E N R Y

P.S. And Merry Christmas to you!

/ • /

Gotham Book Mart: HM had made the acquaintance of Frances Steloff, owner of the bookstore, during his visit to New York in 1935; she was to be a loyal friend and promoter of his work. Hers was also the first bookstore to stock ND books.

20. T L S - 1   Feb. [21 ?], 1940
                                                    New York

D E A R L A U G H L I N ,

. . . I spent a week with Cairns in Washington and met all manner of officials there, all most friendly and sympathetic. I prefer to abide by Cairns's judgement—he honestly has my interests at heart. . . . I think that the most practical and effective thing is to allow the pressure from the reading public to accumulate. Nobody can stop the pirating—that's inevitable under the circumstances. As for Legman, though I shall have nothing to do with him I am rather glad he did what he did. I won't raise a finger myself to prevent anybody from pirating me under present circumstances. . . .

Yours,
H V M .

/ • /

Legman: G. (Gershon) Legman, a specialist in erotica, evidently acting as agent for the publishers of a "pirated" edition of *Tropic of Cancer.* On January 27, HM had written JL, "I can't afford to accept money from Legman's outfit and hope he doesn't go thru with it." But eventually HM did accept royalties. (See Roger Jackson's note in *Henry Miller: A Bibliography of Primary Sources,* pp. 11–12.)

21. CC-1   February 25, 1940

DEAR HENRY:

    . . . If that is your wish, I'll do nothing to prevent the various piracies. Please remember that you wanted me to take this stand and don't blame me for it later.

    I should not like at this time to give away whatever rights I may have in your work. But, in the event that you can find someone to do the books to your satisfaction, you may count on me to be fair and reasonable. I don't want to give up my rights before you have found someone else, because at any time changes might occur in my family which would make it possible for me to take an entirely different line with regard to your books. See what I mean?

    In the meanwhile, I would like to do another book by you this coming Fall. What do you suggest? What have you that we could make up into a good book? . . .

    Hope you are well and happy,

/ • /

family: ". . . I knew full well that if I had brought out those 'wicked' books my family would cut off the funds that supported the business." (JL letter to GW, June 13, 1991) In the *Paris Review* interview, JL spoke fondly of his Aunt Leila, whose home in Norfolk became his office for

ND, but added: "She was very down on certain books I published; she couldn't stand Henry Miller. I was very careful not to undertake the *Tropics,* because I knew it would set the whole family on its ear. She thought he was obscene and an anarchist." (*Paris Review,* 89 ([Fall 1983]), 166)

22. TLS-2   Feb. 27th [1940]
                                                 New York

DEAR LAUGHLIN,

. . . What you say about preserving your rights until such time as I find another publisher is understood. If the time comes that one can publish the books it will mean a private, limited edition undoubtedly. Though I didn't like starting with the present book it is perhaps well, because the important thing, according to the legal view, is simply the building up of a solid body of critical data, proving that my work has literary value. By what means we obtain that doesn't matter. *The Cosmological Eye* apparently unleashed a good number of reviews. . . . I too am hoping that you will be the one to go through with the publications, whether here or elsewhere. We will bide our time for a while.

As to another book, yes, I had in mind giving another collection of essays and portraits to the Obelisk Press—*Plasma and Magma,* which is probably a bad title. But as they are hardly likely to be able to bring out such a book while the war is on, I think you could do it here, if you think it feasible. It would not contain any stories. I have a tentative list of the contents in mind, which I summarize for you briefly. . . .

                                                 Yours,
                                                 H V M

/ • /

list of the contents: All but one of the essays and portraits listed in this
letter appeared in *The Wisdom of the Heart* (ND, 1941).

23. TL-2   Monday, 4th March [1940]
                                              [New York]

DEAR LAUGHLIN,

If you are going to be in town this week I suggest
we meet either at lunch Friday or else some time
Saturday morning. I'm pretty well booked up and
working between times. A note to the Gotham will
be O.K. I live near there, but am keeping my
address secret. . . .

As for informing people as to where to go for the
pirated edition I think that is bad policy. Let them
find out for themselves. The answer I would make
to people who want to know my attitude about the
matter is this, that Henry Miller has heard of the
existence of such an edition but has no interest [in]
it nor did he authorize it, nor on the other hand has
he any objection to the publication.

About the new book, yes I'll begin collecting the
material and will give you most of it before July. If I
can write a story or two I will—I have been thinking
about it. I could write a tremendous one about the
reunion with the family the other night. My father
is slowly dying of cancer of the prostate, after three
operations—74 years old. If you would like to draw
up a contract for the new book do so and I'll take
the advance now, if you can do it. Perhaps when I
see the contract I'll be able to figure out what's coming to me on the first book. I haven't the letter with
me which you sent me to Paris stipulating the terms.

I take it the only deduction to be made against the royalties are the $200 you cabled me and what I owe you for books which I ordered. Is that right?

I told you once I'd never again ask you for anything that wasn't due me. If I say to send me the advance on the next book immediately it's because you say "any time you need funds badly." I want to explain my position about money once and for all. I always need funds badly. I have never earned a living since the year 1924 when I walked out of the telegraph company. I owe roughly about $25,000, at least, which I confidently expect to pay back before I kick off. I owe money to several hundred people, in sums ranging from three or four dollars to several thousand. I think you are probably sensitive about the subject because you are a rich man's son and fear that people will abuse your good nature if you show them a little kindness. It's not my place to tell you how to behave—you'll learn from experience which is the better policy to pursue. You've done me a great injustice in even thinking about me the way you have. But you've harmed yourself even more than me. All I want of you is what's due me when it's due, no more. I have absolute confidence in your honesty, else I wouldn't have entered into relations with you. But, never ask me again if I am in need— I am and will be for a long time. And, if ever you're moved to make a friendly gesture which is not strictly demanded by the rules of the game, as you now see it, I will not refuse to accept your aid in the right spirit. I know how to give and take. Shakespeare put it negatively—he was speaking for the practical man. But the most practical man in the world is the impractical one—he sows and reaps. That's all. I hope we're clear on it, and I say this with the very best of feelings.

There is another little point I wish to make which

may help you to understand what lies behind my attitude towards the publishing of the *Tropics*. Part of my refusal to do anything with Signet is motivated by a great desire to see you, help you, keep the promise you made. People are expecting great things of you—even your rival publishers, I find. Even they have admitted to being disappointed by your failure to publish the books in question. They gave up the battle long ago; they looked to you as a younger man to do what they failed to do. I know all the obstacles in the path and recognize them as real. I think that in years to come, if you let this opportunity now slip out of your hands, you will never forgive yourself. . . . Every day some one tells me that you're just a dilettante. Maybe you are, but you won't be with me because I'm too earnest and sincere to let you be if you wanted to be. What I want, and usually get, is a thoroughly human relationship. We began (with the Pound notes from Italy, you remember) on the right basis and, to the best of my powers, I am going to keep it on that basis. I've made too many blunders myself not to allow for the other fellow's mistakes.

Just drop me a note c/o Gotham saying when and where to meet you either Friday or Saturday. Friday for lunch would be good, if you can. Somewhere in the forties or fifties, say.

Yours,
HVM.

/ • /

reunion with the family: HM's "Reunion in Brooklyn" would appear in *Sunday After the War* (ND, 1944).

Signet: The publisher had expressed interest in publishing something by HM.

24. TLS-2   Friday [April 1940]
                                               N.Y. City

DEAR LAUGHLIN,

I am returning the original copy of contract here-
with in the hope that you will agree to making the
revisions suggested herein—otherwise it will be
impossible for me to sign it. I don't find it at all
generous in spirit; in fact, I've never seen a contract
so thoroughly armor-plated, so full of protective
devices. One would think you were dealing with a
thug or a maniac instead of a sensitive, intelligent
author. . . .

Another thing—if you are contemplating bringing out a second or third edition of *The Cosmological
Eye* I wish you would grant me the privilege of
writing a foreword to the next edition in which I
might explain what happened in connection with
the publication of this volume in its present form.
Would you? Otherwise, if you would do me a real
favor, I would say suppress the book, let it die in its
first edition. . . .

                                               Yours,
                                               HENRY

                        / • /

revisions: HM did not really suggest revisions. Instead, he flatly rejected
or took exception to some eight or ten clauses in the ND contract.

25. ALS-1   April 17, 40
                                         New York

DEAR LAUGHLIN—

Better drop the idea of doing a new book. We see things too differently, I'm afraid, to ever come to any real agreement.

                                         Yours,
                                         HENRY MILLER

26. CC-1   July 3, 1940
                                         Norfolk

DEAR HENRY:

This is to advise you that I have read the draft of your Greek travel book, *The Colossus of Maroussi,* and do not feel that it is suitable for publication under my imprint. Accordingly, I release my option, as provided in our general contract, and you are free to place this book with another publisher, provided always that in so doing you do not enter into any obligation to another publisher prejudicial to my rights in your other, or further, works. In other words, in contracting for this book with another publisher you may not offer him first options on other books.

                                         With best wishes,
                                         JAMES LAUGHLIN

27. TL-3   Jan. 19th, 1943
                                    Los Angeles

DEAR LAUGHLIN,

. . . Thanks for your comments on the *Horizon*
fragment. That has already had tremendous reper-
cussions. It was that particular bit which gave
D.D.&Co. the jitters when they saw the first 200
pages of the book. They did not turn the book
down. I withdrew it, after writing 500 pages, of my
own volition, knowing they would be unable to
publish it as it stood and knowing it was futile to
engage in controversy about it, as we had just
entered the war. My thought was to shelve it until
after the war. Two English publishers now seem
eager to take it. I am debating what to do. Connolly
is publishing two or three more fragments. I would
be glad to give you a fragment for the Anthology—
one he is not using—when and if we straighten out
our misunderstanding about the past debt. I would
like very much to get straightened out with you—it
would do me good, morally. As it stands I harbor a
deep grudge against you. Not only for this transac-
tion but for other things. It would be better if I
could wipe the slate clean, look at you with a fresh
eye. I want to make the effort. There is no one in
this world whom I hate, not even Hitler or Hirohito. Why should I continue to hate you? It's poi-
sonous. . . .

/ · /

the *Horizon fragment:* An excerpt from HM's *Air-Conditioned Nightmare*
had appeared in Cyril Connolly's *Horizon* in November 1942.
D.D.&Co.: Doubleday Doran had given HM an advance to write *The
Air-Conditioned Nightmare* and was to have published the book.

28. PCS   12/15/43
                                         [Los Angeles]

Regrettable that *N.R.* came out just as we effected
our reconciliation. All that belongs to the past. Am
still getting material typed. Will mail you what's
ready before Xmas—the balance can follow later, if
needs be. I'm plagued with visitors and over-
whelmed with mail—also commissions for paintings. When I get back from Monterey I may go
direct to Mexico to achieve quiet, solitude and time
to work in peace. Excuse card. Am in a rush. More
later.

                                              HENRY

                          / • /

N.R.: On December 6, 1943, *The New Republic* had published an open
letter from HM, complaining that JL had failed to publish his banned
books and had been anything but a champion and benefactor. The
open letter was published along with two others in a pamphlet entitled
The Plight of the Creative Artist in the United States of America (Bern Porter, 1944).

getting material typed: For the new collection, *Sunday After the War*
(ND, 1944).

29. AL-1   2/5/44
                                         [Los Angeles]

DEAR J.L.—

Here's a letter from R.&V. to which I responded
by telegram saying I was certain everything was
clear between us & to telegraph me the money, as I
need it. I assume you have already signed contract &
put it in mail.

I don't feel the least worried about future dealings with you. I trust you absolutely. And I want to repeat that I admire your change of attitude—i.e., what it took to bring it about. It was much harder for you than for me, for the reasons we both now understand.

That was a wonderful card you sent me from Salt Lake City. I like getting such things—for my wall.

The *Angel* book is now on its way to you, I understand. I hope you like it. Orders & promises of orders are coming in slowly but steadily. I think it will be something of an event in the literary-painting world. The most significant thing is that you should have been the first to order a copy. . . .

It may seem that I am now trying to push you into publishing everything. That is not the case, precisely. I am urging you, yes, but for your own sake, your own reputation, largely. I know now that I can get *everything* published, either openly or privately. I am going like a dynamo, carrying on like a promoter, in order to make this a phenomenal last year in America.

/ • /

R.&V.: Russell & Volkening, HM's literary agents, had been holding an advance from ND on *Sunday After the War* until differences between author and publisher could be resolved.

the Angel book: *The Angel Is My Watermark,* a limited edition including photographs of the artist at work, reproductions of his paintings, and texts, e.g., the title piece from *Black Spring,* photographically produced by George Barrows and Norman Holve in 1944. An original HM watercolor was bound into every copy. "Gave them a little beauty of an aquarelle for your copy," HM wrote to JL in an earlier note.

30. ALS-3   2/8/44
                              [Los Angeles]

DEAR J.L.—

. . . About "Selected Writings"—O.K. Entendu
[Agreed]. I always have my finger on the public's
pulse. Get from 75 to 100 letters a week, from readers. In addition, get the gossip from bookstores.
And—from the professors—and better still, from the
professors' students. Many of these two classes
write me—the students much more keenly than the
professors, I find. . . .

One day, when I get a clear breathing stretch, I
may tackle *Season in Hell*—not to *translate,* but to
improvise, giving my own flavor and savour, what
I *imagine* it is, and not what it actually reads. I think
that is the only way to do Rimbaud in another
tongue. No translation ever sounds right to me,
especially if it is merely correct. . . .

The fact that our relations are now solid and last-
ing relieves me tremendously. My future trouble
will not be how to get printed but rather to deliver
the goods, as it were. And shut off (how?) the flood
of correspondents who pester me.

The last book I am interested in seeing published
here in America is the *Hamlet.* I don't *press* you to
say yes. I say, as with the others, that in the end you
will not regret it. I may often sound too positive in
my assertions about my own work—but I can judge
from the letters & conversations I have what's what.
With each book there are always some who adore &
some who hate. The book most universally accepted
& praised was the *Colossus.*

Now a young friend in Berkeley (George Leite)
talks of bringing out *all* the letters I have saved from
readers—beginning with the *Tropic of Cancer* (which

drew the biggest response). If he does that it will give great impetus to the sale of all the books. And perhaps lay a base for the future "trial" of my case.

HENRY

/ · /

"Selected Writings": On June 10, 1944, HM sent JL a list of selections from his major works to be published in ND's "Dollar Series." This project languished for years and eventually emerged in a very different form as *The Henry Miller Reader* (ND, 1959), edited by Lawrence Durrell.

Season in Hell: HM was to be obsessed for a number of years by *Une Saison en Enfer* (1873), the confessional work of French poet Arthur Rimbaud.

George Leite: Editor of *Circle,* a literary magazine which published several of HM's essays.

31. TLS-1

Sunday [March 5, 1944]
c/o Lynda Sargent
Big Sur, Cal.

DEAR J.L.

Will be here till I find a vacant house to take over. Love this country—Big Sur. Just like Jeffers' poems. Exactly. He and Faulkner are [the] only two American writers, since Twain and Whitman, who give the real American feeling. Met Jeffers the other day. He's O.K. In fact, he's fine—like a good hound. A trembling rock. There are great characters round about here, and I am meeting them all gradually. . . .

H.M.

/ • /

Lynda Sargent: A writer who lived in a log cabin in Big Sur and invited
HM to stay with her until he found a place of his own.

Jeffers: The poet Robinson Jeffers (1887–1962) built his house on the
coast at Carmel and wrote many poems about the rugged Big Sur landscape.

32. ALS-1   Wednesday [March(?) 1944]
                                     Big Sur

DEAR J.L.—

. . . Write me here till I advise differently. May
take a job as overseer of the Sulphur Baths establish-
ment 16 miles down the coast. That is, if I get free
rent. Depends on how much work I'd have to do. I
can't make any solid plans for going to Mexico until
I get a more regular dependable income. But with
all the books now being printed maybe by the end
of this year I'll see daylight.

                                            HENRY

Do bear me in mind about water colors. Will always
make one for anybody at any price they wish to pay.
This is mainly what keeps me going.

33. TLS-2   [April 1944]
                                         [Big Sur]

DEAR J.L.

. . . If I move I will leave forwarding address. I
am out scouting every day for a place of my own in
this vicinity. They are hard to find, livable places. It

is a rich man's terrain. Firewood costs about $25.00 a month. I may take over an ex-convict camp at Anderson Creek, where Varda once lived. But it will be tough there—not a stick of furniture, etc. If I had no books to write or pictures to make, I could live under any conditions. It's always a great temptation for me to give up all work and just idle away my days. I have friends all over the country; I could have a wonderful time of it, just wandering about. But I don't think I shall succumb to this temptation. I'm not proud of my not succumbing, either. I loathe work. It's a vice.

. . . If I get a shack here, say for 15 or 20 a month, I'll find my own firewood, cook outdoors, if necessary, and sleep on the floor. The mailman brings you the food three times a week. Nearest town would be 35 miles away. Sulphur Baths four miles away. I like the prospect⟨. . . .⟩Up the hill nearby is a stone house where Jack London and Sterling lived for a while. London used to ride down from the Valley of the Moon on horseback. You still need a horse to get up there. That's what I like about this country. Well enuf. Good luck to you. I feel very fine about our having settled our differences. We'll never see eye to eye, I know, but we can have faith in one another.

HENRY

/ • /

Varda: Jean Varda, Greek artist living in Monterey, the subject of a portrait by HM, "Varda: The Master Builder," first published in *Circle* in 1944 and reprinted in *Remember to Remember* (ND, 1947). It was Varda who introduced HM to Big Sur.

Jack London: (1876–1916), American novelist and short-story writer.

Sterling: George Sterling (1869–1926), American poet, friend of Jack London.

34. ALS-1   4/12/44
                                      Big Sur

DEAR J.L.—

. . . Found a fine place to live 4 miles down
road—up high & quite inaccessible. All set. Address
always—"Big Sur"—just that.

Any time you write (and think of it) enclose some
postage stamps. Always need them.

Yours,
HENRY

35. ALS-1   Sunday [Spring 1944]
                               [Big Sur]

DEAR J.L.—

Lynda [Sargent] was telling me you wanted to
give her a hatchet. If you don't need it, don't use it,
send it to me, will you? I need one badly. Also, if
you have any old phono records send them along. I
have an old machine now, but no records. And if
you have an extra thermos bottle throw that in too.
The problem here is to *not* make a fire more than
necessary. If I had the thermos bottle I wouldn't
need to make fresh coffee in the morning.

Yours,
HENRY

36. TLS-1   Wednesday [Spring 1944]
                               Big Sur

DEAR LAUGHLIN,

Forgot to say something in letter just posted.
About Rimbaud⟨. . .⟩You never sent me *Season in
Hell*. Will you, please, and soon? The idea of a free
translation intrigues me more and more. I wish you
wouldn't advertise that I am going to do it, however, or count on it for a certain time, as for instance
in the next Anthology. I want to do a glorious job
of it. It's something I shall do slowly, in the eve-
nings when I am all alone, and get slightly cuckoo.
Towards two A.M., that is. I figure now that being
up there on the hill in the great silence, surrounded
by walls decorated with my own creations, seeing
no one for days on end (and I wish it could be
months!) I will get to talking to Rimbaud in the
beyond. What I shall do will not be altogether liked,
you know that, I hope. It will be in English what
Rimbaud means or suggests to me, not in any sense
an "improvement" on existent translations. But he
has done so much to me, I want to immortalize the
impact, as it were. And also, kill him off! He's my
only adversary in the whole realm of literature. He's
the dragon I have to slay. . . .

                                        HVM

37. TLS-2   July 2nd [1944]
                                   Big Sur

DEAR LAUGHLIN,

. . . I got an idea in the shower yesterday and am
writing three great legal minds about it. To wit:

possibility of publishing banned books with blank spaces (on my own, if necessary) and saying in foreword that if reader is curious he can write the author about said blanks. We are keeping within the law, observing the four freedoms, etc. etc. Then when they write send them a printed slip to paste in book, revealing deleted passages. But this plan is only *if it is legal.* My aim is to defeat the law, the censors, and attain my objective too. Will add that if illegal to mail such slips, what about sending them through American Express. I lie awake sometimes wondering how I could get these books published openly, keep within the law, defeat them on their own grounds, and play a good prank at same time. I hate to think I have to play their stupid, serious, tragic game. . . .

Do you know that Ben will soon have *Aller Retour* out—I read proofs the other day. *Murder the Murderer* (110-page pamphlet—"excursus on war," from the *Nightmare,* also out soon). Every mail brings news of some new publication in an English mag. or anthology. Most of the *Nightmare* will have appeared in print somewhere by time it's published. Have over 500 pages, in well-ordered chapters, done now. Part One finished. Part Two—about 250 to 300 words, I think, will be a wild and wooly bit, completely gaga. I will have to run for my life, I guess. And no obscenity this time! But they will be sore as hell, everybody. I work about six hours of the day doing chores up here. And make water colors at nights. And answer bloody correspondents. I'm right down to bone and muscle.

HENRY

P.S. Do you send copies of my books to
British Museum Library—London
42nd St. Library—N.Y.C.
?
Could you, would you!

/ • /

Ben: Ben Abramson of the Argus Book Store in Chicago had HM's
The World of Sex printed in an "unauthorized" edition in 1941 and *Aller
Retour New York* "Printed for Private Circulation Only" in 1945.

Murder the Murderer: "An Excursus on War from the Air-Conditioned
Nightmare" (Bern Porter, 1944). A much revised version appeared in
Remember to Remember (ND, 1947), which HM considered Part Two of
The Air-Conditioned Nightmare. Presumably he had written 250 to 300
pages, not words, at the time of this letter.

38. TLS-2   July 7th, 1944
                                               [Big Sur]

DEAR LAUGHLIN:

. . . Enclose letter from Jane Grabhorn which
constitutes a release on the *Colossus.* May I write her
now to say you will do the reprint, or do you want
to write her yourself? Let me know. I'm delighted.
I only wish I could afford to buy the plates
myself. . . .

My water colors are improving. I've done some
beauties recently for that show in London. I wish I
could finish with my writing and do nothing but
paint—and write poetry. That's my objective now.
But it will take another two years at least. Unless I
suddenly say what the hell and throw up the sponge.
Which I'm likely to do, because I'm getting quite
fed up with all the detail involved in being famous
and broke at the same time. I have an inordinate

desire to do nothing. Only my iron will keeps me
going—and I despise that. But I know I will keep on
until I've finished the program, even if that means
death at 55. You really don't know me, you know.
Some time you should come and stay with me for
a week or two, talk everything out, get acquainted
really, deeply, truly. We'd both feel better.

HENRY

/ • /

Jane Grabhorn: Editor of the Colt Press in San Francisco, which published *The Colossus of Maroussi* in 1941 after JL turned it down. JL subsequently thought better of the book, acquired the rights, and
published it in 1946. *The Colossus of Maroussi* has outsold every other
HM title published by ND.

the program: HM's grand design to complete *The Rosy Crucifixion*, the
story of his turbulent relationship with his second wife, June Mansfield, eventually written as a trilogy: *Sexus, Plexus,* and *Nexus.*

39. TLS-2   July 28th [1944]
                                        [Big Sur]

DEAR J.L.:

    . . . About my proposal to write in blank spots—
N.G. Just heard from three best lawyers in country
on it—absolutely impossible—means jail.
    . . . No, I haven't started on the Rimbaud yet.
Am still struggling with the *Nightmare* and doing
water colors at night. I'll get started one day,
though.
    I am just rereading one of my favorite books:
Steppenwolf, by Hermann Hesse. Would make a
marvellous movie. . . . Am deep in Keyserling's
Travel Diary now and swooning with delight. First

read it on the S.S. *Deutschland*. That's how I got acquainted with Keyserling. And later came his son in a big fur coat and ate me out of house and home. After dinner was over he began eating again—bread, all there was, all the cheese, all the apples, the nuts, etc. Now dead, I suppose, on the Russian front. Probably all his sons dead. Well, murder the murderer⟨. . .⟩always merry and bright.

HENRY

---

40. PCS   8/12/44
                                              [Big Sur]

Just got release from D.D.&Co. on the *Nightmare*—after a reading of the *Murder the Murderer* excursus. Delighted. (Sent their letter to R.&V. who will in turn send it to you.) Will you then have contract drawn up for *Nightmare,* or, if you have any qualms or change of heart let me know, as Pantheon Press, N.Y. will take it if you won't. But I hope you still want it. Figure another 2 to 3 months to finish with it.

HENRY MILLER

---

41. PCS   12/17/44
                                        [Boulder, Colorado]

DEAR J.L.

Am here at Gilbert Neiman's home with my new (legal) wife Lepska till Jan. 1st when we go to Big Sur. . . .

HENRY MILLER

/ • /

Gilbert Neiman: A writer who with his wife Margaret had provided HM with a place to stay when he moved to Los Angeles in 1942. They moved to Big Sur in 1945 and lived next door to HM at Anderson Creek. Neiman's translation of García Lorca's *Blood Wedding* appeared in *ND 4*.

Lepska: Janina Martha Lepska, twenty-one, a Bryn Mawr graduate HM had met in New York in the fall of 1944. They were married in Boulder.

42. ALS-1   2/8/45
                                               Big Sur, Calif.

DEAR J. L. —

I thought I ought to let you know that I've had a number of letters since the occupation of France by our troops to the effect that all the Obelisk books are prominently displayed in Paris book stores and are selling well—to American soldiers. Also that I heard from the son of Kahane, former director of O.P. that he (the son) is carrying on the business, under the name now of "Les Editions du Chêne," same address—16 Place Vendôme. His own name is changed to M. Girodias.

I mention these things because it occurred to me that you might possibly be able to sell the N.D. books to the Paris book stores, and, if you like, get Girodias to have them translated into French. He asked in his letter if he could publish my books in French too.

It's just a thought.

HENRY

/ · /

M. Girodias: Jack Kahane's son Maurice took his mother's maiden name during the occupation and continued to publish the Obelisk Press books, selling them to German and American troops successively.

43. ALS-2   2/27/45
                                     Big Sur

DEAR J. L. —

The idea has occurred to me to offer you Vol. I of the *Nightmare*—any length you find convenient. The thing is going to be too long for one volume, in these times—cost of paper, etc. Besides, by having Vol. I done this year, I can take it easy with that book—bringing out Vol. 2 next year—and so give myself a chance to finish *The Rosy Crucifixion* and send it to Paris for publication there. (It could not be printed here.) . . .

I wouldn't want this idea, however, to prevent you from doing *Black Spring* (and the *Selected Writings*). . . .

It was good of you to send me those last 25 copies of *Sunday* so promptly. Seeing my long desired wish realized I begin to ask myself if I should hold you to your promise any longer. Believe me, if it is a hardship to give me these 50 free copies, I won't hold you to your word. The gesture is the important thing. . . .

Meanwhile good cheer!

HENRY

44. ALS-2   5/17/45
                                                   Big Sur

DEAR J. L.—

You're quite right about the Rimbaud! I made a mistake. In fact, I got all balled up. I've been thru a private hell over his *Season in Hell.* At this moment—10:30 A.M.—I'm flatly discouraged—with myself. I may snap out of it. I hope so. I'm praying for inspiration. Never felt so defeated. Look—either I'll come thru with it in the next ten days or I'll have begun something else, something I planned for Vol. 2 of *Nightmare,* called "Remember to Remember," which (either of them) will be for your Annual #9. I'll send you a telegram to N.Y. about time you arrive, saying what I'm doing—or Total Failure! So that you can plan your space. . . .

                                                   HENRY

P.S. I worked so hard on the Rimbaud that I got lost! Your words gave me renewed hope. If it breaks, it will be a torrent.

/ • /

"*Remember to Remember*": A long reminiscence of France which became the title piece for the book HM considered Vol. 2 of *The Air-Conditioned Nightmare.*
Annual #9: The first instalment of HM's study of Rimbaud appeared in *ND 9* (1946).

45. ALS-1

July 3, 1945
[Big Sur]

DEAR J.L.—

Here it is at last, the Rimbaud! Despite all the corrections, this is the rewrite. I've been over it again and again—that's why I've held it so long. I can't tell you what work I put into it! I hope it shines through <. . . .>

Now I intend to write another 20–30 pages, showing analogies and affinities with my own life—not out of vanity but for illumination. It may be valuable to other younger writers—anyway, it's a compulsion. This I'll tack on for its final appearance as a little book. I'll let George Leite use it in *Circle*—after the Annual comes out.

I feel as though I had been through a great siege.

HENRY

46. TLS-1

August 18th. [1945]
Big Sur

DEAR J.L.

Just had a long letter from my old friend Raymond Queneau (writer), who is now a person of importance chez Gallimard, Paris, and directs the reading of foreign books. They are interested (vitally) in new books, preferably of an "avant-garde" type, and want to exchange books with an avant-garde publisher here. I informed Queneau that you are still the one and only publisher of that description here. And that I would urge you to send him whatever you think worth while. He says they are starved for good books and have received only the usual commercial hash from big publishers. (Gallimard, incidentally, is now more powerful than ever—this I heard from Duhamel.)

Queneau has written several books during the war, short ones, he says, and perhaps too strong (in language) for American taste, also difficult to translate, but, he adds, if there were an acceptance, he would help in the translation—he knows English well and has done lots of translation. He talks of a possibility of putting three of his books in one volume. At any rate, I told him to send me whatever he likes and I would show them to you. . . .

HENRY

/ • /

Raymond Queneau: (1903–1976), French poet and novelist. ND published a number of his works, beginning with *The Skin of Dreams* (1948), translated by H. J. Kaplan.
Duhamel: Marcel Duhamel, editor at Gallimard.

47. ALS-2   Sept. 26th 1945
                                             Big Sur

DEAR J. L.—

We are trying to dicker with Keith Evans, who owns this house, for the purchase of it. He is due to be released from service towards the end of the year. If he won't consider it, we shall have to find another place. Meanwhile our nearest neighbor has offered to let us buy a small piece of her land, just big enough for a house and garden. Varda and a couple of other friends have promised to build a house for us if we get the land.

Every thing hinges on getting the necessary cash, how much I don't know yet. But it may run to $2500.00. I've just written Caresse Crosby, who is in Paris now, to see if she could trade the francs which Girodias owes me for dollars. If she can't or won't wangle that for me, I wonder if I could work out a satisfactory basis for a loan with you. I can think off-hand of two methods which might appeal to you. One would be to surrender to you my complete rights on one of the books you are handling. This would be a speculation for you, with a good chance that you would recover more than I should want to borrow. The other would be to cede the royalties on all my books (which you handle) until the debt had been paid off—at whatever interest you ask. You could name your own interest rate. In either case, I don't think you run any risk of losing your investment, do you? I am hardly likely to prove a complete flop in the next three years.

I suggest these propositions with some trepidation, knowing your reluctance to mix business with friendship. I know too that your cash must be tied up in various ventures. Nevertheless, you might look at it in a purely business way. If it's a sound and paying proposition perhaps it won't seem odious to you. I don't say this sarcastically. You must realize that ever since we got on an understanding basis I have asked no special favors of you. I merely asked you to treat me justly, and you are, and I am, thoroughly satisfied. Moreover, I feel you have actually been generous with me.

Do think it over and let me know. If you have an alternative proposition, give it to me. I'll be hearing from my landlord in about ten days and will then know exactly what I need. And if Caresse meanwhile puts a deal through with Girodias, why I won't need to call on you.

HENRY

/ • /

Caresse Crosby: (1892–1970), American editor of the Black Sun Press in Paris in the 1920s. HM first knew her there, then stayed in her New York apartment and on her Virginia estate when he returned to the U.S.

48. ALS-2   11/10/45
Big Sur

DEAR J. L. —

. . . We plan to live at Anderson Creek soon as Keith Evans returns. I'm getting Varda to fix up George Leite's shack a bit—install a hot water system & bath tub—maybe build a wing to it. He says he can do it. I've also got a studio (formerly a horse shed) next to Emil White's cabin on the road. Am living in it *now*—as Margaret Neiman & her infant are occupying my place. I need a work place & this suits me fine. It's small & cosy—and for the present a hide-out. The visitors are a great pest—like the correspondence.

Just had copy of letter from Heath & Co.'s foreign representative about Girodias. Apparently, all is clear—and even better than I imagined. He hopes to arrange with my lawyer there to get the money transferred soon—maybe 13,000 pounds—before exchange drops. This is big news! I plan to build a house near the Evans one—a neighbor offers to sell

me a big enough piece of her land for the purpose.
This in the spring, if all goes well.

I may need a few hundred dollars very soon—to
fix up the Anderson Creek shack. Maybe less. This
for stove, boiler, materials, a few odds & ends for
household. Will let you know later. But be prepared
for say $200.00, if I ask it suddenly. I'll move Lepska
& the baby in soon as it's livable. I've been using the
sulphur baths to wash diapers already—for Margaret's brat. . . .

Yours,
HENRY

/ • /

Emil White: Austrian-born bookseller, who moved to Big Sur at HM's
suggestion and became his neighbor, faithful friend, and factotum.
HM devoted a chapter to him in *My Bike and Other Friends* (Capra,
1978).

49. PCS

11/21/45
from George Leite's
Oakland

DEAR J.L.—

Just to say baby arrived safely & easily 6:11 P.M.
Monday. I'll be back in Big Sur Monday. If you can
send me some money now I would appreciate it.
Varda has found stove, coils, etc. Is making bath
room, fireplace, fixing roof, adding a wing to
house—at Anderson Creek. All's well. Didn't know
you had two children until yesterday. Congratulations.

The baby's name is Valentine—a Scorpio.

HENRY

Scorpio is my father's sign. I have in it 3 planets in conjunction. "Sex & death" is the symbol.

50. TLS-1   12.17 [1945]
                                             Big Sur

DEAR LORENZO,

That silver spoon gave me the jitters. It is very beautiful and what I would have given the child myself one day. All along I was praying she wouldn't be born with a silver spoon in her mouth—for that would mean a hard life later. The amount and variety of gifts that poured in was staggering. She is about the luckiest child ever born. A very good baby too—sleeps blissfully all day long. Hardly ever makes a sound. Lepska was delighted with the spoon. At the same time came a silver gold-lined mug—we don't know from whom. At any rate, all our thanks! . . .

HENRY

/ • /

Lorenzo: Presumably HM has in mind the Renaissance merchant prince Lorenzo de' Medici, famed for his munificence and taste.

51. TLS-1   1/1/46
                                             Big Sur

DEAR J.L.

. . . This morning I surveyed the spot we are buying from our neighbor—we will get it cheap too. It is magnificent—one of the best sites around here. Next week we move into the Anderson Creek shack for the winter. . . .

I didn't send you anything for Xmas. The truth is, I forgot. But I'd like to send you a water color, if you would like one. Let me know. All good cheer! The baby is thriving. I'm going to take her up on the "property" this afternoon—a fine West wind blowing—and have her bless it. To-day is one of those perfect days after a storm.

HENRY

52. CC-2   January 14th [1946]

DEAR HENRY—

It was fine to get your letter which fairly seems to blow some of the Pacific wind right across the continent. You sound very happy and I envy you.

I wish you would keep your eye open for a little piece of land around there for me to buy. I'm crazy about that country and hope to get down again this year in May. I'd like nothing better than to have a little shack somewhere there that I could come to and camp now and then. If you know of anything, please let me hear about it. . . .

Yes, I'd love to have a watercolor for Christmas. One with blue in it. My lucky color.

as ever

53. AL-3

Jan. 16th '46
Anderson Creek, Big Sur

DEAR J. L.—

Writing in the midst of chaos as we just moved in and have still a lot of work to do about the shack—vital problems. Got your letter of Jan. 8th and am answering. First let me tell you of a project for which I need your consent quickly—by telegram if possible. A painter from Palestine (and France)—Bezalel Schatz—came to me the other day with his paintings to interest me in doing a book with him—largely an art creation—by silk screen process. We need only a small text. He will do the art work on it, print the 500 or 750 copies by hand himself on the screen, and either we will bring it out ourselves (he's to dig up the paper) or if some one offers to publish we may do that. But he does all the labor—a job requiring 5 or 6 months' work. As for text—we are debating as to which of these to use—1) the Jazz Interlude from *Colossus,* 2) "Into the Night Life," 3) "The 3rd or 4th Day of Spring"—the 2 latter from *Black Spring.* We need your consent to use any of these fragments. As it will be a limited edition, de luxe, selling at $15.00 probably, I don't think it could hurt you—may help to advertise the book perhaps. Do let me know, as Schatz is all set to begin. I think it's what the French call *"pochoir."* Even the text will be put thru screen from my handwriting. . . .

[Part of this letter is missing]

/ · /

"Into the Night Life": This text, taken from *Black Spring,* gave the book its name. HM provided a handwritten text, and Schatz spent the next

sixteen months producing the silkscreen work. The cost per copy came
to $73, so the book had to be priced at $100. It took HM 25 years to
sell the first 174 copies. (Roger Jackson letter to GW, Aug. 8, 1993)

54. ALS-2   5/7/46
                                                   [Big Sur]

DEAR J. L.

    . . . Under separate cover I'm sending you the
typescript of the 2nd part of the Rimbaud opus
which Leite is publishing serially in *Circle*. He wants
very much to bring it out when finished—the book,
I mean. I'll probably write another part, maybe two
more. Waiting for critical books on Rimbaud (documentary stuff, etc.) before continuing.

    I told Leite you have first choice, of course. Can
you decide from these first two sections if you'd like
to do the book? . . .

    I'm doing a last big section now for *Nightmare*
(Vol. 2), called "Remember to Remember"—on
France. Then I'll send you the text for that volume.
Then too I'll be cleaned up and resume work on *The
Rosy Crucifixion*. How long that will take to finish
I've no idea. It's just about 20 years since I laid out
the plans for it(!)

                                            Ever yours,
                                            HENRY

/ · /

2nd part of the Rimbaud opus: Published in *ND 11* (1949). The two parts
were published together as *The Time of the Assassins: A Study of Rimbaud* (ND, 1956).

55. CC-2   [May 1946]
                                                [Alta, Utah]

DEAR HENRY—

I've put off writing to you thinking I would be
driving down to California any day, but am still
stuck here so better write.

Those reviews are fine. It can't but help enormously with sales here that those soldiers read the
books there. And the French response sounds good.

Yes, if the Rimbaud is growing to such propor-
tions I think we had better undertake it. It's much
better for you to be with one publisher. Any time
you have it ready I can start on it. . . .

About Queneau. I am terribly keen on his funny
little book *Loin de Rueil.* Did you read that one? It
reminds me of a mixture of Patchen and Nathanael
West. Really very nice. I think we will publish that
one if the translation comes out well. . . .

When I come down there I want to get together
with you and decide on the contents of the Selected
Volume. I have all the books assembled and will
bring them along.

                                            Best wishes,

/ · /

Loin de Rueil: Translated as *The Skin of Dreams* (ND, 1948).

Patchen and Nathanael West: JL probably has in mind the satiric works
of two writers published by ND, the poet Kenneth Patchen (1911–
1972) and the novelist Nathanael West (1903–1940).

56. TLS-1   June 5th [1946]
                                               Big Sur

DEAR J. L.

   . . . Had a long letter from Girodias, and from
my agent in Paris, Dr. Hoffman, regarding my
credits there. Seems they owe me considerably more
than I thought, but, they add, how to get the money
to me they do not know. The Exchange Control
Bureau in Paris has no funds to authorize payments
to American authors and doesn't know when or if
ever they will again. I was wondering if you had any
suggestion as to how to recover the money legiti-
mately and at the legal rate of exchange? I remember
you said you are sending books to Albertine Scarlet.
How do you hope to get your money on these and
when, if I may ask? The only solution they offer me
is to come to Paris and spend the money, or invest
it there in something, which I do not want to do
yet. Some one suggested that I have a dealer buy me
French paintings which I might sell over here at a
profit—but that's complicated too. So do let me
know, if you have any ideas. . . .

   Incidentally, regarding the money due me from
Paris—almost $40,000.00 at the present legal rate of
exchange, and accumulating rapidly with all the
new editions being put out—do you suppose that
any American banker would take up my credit and
dole me out a decent sum at intervals over a period
of two or three years? That to me seems the only
way out at the moment. Please keep confidential the
amount involved, won't you.

   I think that's all for the moment.

                                               Yours,
                                               HENRY

/ • /

Dr. Hoffman: Michael Hoffman, HM's very able literary agent in Paris, would end up handling all his foreign rights, representing ND in Europe, and becoming a good friend of all concerned. "Hoffman became one of the most important and successful agents for handling American books in France" (GW interview of JL, June 16–18, 1992).

Albertine Scarlet: American bookseller in Paris, stocked ND books in her bilingual bookstore near the Café des Deux Magots.

57. TLS-2

7/19/46
Big Sur

DEAR J. L.:

. . . Why don't we act therefore as if you had all you wish, let your agents handle these foreign matters, and thus be free of worry and trouble and further discussion? As I have repeatedly said, the main thing is to place the books in foreign lands. I said once, and I mean it, that whatever any one demands in the way of money I am willing to agree to—I want everyone to feel happy and satisfied. Let's all get rich together. . . . My whole desire is to get out from under all the dither and bother which each new offer from a publisher abroad entails. So let Pfeffer and your other agents deal with these publishers for *you* and I'll deal with you. That seems the simplest, easiest way out. . . .

About Ezra. I doubt that Big Sur would be the place. First off, there is nothing to buy or rent around here. Second, it's too small a place; word would get round instantly and he would be pestered and perhaps further humiliated. It must be a horrible problem for him to find a suitable place to live now in America. I should think he would be much better off in some remote corner of the world—at least for a few years. A place like Ibiza, for instance, or Bali. . . .

HENRY

/ • /

Pfeffer: Max Pfeffer, JL's agent for European publications at this time. The arrangement outlined in this letter ultimately proved unsatisfactory to both HM and ND, and both placed their foreign affairs in the capable hands of Michael Hoffman.

About Ezra: Pound may have hoped to be free to live where he chose in 1946, but he was destined to spend the next twelve years in St. Elizabeths Hospital in Washington, D.C., having been judged mentally unfit to stand trial for treason.

58. Telegram

September 3, 1946
Carmel, California

JAMES LAUGHLIN

WOULD YOU TAKE CHANCE ON RECEIVING COMPLETE SCRIPT FOR NIGHTMARE SOON AND ADVANCE ME NOW TWO HUNDRED AND FIFTY OR MORE ON IT? NEED MONEY DESPERATELY FOR MATERIALS TO COMPLETE HOUSE BEFORE RAINS SET IN. I WONT LET YOU DOWN EVEN IF IT IS NECESSARY TO RETURN LOAN IN CASH. EXPECT HUGE CHECK FROM PARIS MOMENTARILY.

HENRY MILLER

/ • /

ADVANCE: JL promptly responded by sending money, and Lepska wrote soon after: "Henry is still away in San Francisco, trying to raise more liquid cash—and cannot thank you himself for your very swift and generous response to our need. May I thank you warmly for him and for myself."

59. TLS-1   Sept. 29, 1946
                                 Big Sur

DEAR J. L.

. . . According to a recent letter from Girodias, the trial against the *Tropics* and *Black Spring* (!) will come up six months hence. He expects imprisonment, but is not worried about it. Myself, I think it will do a lot of good—clear the air there and over here too, perhaps. I am not disturbed about it.

The only man beside Cossery I think you might enjoy looking up is my old friend Hans Reichel, the water colorist. If you don't know his work you may enjoy seeing them. Find out if he is desperate, because I would help him if I can. I take it you will see Raymond Queneau at Gallimard's. I do hope you can take one of his books for translation. Am curious to know what you think Paris looks like today, and how you think it would feel to live there now under present conditions. . . .

Oh yes, perhaps Girodias has some precious note books which he has not yet mailed me—things I left in his father's safe. If you could bring them with you, even if only two or three, it would be a great help and lessen the risk of loss in transit, which I fear.

And why don't you stop in at Galignani's bookshop, rue de Rivoli—see when and if you can put your N.D. books in their window. They sell a great many of my books and are happy about it, apparently.

                                 Yours,
                                 HENRY

/ • /

Cossery: Albert Cossery (1913–), Egyptian-born French writer whose cause HM took up. His collection of short stories, *Men God Forgot,* was published by George Leite in Circle Editions in 1946; when it was remaindered, HM bought up much of the stock and tried for years to sell copies. ND later published two of Cossery's novels, *The House of Certain Death* (1949) and *The Lazy Ones* (1952).

Hans Reichel: The subject of HM's essay, "The Cosmological Eye."

60. CC-1   December 22, 1946
                                             Sandy, Utah

DEAR HENRY—

I certainly enjoyed seeing you down there the other day. I think you have got yourself an absolutely marvelous wife. I don't know when I have been so impressed with a personality. She seems perfect for you, and you might say that the beautiful little dutch doll baby is an attestion of the fact.

I have been reading through the manuscript of *Remember to Remember* with greatest pleasure. You really do have a wonderful style. And now the overall architecture of your philosophy begins to shape up before me. For a long time there were many parts that I could not join together, but some of these essays fill in the joints. I think this is particularly true of "Obscenity and the Law of Reflection," and I think it's most important that this be included in the book. Shall I put it in any particular place? . . .

We had a fine visit with Varda after leaving you, and also a funny time with the Rexroths. I wish you'd write about him sometime—somewhat in the manner of "Jabberwhorl." He probably doesn't appeal to you much because he doesn't have the inner calm and light. He's all bitter edges. But a fabulous mind. Packed with the damndest stuff.

I shall enclose a contract for you on the *R. to R.* Please note that I have boosted the starting royalty up to a straight 15%. I believe you have this coming to you because your initial sales are now fairly well assured. . . .

Please tell Cousin Jean I was sorry not to get a chance to know her a little bit. Hope to get back sometime. She certainly is not like most of the people in our family—to her great credit. Most of them can't bend their necks.

Merry Christmas,

/ • /

Rexroths: Kenneth Rexroth (1905–1982) and his wife. See *Kenneth Rexroth and James Laughlin: Selected Letters* (W. W. Norton, 1991) for a chronicle of the friendship between the writer and publisher that lasted almost fifty years. In 1987, JL reminisced: "Back in the forties when I was trying with utter ineptitude to run the Alta Ski Lodge in Utah . . . it was a relief to drive down to San Francisco to visit with Kenneth Rexroth. Kenneth was the best talker I've ever heard next to Pound. . . ." (Reprinted in *Random Essays: Recollections of a Publisher* [Moyer Bell, 1989], p. 51).

"Jabberwhorl": "Jabberwhorl Cronstadt," the parody of Walter Lowenfels's speech in *Black Spring.*

Cousin Jean: Jean Wharton, a neighbor and good friend of the Millers. In his book on Big Sur, HM describes her as a spiritual person with great healing powers. Feeling that the Millers' need was greater than hers, she offered them her house on Partington Ridge, which became their permanent home in Big Sur in January 1947.

/ • /

61. TLS-2   New Year's Day [1947]
                                         Big Sur

DEAR J. L.:

. . . It's good of you to give me the 15% straight
off. Thank you. As I tried to tell you when you were
here, I really feel secure now—inwardly, at least—
and am not worried about material things any
longer. Girodias wrote since saying he would send a
very substantial sum, and if he does I will be entirely
free of debt; the house is paid in full anyway, and all
I worry about now (God help us!) is the Income
Tax. That means I am at last a "moneyed" man. . . .

Well, all the best for the New Year! And to your
wife too, whom I liked, even if she had it in for me
or my books.

                                         HENRY

62. TLS-1   May 14th [1947]
                                         Big Sur

DEAR J. L.:

. . . Every book dealer I meet now or hear from
by letter informs me there is a renewed demand for
my books—I suppose as a result of the *Harper's*
write-up and the *Examiner* campaign too. I should
think you would have no trouble in getting rid of a
first edition of 5,000 for the coming book. The situation in Paris grows better and better. That Anti-
Vice League (Daniel Parker and cohorts) seem to be
soft-pedalling the trial, trying to back out of it, from
all reports. Largely because of the strong member-
ship in the Comité de Défense d'Henri Miller, which

André Gide recently joined. Seems Gide had never read me, then was shown a copy of *Printemps Noir,* read only a few pages, and made up his mind at once to come to the defense. . . .

HENRY MILLER

/ • /

Harper's write-up: "The New Cult of Sex and Anarchy" by Millicent Edie Brady, published in *Harper's* magazine (April 1947), a disparaging account of HM's role in the bohemian community at Big Sur.

Examiner campaign: Prompted by the article in *Harper's,* the *San Francisco Examiner* took up the criticism of HM and the "cults" at Big Sur.

Daniel Parker: A French citizen who had obtained a ruling against the *Tropics* and *Black Spring* in France, only to provoke a strong reaction among French intellectuals.

the Comité de Défense d'Henri Miller: The committee included such prominent writers as Jean-Paul Sartre, Albert Camus, and André Breton. HM enjoyed his role as hero of a cause célèbre and later proposed to Maurice Girodias that he publish a history of *l'affaire Miller,* including the enormous file of newspaper articles written in his defense.

André Gide: (1869–1951), French writer. His support carried particular weight in 1947, the year he won the Nobel Prize.

63. ALS-2   8/20/47
Big Sur

DEAR J. L. —

The reason I asked you to send me the semi-annual royalties payment before September if possible was because I am trying to get my old friend Moricand here from Switzerland. He now has his visitor's visa for America—since two months—and is waiting for me to send him the passage money and a bit of cash for traveling expenses. I am expecting to hear from Girodias any day—as he is supposed to try to purchase the tickets for Moricand in Paris out of my French account. But I can not bank on him. By the end of this month Moricand will be flat broke and if he has to linger on I will have to send him money anyway.

What I would suggest is this—that *you* send him $500.00 out of what's coming to me (if there *is* that much due me) by cable or by airmail. . . . I hope you can do it. It would mean a great deal to me.

HENRY

/ • /

Moricand: Conrad Moricand, an astrologer and occultist HM had frequently consulted in Paris in the 1930s. JL sent $500, and Moricand arrived in Big Sur by the end of the year, but soon proved to be an impossible houseguest and a great burden on the Miller household. He thus provided HM with the material for his "Paradise Lost," Part 3 of *Big Sur and the Oranges of Hieronymus Bosch* (ND, 1957).

64. ALS-1   9/18/47
                                                Big Sur

DEAR J. L.—

. . . Have just read, *in German,* Hesse's *Siddartha*—and am profoundly impressed by it. Cannot find out if it has been translated into English ever—doubt it very much.

If you are interested, let me know. Otherwise, I'll recommend it for translation to Kurt Wolff of Pantheon Books, N.Y. Seems like a find to me. . . .

HENRY MILLER

65. TLS-2   Feb. 6, 1948
                                               Big Sur

DEAR J. L.:

   . . . I'm now at page 1100 of the *R.C.* I believe I could write 3,000 pages as easily as 2,000 now. Once you pass a certain point there is no limit. When this book comes out it will be like dropping an atom bomb on the literary world. I only hope I will live to complete it. I am exhausted. Have too much to do; lucky if I can get in two to three hours writing a day. What I need is a secretary who owns a car, who could do my dirty work (correspondence, etc.), take care of the child occasionally, run to town with us when necessary, etc. But where will I find such a person—especially with no compensation in sight? Big Sur is marvelous but the hardest place to work in I have known.

   . . . From what you say about the slow sales of my books in America, the expense of keeping them in print, I should think it might be wise to let them die out altogether. I had always hoped I might have a steady income from them but perhaps I am too optimistic. On the other hand, the rising interest in Europe should have some effect here, don't you think? Do you realize that with all the hullabaloo in France scarcely anything has crept into our papers or literary reviews? Almost seems like a conspiracy of silence. That is why I think it would be a good idea to make a book of the *"affaire Miller"* and give the body of serious reviews, which are really something! in translation. You don't need to issue this at a loss—you could sell them, after distributing a couple of hundred to the press. More in the next.

                                HENRY MILLER

/ • /

the R.C.: The Rosy Crucifixion, the trilogy on which HM worked off and on through the 1940s and 1950s.

66. A L S - 2   2/8/48
                                                       Big Sur

D E A R J . L . —

Since writing you at length this morning have had an idea I've long wanted to propose to you. (Result of spending several long days writing letters— mostly to raise money.)

The bulk of my current expenses goes to our mailman who, as you know, delivers us most every-thing—food, drug supplies, hardware, kerosene, stamps (a big item), etc. We spend practically noth-ing for clothes or entertainment, being virtual pris-oners here, without a car.

This monthly bill averages a good $150.00—and it's rare that I have this sum when he presents the bill. Usually I go thru agonies the whole month try-ing to eke out this ridiculous sum. I depend a great deal on sales of water colors—and windfalls.

But I am getting weary of this daily struggle to keep my head above water. My situation would be tremendously eased if I knew for certain I would have the first of each month the $150.00 for current expenses. It would solve my problem. I own the house & grounds free & clear now, my taxes are almost nil. My only other worry is income tax— which I manage to pay at end of year one way or another.

Monies coming from France I use to wipe out old debts—all personal ones and payable at my conve-nience. As you probably know, I have helped quite a few people in the last few years—materially as well as morally. I have done this at great sacrifice, always raising the cash at the last minute by painful effort.

To cut it short, here is what I propose—let me know as soon as convenient if it is possible to acquiesce. Instead of paying me my royalties twice a year, pay me this sum of $150.00 monthly. I believe my earnings about cover that now—I mean from N.D. books. With foreign publications increasing, there ought to be little risk in it for you. All the proceeds from abroad are cleared thru you—you have the control. (And I think you will admit I made a liberal arrangement with you on this division of spoils.)

Naturally I don't mean that the $150.00 a month should be in lieu of what I earn, but drawn from my earnings. If at the end of the year I owe you money, under this arrangement, I will pay you the deficit— or you can discontinue the arrangement and deduct what is owing you from the following semi-annual payment of royalties. If there is something coming to me over & above the $1800.00, you can pay me whatever it is in a lump sum. Does this seem equitable and reasonable?

Somehow I feel I ought not to be harassed any more by these petty difficulties. It drains my energies, and I haven't a superabundance. To finish the magnum opus is a herculean task in itself. And I do a hundred other things besides.

Well enough. I wait to hear from you.

HENRY MILLER

/ • /

$150.00 a month: JL agreed to this scheme, and hereafter ND sent a monthly check varying in amount from year to year as HM's royalties rose and fell.

67. CC-2   November 17, 1948
                                                 [New York]

DEAR HENRY:

. . . That Polish chap was in here to see me the
other day, and he told me something I had not
known—that at that famous conference in Warsaw,
the Russian delegate had singled you out, along with
T. S. Eliot, Dos Passos, and O'Neill, as being one
of the most menacing of the hyenas of Western literature. How funny. But I suppose that means we
won't be able to publish you at all in any of the Iron
Curtain countries. . . .

                                        With best wishes,
                                        JAMES LAUGHLIN

                        / · /

hyenas: HM answered: "If Dos Passos and O'Neill and Eliot are hyenas, then I'm a praying mantis! What ridiculous stuff this is. Stalin
will meet his Waterloo in France, is my guess. A Waterloo without
a battle."

68. PCS   12/3/48
                                                 [Big Sur]

DEAR J.L.

Thanks for the December check. May Allah protect you in all your enterprises. Seriously—I am
truly grateful for what you did this past year. It was
a godsend to us.

                                        HENRY

69. CC-1   August 25, 1949

DEAR HENRY,

I just wanted to let you know that I had finished reading the French text of *Siddhartha* by Hermann Hesse, and I agree with you that this is a very impressive work which we ought to add to our list if we can obtain a satisfactory translation.

I suppose the Semanticists would throw up their hands in horror at the confusion of philosophical terminology and that our sophisticated friends over at the *Partisan Review* would consider the book very corny and sentimental. Nevertheless, I find it profoundly moving and I think that a great many other people would do so as well.

Now who do you think we could get to make us a good English translation? It seems to me that it has to be done by someone who is definitely in sympathy with the subject matter and who also has a gift for a kind of a simplified quasi-biblical prose. Would there be any chance that you would be able to undertake the work yourself? I know how busy you are, but on the other hand, I really think the book has to be done by somebody who cares about it, and I think it ought to be done out of the original German rather than at second hand from the French text which I have. I think too that if the book were translated by you, it would attract a great many of your regular following who would be sure to buy it, since the fact that you had translated it would be such an indication of your enthusiasm for it.

Meanwhile, I shall be writing Hesse in Switzerland to ask whether by any chance a translation has been made in England which we could get a hold

of, but I think I would have heard of it, if one had
been made.

> Best wishes to you all out there.
> JAMES LAUGHLIN

70. TLS-4

January 9, 1950
[New York]

DEAR HENRY,

. . . Now to get down to the most important
matter of all, which is the question of what book of
yours to do next. I think that we very definitely
ought to get out a new book, because of the way the
sales on the back list have been falling off. After all,
we have got to do something to keep up some reve-
nue for you.

The list of selections which you suggested in your
letter of September 13th, namely: "The Waters
Reglitterized," "The Smile at the Foot of the Ladder," "Maurizius Forever," the piece on Patchen,
and "Mara-Marignan," sounds like a good start, but
I think we ought to put something in there which
would really bring the customers in. What about
some selections from *The Rosy Crucifixion*? [John]
Slocum very kindly brought me over a copy from
Paris, but almost immediately Huntington Cairns
borrowed it from me, and he has now given it to
Arthur Krock. I am trying to get it back from him,
but it doesn't come in.

I think that we have really got to put something
forward which will be a shot in the arm, not just
another selection of odds and ends. The Miller market is slipping a little bit, and we have got to reglam-
ourize it somewhat. How about a book made up of

the pieces you enumerate, with good strong narrative bits from the Paris books interspersed? I should think that might do the trick.

I know that you will be anxious to know what we can do for you this coming year in the way of continued regular monthly payments, and so I shall try to figure up your accounts next week, as soon as I have received the figures from the inventory. Meanwhile, I am enclosing a check for $75 for January 1st. This is just a very crude guess at what the 1950 rate might be. It is based on the rather disappointing showing of the back books during recent months. If we were able to go ahead with a good strong new book, such as I outlined, or some stronger suggestion of yours, we could of course do better than this rate, by including the advance in the monthly payments. . . .

With best wishes to you all out there,
JL

/ • /

The list of selections: Three of the pieces listed had already appeared as separate publications, and "The Waters Reglitterized" would also be published as a pamphlet in 1950. "Mara-Marignan" was one of the two narratives that made up *Quiet Days in Clichy,* written in 1940 for a dealer in erotica but not published until 1956.

The Rosy Crucifixion: The first part of the trilogy, *Sexus,* had just been published by the Obelisk Press in Paris.

Arthur Krock: A highly respected conservative journalist, Washington bureau chief and columnist for the *New York Times.*

71. TLS-1   2/20/50
                                                  [Big Sur]

DEAR J. L.:

. . . I said other day I might have good news.
Here it is . . . Some months ago, when he was here,
Larry Powell put a bug in my head. Asked me why
I didn't write a book about books—my personal
experience with them. It lodged. Jan. 17th I sat
down to do a small book between times. By Feb.
17th I had written 114 pages. And it is still going
strong. . . . Can't say how much I will write, but
know I will go on till I finish—and without break.

The idea is to include an Appendix at end, listing
every book I can recall ever reading—and a smaller
list of those I intend to read some day. . . . I do not
remember ever seeing such a complete list of what
any well-known author has read in his lifetime. Do
you? I think "readers" would enjoy thumbing such
a list. I know I would in the case of my favorite
authors. I now have recalled over a thousand. Doubt
if it will run to more than 2,000—if that many.
Many are "lost" forever!

You will see, in reading script, that I made an
excursus on an old favorite I recently dug up from
memory and reread—*She* by Rider Haggard. . . .

Have two long (deliberately inserted) excursi—
the only ones of this kind there will be!—on Cendrars and Giono—about 20 pages each. The rest is
general, casual, roaming far and wide and full of
"associative memories." This is the deep purpose—
to tie up reading with living. As for me, I am aston-
ished in writing thus far to see what I have discovered about myself, in connection with the books I
have read. You will see. . . .

                                            HENRY

/ · /

Larry Powell: Lawrence Clark Powell, librarian at UCLA, befriended HM when he moved to Los Angeles and established the Henry Miller Collection at the university. *The Books in My Life* is dedicated to him.

Rider Haggard: (1856–1925), Sir Henry. English writer of romantic novels. HM read *She* when he was thirteen or fourteen and was profoundly influenced by its "femme fatale," a figure that later inspired him when he wrote *Tropic of Capricorn* and *The Rosy Crucifixion.*

Giono: Jean Giono (1895–1970), one of HM's favorite French writers.

72. TL-2

March 6, 1950
[New York]

DEAR HENRY,

. . . I am very much interested by the news of the book you are writing about the books you have read. That may be just the thing we are looking for—something to change your luck, and something a little different in vein, which will reawaken interest. Do by all means press onward with it and let me see it when you have it in shape. This encourages me very much indeed. . . .

With very best wishes,
JAMES LAUGHLIN

73. TLS-2

August 9th, 1950
Big Sur

DEAR LAUGHLIN:

Now that I'm approaching page 500 in my book about books I begin to have a different perspective on the work. There is so much more I want to write, and leisurely, over a period of a few years perhaps, that I begin to think it might be better to bring it out in installments, a volume at a time, probably one a year. Assuming that when you read what I've written so far you like the book and wish to bring it out, how many pages do you think each volume should contain—350, 500 or 750? . . .

Perhaps I ought to explain that when I embarked on this book I thought to make it a short one. As I began to receive books (from all quarters), books I had demanded—my old favorites, largely, the thing grew and grew. It is immensely stimulating to reread books which meant something to you in the past, more particularly the distant past. Each old book I read opens new horizons. The basic idea behind all this was to round out, as it were, my autobiographical books. That is, to show the great role which books played in my life, as well as sex and other things. Well, I find that the place which books occupy in my life is much bigger and more important than I originally thought. I am discovering things about myself. Therefore, say I to myself, why curtail the adventure? Why not carry on till exhaustion?

You will see when you read the script how living and reading tie in together—that is what I am striving to point out, at least. And that's why I think it important to give such a book to those who like my work. I have a hunch all book-lovers will find this work interesting, even though they may not agree with my views, my evaluations, etc.

Well, enough, for the moment. I think you have the general idea now.

> All good wishes meanwhile.
> HENRY MILLER

P.S. I open the envelope to add that only at the age of 58 could I have conceived of such a work. A certain feeling of "ripeness," plus a genuine enthusiasm for my subject, goads me on.

74. TL-1

August 16, 1950
[New York]

DEAR HENRY,

. . . I think that I agree with you about the advisability of bringing out the book about books in several installments, if it is going to run so long. It seems to me that an enormous big tome might frighten off some readers. So why don't we think and plan about it in that light.

How is it coming along? I don't want to hurry you, but it would be nice to think that we could have another Henry Miller book on our list in 1951.

I am not sure that the excerpt from the book which you sent me for *New Directions* sits too well in that form. It seems to me that this is something which needs space to turn around in.

Do you have perchance any short excerpts from the work in progress, or anything of that kind that you could let me consider? I do definitely want to have something by you in the annual, but I'm not too certain that the book about books excerpts well. . . .

With best wishes,
JAMES LAUGHLIN

/ · /

Do you have perchance: In response, HM sent two passages from Book Two of *The Rosy Crucifixion,* and on September 7, JL wrote again: "I received the two excerpts from *Plexus* safely, and like them very much.

They are excellent. In your best vein, and very stimulating and beautifully written." They were published in *ND 12*.

75. TL-4   April 2, 1951
                                        [Alta, Utah]

DEAR HENRY,

I have now completed my reading of the new
book, and am very much impressed with it. I think
that it might profit by a little cutting here and
there—you have a tendency to repeat yourself, saying the same things in different chapters—but
knowing your methods of work, and reluctance to
rewrite, I hesitate to suggest such a procedure. It
doesn't really matter much anyway, as the book
does not intend to be architectural, and the good
thing about it is the sincerity and genuineness of
feeling. And, of course, the ideas expressed. So
please don't attach any more weight to this criticism
than you want to. . . .

                    With best wishes and many thanks,
                    JAMES LAUGHLIN

                        / · /

tendency to repeat yourself: HM underlined this phrase and wrote in the
margin: "Tell me!"

76. TL-2

April 10, 1951
[Alta]

DEAR HENRY,

Thanks very much for your letter of March 17th which has reached me here in Alta. I am writing right away to say that I don't like the title "The Plains of Abraham" at all. It doesn't seem to me suitable for this book, and rather misleading, and I don't think it would help sales much. "The Quick and the Dead" is certainly much better. Possibly, however, something really "corny" like "The Books in My Life" would be better for reaching the people whom we want to reach. You know, this book is not going to appeal at all to the literary crowd. They are going to scoff their heads off at your approval of writers like Rider Haggard, etc. We might just as well wash our hands of them from the start. If we can just get this book across to a wholly different type of reader—what I would call the non-academic reader—I think it may have a very big influence. That is why I suggest a corny title. What do you think about this line of reasoning? . . .

You will be glad to know that Hesse's *Siddhartha* has gone off to the printer. I didn't have time to work over the translation myself, but I got a highly intelligent girl who is working out here at the lodge to do so, and she fixed it up in fine shape. She was deeply moved by the book herself, and I think we will find this experience repeated pretty widely. . . .

With best wishes, as ever,
JAMES LAUGHLIN

/ • /

"The Books in My Life": Earlier JL had written: "You are always awfully good on titles, and I hope that you will come up with one

that will arouse curiosity." But in this case HM had not succeeded in producing a satisfactory title and, dissatisfied with JL's, continued to "spend sleepless nights" trying to find one he preferred, to no avail.

77. TL-3

May 2, 1951
[Alta]

DEAR HENRY,

. . . I am hoping to get down to San Francisco in about a week or ten days, and if it is agreeable to you, I will come down, bringing the manuscript with me, and we can work over it together at your place. Probably I can find some place to stay there in the neighborhood. We can go over everything carefully together, and in detail, and then rush the manuscript off to England to get it started on its way. . . .

I agree with you entirely about the importance of giving a truthful account of what books really influenced a person. The only thing I was trying to get across to you was that you must expect to take quite a rapping from the magazines like the *Hudson [Review]* and the *Partisan [Review]*. But I'm sure I don't care, and I hope you don't. After all, I have never thought of you as a highbrow writer anyway. To my mind, you belong in the great popular tradition of Cervantes, Rabelais and Balzac.

These fellows with the new criticism, in their high-powered little cult around New York and the university towns are only a thing of the moment. The masses will be reading you when they are all forgotten. . . .

I have had a very favorable letter about you from Weybright of the New American Library. He swears up and down that he is determined to go ahead with the project of making up a selection from your works for 25¢ reprint. I am arranging now to borrow copies of the *Tropic* books for him, so that he can see if there are possible selections there. I have made it clear to him that you don't want anything cut. But I am confident that we can find passages which will go as they are, and which stand up well by themselves. If we can put this across with the New American Library, it will be a tremendous step forward in your situation. As I said above, I am convinced that you are really a "popular" writer and could have thousands of readers if we could only reach them some way. The plain fact is that there are thousands of what I would call "natural" readers all over the country who never go near a bookstore. . . .

Well, enough of this for now, and I will hope to be seeing you soon.

> With best wishes,
> JAMES LAUGHLIN

/ • /

Weybright: For over a year JL had been after Victor Weybright and others at New American Library to publish a selection from the works of HM and had even made very specific recommendations on what works might be included, but it would be another four years before NAL published *Nights of Love and Laughter.*

78. ALS-2   5/10/51
                                               [Big Sur]

DEAR J.L.—

Sorry to hear you are going to the hospital. Also very sorry to tell you this—that I'd much rather you didn't come down to see me. Has nothing whatever to do with *you*, I hope you understand. I'm in a bad mood, a bad situation, and I don't want to see any one. I think every thing to be discussed is virtually taken care of. . . .

Please don't be offended by my request not to come. I can't explain further now. And I *was* looking forward to seeing you.

As ever,
HENRY

79. TLS-1

May 12th [1951]
Alta, Utah

DEAR HENRY—

Just got your letter about not coming to Big Sur. I understand what you mean. I am a moody person myself and often don't feel up to seeing people, even good friends. It's quite all right.

But I don't see how we can get the book in shape without a meeting. In putting the index in shape the girl found a great number of lacunae which nobody can fill in but you, and you will probably need your books at hand to answer the questions.

Would it be easier for you to meet somewhere else, say perhaps at Powell's library in LA where we could chase down the missing titles? I really don't see how the queries could be answered by mail. . . .

I'll probably be starting for San Francisco early in the week so you can write me care of Marie Rexroth at 3524 Clay St. I will be driving down the coast road anyway—have to see Kenner in Santa Barbara—so we could meet anywhere.

Best luck,
JL

/ • /

Kenner: Hugh Kenner, author of *The Poetry of Ezra Pound* (ND, 1951)
and *Wyndham Lewis* (ND, 1954).

80. PCS   5/15/51
                                                [Big Sur]

DEAR J. L. —

O.K. Come anyway—it will be all right. I may
be out (in Monterey) Thursday of this week. Otherwise I'll be home.

                                        HENRY

81. TL-3   December 5, 1951

DEAR HENRY,

. . . You may recall my telling you that I was
going to pick up some overstock of *Sunday After the
War* and *Wisdom of the Heart* from an English publisher, who was remaindering them in London. I did
this, but the other day when the books arrived in the
Port of New York they were seized by our Customs
as "obscene." We have protested this, of course, and
they are holding the books and will get a ruling on
it from Washington. Actually, I think this is just a
case of mistaken identity. Or perhaps a precaution
on their part. They doubtless have your name down
on their black list for the Paris books, and no one in
the Port has authority to distinguish that *Wisdom* is
harmless. If, on the other hand, Washington should
rule that this book is objectionable, this would
please me very much, as it would give us an oppor-

tunity to fight a case which we could surely
win. . . .

> With best wishes, as ever,
> JAMES LAUGHLIN

82. ALS-3

DEAR J. L.—

. . . I hope Weybright comes through with a contract and a decent-sized advance. I can use that
money to advantage. Have to add another wing to
this place—for the children and a "domestic." Lepska and I separated recently. I am keeping the children. That is what set me back the last few months.
Only getting back to normal now.

> Yours ever.
> HENRY MILLER

/ • /

the children: Valentine, 6, and Tony, 3.

83. ALS-1

DEAR HENRY—

I was so sorry to hear about Lepska. That's awful.
She seemed so wonderful. I can't understand it. But
life is full of puzzles. Glad you are able to keep the
kids. They will be company for you and you can
educate them. I miss mine a lot.

Will answer business matters soon on the machine, but just wanted to tell you personally of my sympathy in your difficulty.

As ever,
J L

84. TL-3   March 18, 1952
                                                    New York

DEAR HENRY,

I hope you will forgive me for not writing for such a long time. I have been terribly busy working up plans for the new magazine, *Perspectives USA,* which you may have heard about. It is a very exciting project, and one which I feel can do a lot of good. The work will dovetail very nicely with my New Directions work, and will give me, at last, the feeling that we are getting some readership abroad, which was not possible as things were, because of the dollar shortage. But printing the new magazine abroad, and having the Ford Foundation back of it to subsidize it, it will be possible to sell it in the local currencies, at low prices, so that our writers will really be read over there. . . .

Best wishes, as ever,
JAMES LAUGHLIN

/ • /

Perspectives USA: A quarterly magazine funded by the Ford Foundation with JL as publisher, designed to bring new American writing and ideas to European readers.

85. TLS-2   May 9, 1952
                                               New York

DEAR MR. MILLER,

I will try to answer your several cards at once, but
first wanted to tell you the situation on *Books in My
Life*. I think that when I wrote you last, I mentioned
that they had arrived from Ireland, or rather the
sheets had, in an enormous van, which is the most
ridiculous way of shipping anything like this that
can be imagined. After considerable telephoning,
and considerable added expense, the van was trans-
ported to a special warehouse which could handle
such a monstrosity, and I believe that the Customs
inspectors were "cracking" it open. It will probably
be another week before we can get it unpacked, and
the sheets delivered to the bindery here in New
York. They promise books about three weeks after
they receive the sheets. We are not setting a definite
publication date, however, until everything is
cleared with Customs, but I will let you know what
it is when we are more definite.

I think you realize that the Customs people are
particularly snooty about anything that bears your
name. I went to see two of them yesterday, in an
effort to try to get the duty they are planning to
charge reduced, and they were listing off the titles
of those of your books published only abroad, as if
they had just written a bibliography. Of course they
are just simple men doing a job; they have never
read any of your books. . . .

As for *Perspectives USA,* I will tell you what little
I can. As he bounced around Europe, J noticed, as I
believe others have increasingly in the last few years,
that European intellectuals tended to regard
America as a completely materialistic culture.

Although this is probably true in a larger proportion than in certain European countries, the good writing and good thought that is being published in America did not reach these intellectuals, partially because of currency restrictions, and the fact that the Little Magazines and serious quarterlies are just not known. I think that originally J's idea was to have a reprint magazine entirely, but as the idea grew, and more people became involved in it, it seems that they are actually publishing some completely new stuff. Perhaps the best way to tell you about it is to send you a copy of the prospectus, which J prepared last fall for the Ford Foundation trustees. After the idea was accepted by them, many of the details were changed, but the main idea and the purpose behind it is still the same. . . .

I am sending you, under separate cover, the three copies of *Siddhartha*. Although I was involved with New Directions at the time that it was published, I did not at all know that you had had anything to do with its preparation. This seems to me to be another example of the tremendous number of things J was doing quietly and well without my slightest suspicion. As I try more and more to take over his work, I am increasingly impressed with what an amazing guy he really is. I will probably find many other things I had no knowledge of. Will you have patience with me?

> With best wishes,
> BOB MACG

/ · /

Bob MacG: RM now took over most of the editorial responsibilities at ND and most of the correspondence with HM as JL devoted himself to his work with the Ford Foundation.

86. TLS-1

August 25th, 1952
Big Sur

DEAR BOB MAC GREGOR,

Thought I ought to let you know why I am so feverish about getting my copies of the new book quickly. In the last few days I've written cards by hand to about a hundred friends, asking them to give me their orders, if ordering. I'm getting immediate responses, as I expected. Now I'm having a friend print up these post cards for me, mentioning other titles (other publishers) which are available from here. I have had to do this because I am flat broke and don't know when the next remittance from Europe will be coming, though it will come eventually. These five dollar orders mean a lot to me at the moment.

Since I'm asking you to charge these copies up to me against royalties, at 40[%] off, you might regard this effort of mine as a bit of helpful promotion—consider me as another book dealer, in short, which is what I am for the nonce. If I get to ordering too many, on this basis, why I'll pay cash for the books at 30-day intervals, if obliged to. But I hope you won't find it necessary to exact this of me. . . .

Cordially yours,
HENRY MILLER

87. TLS-2   Sept. 20th, 1952
                                     Big Sur

DEAR BOB MAC GREGOR:

Got your letter of a week or so ago and meanwhile the books came, seventy thus far. Have now
raised order to 100, as I have orders for almost
eighty already and many still to hear from. Excellent
results, from mere post cards, I think. And reactions
to contents excellent too. Believe this book is what
I think, a good seller for you. Besides one that will
make me many new friends. . . .

It hurts me to think that so many copies of the
book went out to reviewers. You'll only get about
fifteen or twenty half-assed reviews out of it all,
wait and see. Laughlin's theory, of course, is that it's
cheaper to send a book and get a brief mention than
to pay for publicity. Maybe true. But I don't believe
any publicity is needed or worthwhile even in most
American newspapers. I don't know of more than
half a dozen fair to middling literary reviews in the
whole country. Every week I get French literary
reviews. Even the poorest of them are far above our
best. And the French buy books. . . .

                              Well, all the best.
                              HENRY MILLER

88. ALS-2   10/12/52
                                     Big Sur

DEAR BOB—

. . . I am getting enthusiastic letters every day—
and orders every day—and amazing *gifts* of one kind

or another (like a movie star?). Now have friends drumming up orders for me. More new names, more work. But it's fun—and especially getting the extra monies—"for a good bottle of wine" or for stamps or for this or that. I think I'm doing more to promote this publication than all the publicity hounds. I don't care what the reviewers may say—I know the readers love it. . . .

Haven't seen a review of book yet. Suppose it's just as well—it's always sad news.

Cheerio!
HENRY MILLER

89. ALS-2   3/20/53
                                                Vienne (Isère)
                                                [France]

DEAR BOB MAC GREGOR—

. . . *All Europe* is alive & enthusiastic about my work. Only America lags. *Q.E.D.* Everywhere I receive a *royal* reception. My name could be Charlot just as well. *And*—these people really know my work—all classes, the wine merchant, the worker, the Communist, the Catholic. What a difference! *The Smile* is coming out in French soon. And Corrêa is dickering with Fraenkel now about the *Hamlet* book. Corrêa is *much* interested in everything I do. . . .

Thanks for work on *Semblance*. What stupid delays! Well, one day—.

As for my trip—it's too full to recount by letter. I enjoy it thoroughly. I can go back now and die in peace. . . .

Best to J.L. wherever he is.

Sincerely,
HENRY MILLER

/ • /

Charlot: French nickname for Charlie Chaplin.

The Smile: HM's *The Smile at the Foot of the Ladder*. First published by
Duell, Sloan & Pearce in 1948, this little book went through a number
of incarnations, including the bilingual edition published by Corrêa in
1953 and the edition published by ND in 1958.

Semblance: In 1945, Bern Porter published *Semblance of a Devoted Past,*
combining a text drawn from HM's letters to Emil Schnellock on the
subject of painting with reproductions of HM watercolors. In 1952,
when Porter quit publishing, the remaining sheets were sent to the
bookseller Frances Steloff with the idea that she and JL would have
them bound and market them. To HM's great frustration, this plan
was never carried out.

90. TLS-2   22 May 1953
                                                        New York

DEAR HENRY,

. . . We all think it is simply wonderful that you
are getting such a reception in Europe. Would that
the same thing could be done here, but perhaps it is
the fate of a genius like you that recognition in your
own country is delayed. Certainly the sale of *The
Books in My Life* here is nothing to encourage you to
return to this country. The volume of course will
sell steadily for years to come I am convinced, but
its total sale in 1952 was only 1201 copies. . . .

I hope that the reception is continuing, that you
are in great good health, and that all goes well.

Yours ever,
BOB

91. ALS-1

DEAR BOB MAC GREGOR—

. . . Both [Michael] Hoffman and I believe it would be more feasible and practical if he acted as agent for all foreign publications. He is thoroly conversant with foreign situation, and is reputed to be the best agent in France. I found him a most loyal, capable, intelligent man, who is taking care of my interests exceedingly well. Many inquiries come in for *several* of my books; it complicates and delays matters when it is divided thus. J.L. is probably very busy now with other matters. For you it's a tangle. All that's involved is a sacrifice of 10% + / − on J.L.'s part—he takes 50% instead of 40 for foreign placements. Please speak to him and see if he agrees. . . .

Sincerely,
HENRY MILLER

/ · /

Hoffman: RM spoke with JL and found him "quite agreeable to allowing Hoffman to handle the foreign rights to the books published by New Directions, provided that all monies received, minus Hoffman's ten percent of course, are paid directly to us, with us in turn paying you. This is evidently necessary, at least as things are going along now, for us to be able to continue to send the $75.00 per month. At present the foreign advances and royalties underwrite this monthly check to a certain extent." (RM to HM, Oct. 7, 1953)

92. ALS-1   Jan. 26th 1954
                                               Big Sur

DEAR BOB MAC GREGOR—

Want to tell you that the case for the *Tropics* books
(fought by Civil Liberties) was defeated a second
time in Court of Appeals, San Francisco, a few
weeks ago. The language of the "decision" was even
more scathing and condemnatory this time than last.
Thought you had better inform Weybright and
Laughlin so that you will be prepared for trouble,
should you and Weybright bring out that collection
of my work this year. You could play safe, of
course, and cut out any offensive passages. . . .

                                    All good wishes.
                                    HENRY MILLER

93. TLS-1   May 7th [1954]
                                               Tokyo, Japan

Dear Henry—

Just a line from Tokyo, a strange and fascinating
place, as I thought you would like to know that
your Paris books are all over town and seeming to
be very popular. *Black Spring,* both *Tropics* and two
volumes of *Sexus,* retailing at price around two to
four dollars. Put out by a firm called Kemeisha,
apparently offset from the Paris volumes, and I hope
they pay you.

I'm sorry not to have written for so long. This
job I have is very time and energy consuming. At
times I get fed up with the restrictions they impose
on me editorially, but I think we are doing some
good, and at least I have seen the world. Had

another month in India, the most marvelous country, and then all over South East Asia.

I hope that Bob is taking good care of you and that all goes well.

Best wishes,
J L

94. ALS-1

2/8/55
[Big Sur]

DEAR JAMES LAUGHLIN—

Huntington Cairns will be visiting us in a few days. I am going to speak to him about *Plexus*— whether, if the two or three offending pages were cut, he thinks it might safely be published here. If you have a copy of the book, would you please look it over in your spare time and tell me what you think—i.e. if *you* would care to publish it, properly cut. (I don't want to cut words and phrases here and there—just those pages dealing with Ulric and his former school-teacher—somewhere along the middle of the book.)

You don't need to feel *obliged* to bring the book out. I'm writing to you first because you are entitled to first choice. . . .

Hoffman (Paris) is engaged in a long-winded arbitration proceedings with Hachette over a few million francs they are trying to do me out of. Money is tight. I hope I don't owe N.D. anything when the year's reckoning is made out!

Don't know where you are at the moment—hope this finds you in good time and in good shape.

Sincerely,
H e n r y

/ · /

Ulric: Character based on Emil Schnellock, HM's boyhood friend and longtime correspondent, recipient of the *Letters to Emil* (ND, 1989).

95. TLS–1

March 15th, 1955
Big Sur

D EAR J AMES L AUGHLIN,

About *Plexus*⟨. . . .⟩I don't altogether like the idea of a limited, expensive edition, castrated. My only thought in bringing it out with expurgations was to enjoy a good sale. I forgot to tell you that when our friend from Washington was here and I discussed the situation with him, he gave me to understand that the Post Office authorities are still difficult and very much opposed to *me,* the head man being a bigoted Catholic and reactionary. He added that it was a mistake, in his opinion, to ever let the banned books come to trial in this country—because there was no hope of ever getting a fair trial.

If all this be true, I would not only have to delete long passages (several pages) but words and phrases here and there, since the book is already on the list of banned books and it would be combed through thoroughly by the officials. To do this, I mean, give the book a thorough pruning, goes against the grain. I am not even sure, knowing these birds, that removing the offending passages, etc. would be sufficient. They might still find the tone of the book, or its purpose, "immoral." I don't trust them!

I write this after sober reflection. Perhaps I was too hasty, too optimistic in writing you about it. Let it rest a while.

As for the *Colossus,* yes, nothing would please me more than to see it come out in an inexpensive edition. It ought to be a pocket book, but apparently I can convince no one of that. There are just two books on my list which have had universal approval—the *Colossus* and the *Smile at the Foot of the Ladder*.

Japan! The books are selling like hot cakes, I hear, but so far no royalties on sales. They'll come eventually, I suppose. I enjoy dealing with the Japanese—they're unpredictable. But they do get things done—and how! . . .

All the best to you. Are you gradually withdrawing from New Directions? Rumor has it that you will give it up soon. Frankly, I don't know how publishers survive these days. Only pocketbooks seem to sell in any quantity—and even that market is glutted, they tell me.

HENRY

96. TL-2   March 31, 1955
                             [Vermont]

DEAR HENRY,

. . . I suppose you are right about *Plexus*. Probably in order to put the book in such shape that we could win a case, if challenged, it would be necessary to cut a good deal of what you consider essential.

I think, however, that we ought to keep our fingers on the pulse, so to speak, of the censorship situation and plan at some future date to try the book when the climate seems right for it. Please, in any case, give us the first opportunity to do so if it becomes a possibility.

I think also that we ought to reconsider the idea

of doing your Rimbaud book at the present time.
Even supposing that Bob is right in his conjecture
that there would be only about 1,000 readers for it,
and I think this may be perhaps unduly pessimistic,
it still seems to me that there would be some way to
price it so that we would come out on top of the
deal with that many readers. . . .

No, there is no truth at all in the rumor you have
heard that I was gradually withdrawing from New
Directions. To be sure, while I have held this temporary job with the subsidiary of the Foundation I
have had little time for other aspects of New Directions than the editorial side, and have been lucky
indeed to have such an outstanding business man as
Bob MacGregor to help me, but the work at Intercultural will be tapering off the end of next year and
I hope then to devote myself almost exclusively to
New Directions. I shall do my best to persuade Bob
to continue along with me and I think that between
the two of us we can come up with some very interesting new plans and ideas for meeting the increasingly difficult problem of marketing the unusual
type of book. So please don't feel for a moment that
we are going to sleep on you. This has been a transi-
tional period—with the paperbacks taking over a lot
of our old readers—but I am sure we can find the
right formula to get into that field in some way
without materially sacrificing quality.

With best wishes,

As ever,
J. LAUGHLIN

/ · /

the work at Intercultural: Intercultural Publications, Inc., established by
the Ford Foundation to publish *Perspectives USA*. JL was both president of the subsidiary and publisher of the magazine.

97. TLS-1 · April 6, 1955
Big Sur

Copy for MacGregor
DEAR JAMES LAUGHLIN,

Sending this to N.Y. office not knowing where exactly to address it. Got your long letter of the 31st and was pleased to read of your intentions. Perlès just had a letter from Neville Spearman, his publisher, who is delighted with the book he has written about me and thinks he will have a success with it. He is eager to publish something of mine there. I wrote him he might get in touch with you about doing the Rimbaud together—as you've done other books—simultaneously, that is. Only, if you do print it over there, please make sure the type is readable, won't you. I think, aside from the high price, the type used in *Books in My Life* has helped to keep sales down. (I am going to try to re-stimulate interest in this book since it's one of the best I ever wrote, in my humble opinion.) Anyway, I do think the Rimbaud book would be worth the venture. . . .

Sexus, Vol. 1., Japanese translation (with all obscene passages in English) has just been seized and suppressed in Tokyo. Good news. The publishers are going to fight the case, they say.

As for *Plexus,* yes, I will keep it open for you, should it ever prove feasible to do it over here. But I grow more and more pessimistic with respect to these books. The climate here is not improving, that's a cinch.

I have just received the six months' royalty statement and see I am in your debt to the tune of $411.70. This marks a new H.M. low! But since I am expecting a good check from France any day now I will send you my check for this balance very soon—unless you have some other suggestion to make. It just hurts me to see that only 39 copies of *Books in My Life* were sold these last six months.

All good wishes to both of you!
HENRY MILLER

/ • /

Perlès . . . book: My Friend Henry Miller (1955).

98. TLS-3   June 18, '55
                                               Big Sur

(Bob MacGregor—please read!)
DEAR JAMES LAUGHLIN:

I have a delicate proposal to make you. If you can't give your assent to it I won't hold it against you. I ask only that you try to put yourself in my place when reading this. Here it is.

A few weeks ago, thinking to revive an ancient unpublished script of about 28 pages (1946—Anderson Creek) called "This Is My Answer," I suddenly found myself writing a *book* about Big Sur. The title (which inspired the bloody thing) is *Big Sur and the Oranges of Hieronymus Bosch*. Thus far I've written almost 200 pages, and may do another 100 or more. I thought it would be a "local" thing, but it's turning out to be a "universal."

I haven't written (a book, at least) for three years. Now I'm passionate again and going strong—flows out like milk. And nothing censorable in it that I can detect. Deals with my life here at Big Sur these past eleven years—the inner and the outer life, the visitors, the letters, the work, the thoughts, plans, etc.

Has four sections: 1.) "The Oranges of the Millen-
nium," in which I talk about Paradise here and now.
2) "Peace and Solitude: a potpourri," in which I go
into my "anecdotal life" here, and that of my
friends, neighbors, freaks, nuts and fans, in free far-
rago. 3.) "Paradise Lost," in which I tell the story of
Conrad Moricand's disastrous stay with me. 4.)
"This Is My Answer." I may add an Appendix for
information of one sort of another. The body of the
book—far outnumbering the pages of the other
parts—is "Peace and Solitude"—which the reader
will discover is anything but.

I *know* the book will appeal to my foreign readers.
And I even venture to believe it will have an appeal
for the American reader. I hope to be finished with
the first draft in a month or so, easily.

Now then—. This time, it seems to me, I have
something which could sell. But, from past experience, I doubt that New Directions is the publisher
to do that. My impression is that nothing you publish ever sells well. Perhaps I am wrong. If so, correct me. But if I'm not mistaken in my judgment,
then I should like to ask if you would consent to
letting me try a few of the other big publishers first.
It may be my chance—my one chance—to rake in
some *dollars*. (What I am earning in royalties from
all the American titles in print is a joke. A hack
writer earns more from one short story than I do in
a year from all these books.)

Despite the flattering overtures which are made
me from time to time by the big publishers, it may
be that even this book, which I think has a wide
appeal, will prove unsuitable for them. In which
case I would offer it to you, should you think it
advantageous to your interests. I would then resign
myself to a restricted sale at home and look to other
parts of the world for a wider outlet—in transla-

tions. And thus, if you didn't profit much from the American sale of the book, you could bank on the income from foreign sales.

Well there it is. I'm being frank and honest with you, but with no thought of arousing your suscepti-bilities. Do let me know what you think. And, if you'd like to see some of the work in progress before coming to a decision, I can send you a sizable number of pages shortly. A matter of getting them retyped, that's all.

With good wishes to you and Bob MacGregor, and with assurances (genuine) that I know you are always doing your best by me, I am

as ever,
HENRY MILLER

99. TLS-2   July 1, 1955
                                            New York

DEAR HENRY MILLER,

. . . I have hesitated, Henry, about making any comment on your letter of June 18th to JL. He is still in India, as you perhaps know, and will not be back until early in August. I am sending a copy of your letter airmail to him, but cannot guarantee that he will get it immediately. His Intercultural Publica-tions office tells me that he has completed his job there, and I expect therefore that he will be starting back, possibly before my most recent letters will have reached him. Of course I have no notion of what his reaction will be; he is sometimes generous toward authors to the point of fault. I can tell you however that he was hurt when Paul Bowles and William Carlos Williams were tempted away by

Random House. Incidentally, Bowles has not done any better there than he did with us, not as well in fact, although he has certainly cheapened his writing and standards to their demand.

Williams' situation would seem to me to be much more similar to yours. JL kept him in print for many years when no one else would publish him, and New Directions published what he wanted whether it was saleable or not, because we believed in his innate and important quality. Random House dangled large advances in front of him, and his wife and others around him made him accept, somewhat against his will I'm sure, because he is also an honorable man. These advances have not been earned I gather, and the good doctor may well end up in a nasty situation there.

Be this as it may, if *Big Sur and the Oranges of Hieronymus Bosch* has a large sales potential in this country you could as well ruin it by moving to another publisher as by staying with New Directions. Your impression that nothing we publish ever sells well is indeed wrong, or I rather doubt if we would still be in business. Your impression is understandable because most of the books you perhaps know about have not done famously, Rexroth's, Patchen's, some of your own, but these books have been paid for by others that have done well: Fitzgerald's *The Crack-Up,* around 70,000; *A Streetcar Named Desire,* over 60,000; Thomas Merton's *Seeds of Contemplation,* around 90,000; *The Collected Poems of Dylan Thomas,* almost 35,000.

You may think that these sales are accidents, that the Thomas for instance would never have sold that way except for a myth that grew up around him and particularly his death. But I can tell you that six months before his collected poems were published and therefore almost a year before his death, we decided that the time was ripe to push Thomas, to build him up as a poet who could reach out far beyond the usual public for poetry. We let loose a publicity campaign that I think no other publisher could surpass. Our releases on Thomas took every form; directed not at the general public but at the newspaper and magazine people. We made use of everything that came to hand and everybody; we even healed breaches within the ranks of the Dylan Thomas followers. Always however, as in a successful campaign of this kind we stayed in the background. Long before Dylan Thomas's death he could have been at the top of any list of poetry Best Sellers if such existed; and something of the Dylan Thomas myth was therefore of our doing. . . .

Please excuse my typing and end-of-the-week tired brain.

Yours ever,
BOB

/ • /

Paul Bowles: (1910–), American novelist. ND published his first novel, *The Sheltering Sky* (1949), and three of his stories in *ND 10, 11,* and *12. The Sheltering Sky* sold 25,000 copies.

100. TL-2   August 1, 1955
[Madras, India]

DEAR HENRY,

This letter will come to you from the New York office, but I am dictating it from Madras, on one of the last days of my fascinating visit here. I have had a marvelous time in India—it is a great country—

and will be sorry to leave, but of course there is much work to be done back in New York. . . .

That is most exciting news about your new book. It sounds absolutely great and I am most eager to see it. Needless to say, as Bob MacGregor has already written you, we are most eager to publish it, and will do everything we possibly can to make it a big success. While I sympathize with the feelings which prompted your letter—it must be very discouraging for you at times to see your books doing so much better in other countries than in your own—I'm sure you will understand that it is necessary for us to have each year a book that is really a good seller in order to carry the many others we undertake which do not have a large sale. I have every hope that your new one will be our big sales leader for 1956.

I think that Bob has given you a rundown on some of the fine sales figures which we have achieved in recent years. There is no question that we have the machinery and the outlet to do a good job if we just get a break on the reviews and word-of-mouth publicity. If we can just get your new book into the hands of a new group of reviewers—not the old bunch of sour-pusses who seem to suffer from perpetual jaundice—I am sure that all will go well. I think a good deal can be done along this line by personal contact work with the people who assign books for review in the major media, a job at which Bob is very good.

I think too the time is ripe to get out a new special circular about you for bookstore use which will have some provocative quotations both from the new book itself and from things that people have said about you. Perhaps you have a new photograph or a drawing of yourself done by some artist which would suit for this. . . .

It is really wonderful news that you have this new book coming along and I shall hope to have a look at it as soon as you have some of it ready.

With best wishes,

As ever,

J. LAUGHLIN

P.S. What would you think of our experimenting with a special Indian edition of some of your characteristic essays and pieces? . . .

101. TLS-1   8/7/55
Big Sur

(copy to Bob Mac Gregor)
DEAR JAMES LAUGHLIN,

Your letter of August 1st, from Madras, carries a sincerity and honesty I can't ignore. Yes, I will send you some of the script as soon as I can get round to recopying. At present I am going ahead with it so fast I have no time for that. Can barely make corrections in off moments. The book is growing—taking me over. I have now almost 400 pages and the end is not in sight. No doubt this, the length, will raise new problems!

As for showing something to an Indian publisher, I am all for it. Have been hoping for something like this for years. And I can send photos, new ones, as well as some more testimonials. There is a letter from Powys to Dante Z. in Fred's (Perlès) book which I hope you can use—part of it, at least. The best send-off I ever received—and from the man I most admire, respect and adore.

Yes, Bob Mac Gregor did give me full details about sales and all that. I was surprised and pleased—for you. Revolving the situation in my mind I've come to look at it with more detachment. With regard to most everything now I've adopted an attitude of complete acceptance. Why should I not with regard to my work? I'm not a sacred cow. And it is possible that the vast majority of Americans would not like my work, even if they had access to all the books. I can bide my time. Certainly, the question of getting full material rewards should be the last consideration, considering that in some peculiar and mysterious way I am fully protected, no matter which way the wind blows. I would certainly blush if I thought I had given you the notion that I intended to desert. Asking for a release is another matter. And now I don't even think of that. I am passionate about the book and possibly let my ego run away with me. The important thing is what I put into the book, not what I get out of it.

You will find, when you come to read the script, that there is a generous section on Jean Wharton. It should interest you very much.

I had hoped to be able to make a trip to Japan and India this Fall, but have to put off definite plans till I finish the book. India means so much to me. I wonder sometimes if I shall ever see it. Somehow I feel it must have influenced me in a subtle way.

Don't worry about finding special new reviewers for me and all that personal publicity you feel you ought to go into. Let the book speak for itself. I'm quite reconciled to my fate.

The reason I mention the Powys letter so warmly is because he was the first great literary influence in my life. A lapse of thirty odd years and then I write him—to thank him. Then a hurried visit to his home in Wales—1953. Much correspondence. And, after all the encomiums, his strikes me as the highest and most direct—and it comes from a veteran, from a Britisher, from an octogenarian! Of all the men I've known in my life he is the most alive, the most radiant, the freest. What an achievement! I hope I can follow in his footsteps⟨. . . .⟩

All the best meanwhile.
H. M.

/ • /

Powys: John Cowper Powys (1872–1963), Welsh writer HM had admired since his early twenties when he heard Powys lecture at the Labor Temple in New York. HM discusses Powys in *The Books in My Life.*

Dante Z.: Dante T. Zaccagnini, American fan of HM who had written to Powys and elicited the apologia for HM that appeared in Perlès's biography.

102. TLS-2   October 7, 1955
New York

DEAR HENRY,

I am sorry not to have answered your good letter of August 26th before this, but there has been such a big sweat of work here around the office, so much stuff accumulated while I was out in India, and great piles of manuscripts to read through.

I have written to John Cowper Powys as enclosed, and hope he will let us use the letter in our circular. It is a corker. . . .

We should be eager, of course, to assist the John Day Company in any way we can, such as mailing lists, with the promotion of the Perlès book. I think it is rather good in a way that it is coming out with another publisher—which will make it look less like an inside job—but anything that helps to build you up in a good way we want to give our support to, and I hope you will pass this word to your contact at the John Day Company, as I don't know anyone there.

It has not been decided yet just what kind of mailing card we might get out for the Rimbaud book because we are still working on the design of the jacket, which, if my plans can be realized, will be quite something. I wanted to hit on something which would be really unique for this, and maybe we have. It now remains to be seen whether technically it can be accomplished without inordinate expense. Roughly, it calls for a cover with holes in it through which your eyes and those of Rimbaud will peer out from a kind of second cover on the end papers. It may be hard for you to visualize it from the description, but I think it will be quite an eye-catcher, if we can get it right. . . .

With best wishes,

As ever,
J L

103. ALS-1   October 31 [1955]
                                          Jones Mill, Pennsylvania

DEAR HENRY—

Just a line to tell you that I am delighted with the Moricand sketch—really wonderful—one of your best portraits. Some magnificent passages of prose in it, and the whole thing moves right along holding one's interest all the way.

Bob is reading the other volume—I'll exchange with him when I return to New York tomorrow.

Best!

J. L .

/ • /

the Moricand sketch: Part 3 of *Big Sur and the Oranges of Hieronymus Bosch* (ND, 1957), recounting the trials and tribulations endured by HM and his family in dealing with Conrad Moricand as a house guest.

104. TLS-1   11/8/55
Big Sur

DEAR JAY AND BOB:

   . . . Things go in waves and cycles—*everything.* In my own life I am extremely aware of these ups and downs. It happens with wives, friends, money, writing, translations, sales, etc. etc. I am now entering once more on a good period. I felt it in my bones when I started the *Big Sur* book—one I had never intended to write!—and since then, from three different sources (occult and astrological) I have received, unsolicited, confirmation of this "good ripe period"; according to these birds, it is to last for a considerable time. Myself, I don't care very much how long it lasts. I'm a "veteran" now, as far as setbacks go. I can weather them. But, if I were reckoning in dollars and cents, I would gamble on myself. I hope this doesn't sound vain and presumptuous—it isn't meant to be. . . .

All the best to you both!

HENRY MILLER

105. TLS-4   12/12/55
                                                Big Sur

DEAR BOB MAC GREGOR:

Thank you for your long, informative letter.
Sorry indeed that you are put to so much trouble.
Seems to me you could use more help in that office!

Now about your proposal for a paperback edition
of the Moricand chapter. I've pondered over your
letter several days, to look at the proposal from
every angle. I must say finally—No! You see, to
begin with, you are asking me to cut out, like a sur-
geon, one of the best and most solidly constructed
parts of my book. And a significant part, too, since
it deals with the "rejection" of this potential paradise
(Big Sur). It's like asking Milton to cut out his Satan
in *Paradise Lost.* The *lost* part serves to point up the
found, don't you see? And then too, to take a chapter
like that and re-write it with the insertions you suggest (lifted from other parts of the book), no, that
goes absolutely against my grain. I don't say that it
could *not* be done! There are writers who can do this
sort of thing, and skilfully, and it is all right. But
not me. Whatever disorder, illogic, irrelevancies,
etc. one may find in my works—and they exist,
viewed objectively—they nevertheless belong and
form an integral part of my books, because they are
always facets of *me.* And my aim, from the beginning, has been to give myself—totally. No evasions,
no compromises, no falsifications. Distortions and
exaggerations, yes! But for aesthetic reasons, to
make the truth more truthful. To put it another
way, I put down what comes to me in the way it is
given. I don't question how it is given or by whom.
I obey, I yield. I know "it" knows better than I. I
am the receiving station. This is my "purity," if you

like. And my credo, as writer. Or—"my watermark."

I don't reproach you for the suggestion, mind
you. I know what you are up against, as publisher.
But—I can not allow these considerations to enter
into my thoughts: they would affect my work, my
approach, my style, my goal. Perhaps I made a mistake in showing you the work before reaching its
final stage. But I had a strong feeling it would be
liked by you both and I thought, from the few hundred pages submitted, you could reach a decision—
yes or no. Actually it is not terrribly important, this
decision. Whatever it may be, it is all right with me.
I can only think of doing what I plan to do, doing it
as I see fit. Then take my chances.

That middle part—"Peace and Solitude"—of
which you read portions only. Yes, it is "diffuse,"
as you say. More than that. As I explained originally, when sending the pages, this part is meant to
convey the sense of turmoil, disturbance, interrup-
tion, chaos, if you like. The preceding part
("Oranges") is calm, almost philosophic, and gives
an over-all picture of the situation here. Then we
dive off the deep end. We get lost. We get annoyed,
irritated, perhaps. And we laugh and we weep and
we shake our heads in perplexity. ("We," the readers, supposedly.) When we come to the end of this
song and dance, we say: "What a life!" Another man
might succeed in giving this effect with less ver-
biage. But I am not that other man. I am dishing it
out as I got it. (As Balzac wrote his whole *Comédie
Humaine,* because if he hadn't vomited it out, he
would have gone mad! All the result of being locked
in the college library and reading those bloody
books!) So, in a way, is it with my life, since I have
been here. What preceded it—the years in New
York, in Paris, etc., were even worse—and they

came out so, in the *Tropics,* in *Black Spring,* in the *Hamlet,* etc. etc. Do you see what I mean?

Now supposing, when I began my career as writer, I had weighed all these (irrelevant) considerations: finding a publisher, being banned, displeasing public taste, telling my own story instead of ⟨that of⟩ some imaginary novelistic hero, waiting ten or fifteen years to be recognized, and so on. Do you think I would ever have written those books? "There is only one man in the world who may possibly print your *Cancer,*" said the Paris agent, when he had read the ms. "That man is Jack Kahane of the Obelisk Press." It was true. And Jack took the book, and then got cold feet, and I waited almost three years before he had the courage to bring it out. You have to think of such things, my dear Bob, because they all form part of the chain that brings us to the present moment.

And now, in two weeks, I shall be 64. I *am* known, at least abroad. And respected there. More than that. And I have never yielded an inch. Am I now, with death upon me, to mock the past, to give heed to publishing considerations? Supposing the book grows that big that it demands two volumes, to be printed simultaneously? Will that give you heart failure—or Jay? Should it? What did Tolstoy's publisher say when Tolstoy handed him *War and Peace?* I wonder. (No, I am not Tolstoy! But does it matter? I'm Henry Miller and I speak for Henry Miller.)

When I spoke of the Moricand chapter as being a thing in itself, I meant that I could visualize ⟨it⟩ coming out as a pocket book—just as it is. I hadn't thought of you as publishing paper-backs. I thought of Signet and those others. But it was only a thought! Actually, I see no reason why it couldn't come out as such, under your imprint, due reference being made to its place in the big book. Years ago I suggested to Jay that he consider bringing out certain texts of mine, embedded in these collections of miscellany, as separate tracts. I proposed that he run off extra printings of certain stories and essays which I felt people would like. My thought was that some people, reading those fragments (finished in themselves) would then demand the books from which they came, or at least want to know what else I had written. Jay turned it down, for what I consider an invalid and short-sighted reason: namely, that it would militate *against* the sale of the books. I am still convinced that he is wrong. And now that the Signet book is out, I have proof in a way, of what I say. I am getting many letters from readers of *N of L.&L.* and of the single stories in the others, asking for the other books. So are the bookstores hereabouts. . . .

Oof! Forgive this long letter. Take it home with you to read. "Read it again, in your spare time," as Mohamed Ali Sarwat once wrote me—I quote his letter in the *Oranges*. What a letter!

And don't let anything I say ruffle you. You don't have to defend yourself, or Jay, or anybody—with me. I accept you, no matter how much we may fail to see eye to eye.

And don't think I am getting ready to die. It's just that I know that every day I hang on is another day of "grace," and I enjoy them more and more, live with them more and more fully, and finally feel utterly justified in having lived my own life the way I led it⟨. . .⟩and why not continue? . . .

Anyway, to relieve any aches or tensions, which I may have caused by this long tirade, do read—if nothing else—the citation, in old French, from Rabelais which you will find in the Perlès book when it comes. And bless ole Sam Putnam for finding it there! It's a passage I copied out into my Paris notebooks years and years ago. It is for the belly— to make it jiggle with laughter.

Yours ever, and warmly,
HENRY MILLER

/ · /

the Moricand chapter: Eventually HM agreed to let the section called "Paradise Lost" in *Big Sur and the Oranges of Hieronymus Bosch* be published separately by Signet as *A Devil in Paradise* (1956).

N of L.&L.: Nights of Love and Laughter, the selection from HM's writings that Signet had been hesitating to publish for years out of fear of being tried on obscenity charges. Kenneth Rexroth wrote the Introduction.

Mohamed Ali Sarwat: Egyptian student in New York City during the early 1920s. He addressed a long, fulsome letter to HM, then employment manager at Western Union, asking to be reinstated as a messenger.

Sam Putnam: (1892–1950), American translator and writer in Paris, editor of *The New Review*.

106. TLS-2

January 17, 1956
[New York]

DEAR HENRY,

Thanks for your good letter of the 13th. I am very sorry to hear about your mother. But it would certainly be fun to see you again, and there are various friends here who are eager to meet you. Speaking of astrology, I think you would enjoy Santha Rama Rau, the Indian writer. She has some wonderful tales to tell about astrology in India. Let me know a little bit ahead when you are coming so that we can set up an evening.

I am extremely pleased, and I know Bob will be pleased too, that you approve the idea of a combination plan for doing the Moricand separately as a pocket book at the same time that the big complete work on Big Sur is brought out. Moricand, as a paperbook, could not fail to get a large number of readers interested in the big book who otherwise would not even hear about it. . . .

Do you have any pieces around in your manuscript box that might be suitable for *Perspectives?* We will be winding up the magazine with Number 16, and I feel very badly about the fact that you have never been included in it. For reasons that I am sure you can understand, we had to go rather cautiously—Foundations are, by nature, like old maids—but I would like to let fly a bit in the last number.

With best wishes,

As ever,
JL

/ · /

your mother: HM had written, "I may have to go to N.Y., as my mother seems to be getting ready to die—of sheer old age, no malady."

107. TLS-1   May 4, 1956
[New York]

DEAR HENRY:

I hope that you and Eve had a good trip back to the coast and that everything is working out harmoniously for you.

It was a great pleasure to see you and Eve while you were here, though I am sorry that your mission was such a sad one. I enjoyed the times when we got together very much and only wish there could have been more of them. Eve certainly is a marvelous cook, and such a wonderful person, I think.

I went down yesterday to see Abe Rattner and got terribly excited about those drawings that he did on his trip with you. They are really extraordinary. I think we must make a big effort to publish them in whatever turns out to be the most effective way.

For the moment I envisage a sort of small portfolio, with as many of the drawings as we can afford to do—that will depend on the cost—reproduced on unbound sheets by collotype or heliogravure or some such process, and then your part of the book printed up as a large-size pamphlet to go in the front of the portfolio.

How does this strike you? I thought that the little introduction you had written was fine. Very fine, in fact. Right on the button. Then perhaps if you felt like doing some little prose poems, suggested by various of the drawings which will actually be used, free reminiscence, as it were, something along the lines of Rimbaud's *Illuminations,* but in your own vein, of course.

How does this appeal to you? I think it can be quite a knockout. The drawings are really marvelous, and such variety in them. Your contribution would make it a rounded and very unusual whole. Abe says that we could use one of his portrait sketches of you as well, which would be all to the good.

With best wishes to you both,
JL

/ · /

Eve: Eve McClure Miller, the sister-in-law of Bezazel Schatz, had been living with HM since April 1, 1952, and had married him on December 31, 1953.

Abe Rattner: (1895–1978), American artist, friend of HM in Paris, accompanied him on part of the trip across the country recounted in *The Air-Conditioned Nightmare,* making sketches to illustrate the text. HM paid tribute to him in "A Bodhisattva Artist," in *Remember to Remember.*

108. TLS-1

7/21/56
Big Sur

DEAR JAY:

. . . I sent Girodias a highly censorable script, which I fear will be suppressed immediately it's out (in English): *Quiet Days in Clichy.* The scripts (two) were lost for over ten years. Turned up miraculously—where I won't say now—and I rewrote. Was written in 1940. Only a hundred pages. May be out this August.

In September that Hebrew edition will come out in Israel, with illustrations by Schatz. Meanwhile I'm waiting to see copies of the Spanish *Colossus* and the German one, and the Italian edition of *Plexus* (Longanesi). Also wonder what happened to the Swiss edition of *Remember to Remember* (Schifferli). Did you ever get a copy of the Guilde du Livre's edition of *Aller Retour New York,* in French—with preface and postface *inédits.* And did you see the French ed. of *Hamlet* (Corrêa)?

Seems like things are at the boil this year.

Meanwhile all the best to you, and forgive my silence.

HENRY

/ • /

Quiet Days in Clichy: Composed of two narratives originally written
in 1940 for a New York dealer in erotica. The 1956 edition was published by Maurice Girodias's Olympia Press in Paris.

109. TL-2   September 17, 1956
                                                     [New York]

DEAR HENRY,

Bob has just shown me the introduction which
you did for Abe Rattner's drawings, and I want to
tell you that I am most enthusiastic and appreciative.
It reads beautifully and will make people think. I
also like the way you have brought out the rare
quality of Abe's personality. I shall really get busy
on this now and push it through. We will write you
in more detail about the plans and financial arrange-
ments when we have been able to study them
through more carefully. I hope that we can find,
possibly in Japan, a printer and a process for doing
the plates both faithfully and economically so that
the thing won't have to be priced out of the range of
the average person. Perhaps the solution may be to
have a limited quantity of signed portfolios on fine
paper for the collectors, followed later by a trade
edition book on ordinary paper at a modest price.

My copy of *Quiet Days in Clichy* came through
from Paris last week and I have already told half-a-
dozen people here about the book and informed
them how they can get it through from Paris before
our friend in Washington lowers the boom on it, as
I am afraid he will have to do. Reading, I was carried
back to the old days in Rapallo when I first read
Tropic of Cancer. It has the same wonderful fresh-

ness, almost a pastoral quality, if that isn't a contradiction in terms. The Brassaï photographs are also very fine. All in all, quite a wallop. . . .

With best wishes,

As ever,
J. Laughlin

/ • /

our friend in Washington: "the censor," Huntington Cairns.

Brassaï: Pseudonym of Gyula Halasz (1899–1984), Hungarian photographer of Paris nightlife. HM accompanied Brassaï on his rounds in the early 1930s and paid tribute to him in "The Eye of Paris," originally published in *Max and the White Phagocytes* and reprinted in *The Wisdom of the Heart* (ND, 1941).

110. TLS-2   September 20, 1956
                               [New York]

Dear Henry,

Thanks for your note of the 13th about the manuscript of your *Colossus*. I am afraid I can't help much. I don't have any recollection of ever having seen a typescript of that one. I think, as you suggest, that we must have worked from the Colt Press first edition. . . .

Generally speaking, unless there is some specific provision in the publishing contract, the author's manuscript remains his property after the printer and publisher are finished with it. It is usually our practice at New Directions to deposit the typescripts with the Harvard Library unless the author requests them back from us. I imagine that there must be several of your typescripts up there at Harvard now.

Should you ever wish to realize some cash from the sale of them, I feel sure that Harvard would release them, since they clearly belong to you. I imagine, however, that they would want the ultimate purchaser to reimburse them for the very handsome slip cases which they have made to protect them.

Unless you have a purchaser lined up, I would suggest that Harvard is a good safe place for them to stay. Their subterranean vaults are bomb-proof, air-conditioned, temperature thermostatically-controlled, and every six minutes Schubert's *Ave Maria* is played over a loudspeaker by Muzak. Properly qualified professors and Ph.D. candidates are allowed to inspect the manuscripts provided that they wear white cotton gloves and do not chew gum. It is all very hygienic and slightly redolent of Grant's Tomb. But you are in good company, as they have almost everything that Henry James ever wrote, the diaries of Emerson, and dozens of others.

As ever,

JL

111. ALS-2   Nov 2nd 1956

DEAR HENRY—

. . . I have given your address to the Indian novelist R. K. Narayan who will be with Stegner at Stanford for 6 weeks. Do see him if you have the strength. He is the best novelist in India and a fine and lovable human being—gentle, humorous, life-loving in the best sense. No fakery. Secluded in India, he knows little of your work but I sense that it might be a deep friendship between you two. I have put him in touch with the Rattners as he is stopping in Michigan. Drop him a card as he is shy.

Best to you both!
JL

/ • /

Stegner: The novelist Wallace Stegner (1909–1993) was director of the creative writing program at Stanford University.

112. TL-2 January 23, 1957

DEAR HENRY,

What a crazy life! I had thought that my work with Intercultural would be winding up about this time, and that then I would be free to concentrate on New Directions, and especially on the various projects which you and I have discussed, but now, all of a sudden, and most unexpectedly, they have asked me to go out to Burma for three months to organize a "Perspective of Burma" supplement to the *Atlantic Monthly*.

It's annoying, but then, of course, Burma is a wonderful place, the heart of Buddhism, and I can't really complain. But I must say I do have a very bad conscience about having procrastinated so much with you on our various projects.

I don't want to let them ride over until my return, so I am going to ask Bob to try to move forward on them with you while I am away. . . .

Do you have any writer contacts in Burma? I'd like so much to meet them if you do, and my address out there will be c/o Ford Foundation, Box 1397, in Rangoon. Actually, we won't be getting to

Rangoon until about the middle of February, as I am making a few short stops in Europe, and then taking a two-weeks holiday in South India, a country which I dearly love.

I hope that things will go well for you and Eve this winter, and that we'll be able to see you again next summer.

As ever,
J. LAUGHLIN

113. TLS-1   February 20, 1957
                                 Rangoon, Burma

DEAR HENRY—

Here we are in the "golden land" of Burma and it appears to be a most attractive place. The people are extremely witty and affable, and they have figured out how to enjoy life, perhaps thanks to Buddhism, and perhaps just because they are smart and not overpopulated. Nothing gets done today that could possibly get done next week and everybody has a fine time about it.

We had ten days in India and it was wonderful as ever. Entirely different temperament from the Burmans, everything very go ahead, five year plans, etc etc.

I talked with Mr Mehra of Rupa & Co in Calcutta, who distribute for us in India. He is a great admirer of your work and has read quite a few of the books. He says he can't sell many in India because the prices are just too high, but I think he is rather eager to become a publisher himself, and if you could work up a little 128-page selection for

him, by printing it right there he could retail it at
Rs. 1/8 or Rs. 2, and sell quite a few, I think.

How does this strike you? I don't see what you
can lose by it, and it might start something going
that would end up big for you. India is so calvinist
(influence of Gandhi), they have prohibition most
places, etc, etc, that I don't think the Paris books
could ever be done there, but certainly the others
could if interest were built up.

If you like this idea, please give some suggestions
on the make-up of such a little book, essays drawn
from the older books that deal with Indian or mysti-
cal subjects and related topics. . . .

Hope you are all thriving.

As ever,
JL

---

114. ALS-1   3/3/57
                                                      [Big Sur]

DEAR JAY L.

. . . Are you quite certain the Indians want the
very "serious" stuff? Don't they get too much of
that chez eux? . . .

Envy you so much, your being in Burma of all
places! Expect confidently to get there before too
long. India too of course. *And* Java!

All the best meanwhile. Thanks for *Justine* (Durrell). Magnificent writing. Too bad you lost out on
American edition.

HENRY

115. ALS-1   May 2nd '57
                                                Big Sur

DEAR BOB—

   I've been wondering—would it be possible for
you to allow me more than the usual number of
author's copies (Big Sur book) this time? I have to
give away a slew of them, because it's a *local* book.
Could you look at it this way—every one you give
me is as good as a "review" copy in pulling power.
(That is, if you consider jerk 3rd rate newspapers
who print a tiny few lines.)
   I won't press the point. . . .

                                                In haste.
                                                HENRY

116. TLS-1   May 15th [1957]
                                                Big Sur

DEAR BOB:

   . . . The people I wanted free copies for are a
mixed group, not all writers. I was approaching it
from another angle, not of getting even minor
reviews but of spreading the word by word of
mouth. Many of the people to whom I've given gift
copies in the past have brought me untold luck—
orders, gifts, new friends, etc. It's intangible, unde-
finable, not something to put in a ledger. You may
not agree with me; I know it works. But it's imposing on your kindness to ask it. Do whatever you
think fit. If you agree, send me 20 extra ones and I'll
mail them out. . . .

Your query about Watts—Zen—is one I've asked myself too. He's quite a wonderful chap, very easy, natural, understanding, and has a marvelous lucidity. His new book on Zen is excellent. But he works like a dog, and that's not Zen. Work is a sin. And I'm a great sinner too. . . .

Well, carry on!
H ENRY M ILLER

/ • /

Watts: Alan Watts (1915–1973), English-born philosopher and author of books on Oriental thought. In two previous letters RM wrote that he had attended lectures on Zen Buddhism given by "your friend Alan Watts" and wondered if Watts, who seemed very anxious, was able to practice Zen himself.

117. TLS-1   October 13th, 1957
                                            Big Sur

D EAR B OB:

I can't tell you how amazed I was to get your letter with the changes and deletions suggested by Heinemann for *Big Sur and the Oranges. C'est écoeurant,* as Céline would say. If it were not for the details you give me regarding Frere's and Warburg's fight against the English censors, I would be inclined to say "to hell with an English edition." It's precisely because the corrections suggested are *trifles* that I am enraged. All this nonsense about swine instead of bugger, bastard instead of prick, and stuff instead of fuck . . . and "paraffin lamps" instead of Aladdin lamps—ye gods! Can't stand the truth even about a lamp! Well, it's a bloody, bleeding mess, and it makes me despise the English still more.

I'll go along with them this time, mostly for your sake—I realize they must be warm friends of yours—but never again. . . .

Sincerely,
HENRY MILLER

/ • /

Céline: Louis-Ferdinand Céline (1894–1961), French writer. His first novel, *Voyage au bout de la nuit* (1932), made a tremendous impression on HM. ND published Céline's *Death on the Installment Plan* in 1966.

fight against the English censors: A. S. Frere, chairman of the board of William Heinemann, and Fredric J. Warburg of Martin Secker & Warburg had both been on trial at the Old Bailey in London for publishing an obscene book; the trial made history when they were acquitted.

Aladdin lamps: In his letter of October 8 announcing the changes required by Heinemann, RM explained: "Seems that Alladin [sic] lamps are manufactured in England, and it seems that an author and publisher there once had to cough up 8000 guineas (a pound and a shilling each, as you know) because of some slighting remarks about an Aga cooker. Libel is of course much stricter and stronger in Great Britain. Heigh-ho!"

118. ALS-1   12/14/57
                                                [Big Sur]

DEAR BOB—

The Smile at the Foot of the Ladder—Greenwood Press edition, limited, is nearly exhausted. Would you care to bring it out in a paper back or hard cover? If not, let me know soon, as I can get it done on a private press. It's well liked, like the *Colossus*.

But very slim in size. And I don't want to fatten it with other material.

Yours,
HENRY MILLER

[At the bottom of this letter RM typed the following note to JL]

⟨12/16/57⟩

JAMES,

Why don't we [do] in a limited way, maybe a smallish limited edition, like the Greenwood Press one. I'm told it originally had quite a children's book sale—at Duell, Sloan and Pearce—and certainly there is a steady demand for its translation. We might be able to work out a deal whereby we would share in all future translation rights ⟨and do all right⟩.

BOB

119. TL-1   January 9, 1958

DEAR HENRY:

Happy New Year! I hope that 1958 will be a good year for you, and now that I have gotten finished with my work on "Perspective of Burma" I hope to be able to devote more time to your projects and bring some of them to successful fruition.

Bob has shown me your letter to him of December 14 about *The Smile at the Foot of the Ladder,* and I have read it again and think it is a very moving little piece. I agree with you that it would stand best by itself, and I think we ought to go ahead and do a fine little edition of it which would be suitable for gift sales. . . .

> With best wishes to you both, as ever,
> JAMES LAUGHLIN

/ · /

The Smile at the Foot of the Ladder: ND published the book in 1959, with HM watercolors and drawings as illustrations.

120. TLS-1   February 25, 1958

DEAR HENRY:

. . . Have you written, or are you thinking of writing, anything about the present "international" situation? By that I mean this crazy missile race and the competition for seizing outer space? I can't think of anyone who could make it look more ridiculous than you, if the mood hit you, and ridiculous is certainly what it is. There have been a few good pieces on the subject, especially in *The Nation,* cries of dissent you might say, and I am looking about for a few more, with the hope of getting out a little collection of them.

> With best wishes, as ever
> JL

121. ALS-1   3/1/58
                                              Big Sur

DEAR J.L.—

. . . I've thought a lot about the missile biz—and
devour everything on it—but can't see how (yet) to
approach it effectively. What is needed, I fear, is a
truly great soul who can awaken the world. None
in sight so far. (I don't think *writers* can offer anything—especially not through ridicule.) . . .

                                              Good cheer!
                                              HENRY

122. TLS-1   April 9th [1958]
                                              Big Sur

DEAR BOB:

Here's a proposition I hardly expect you will find
acceptable, but I give it so that I may soon get your
refusal and pass it on to other publishers. It's something [that] has been in my mind for several years,
and now I feel like doing something about it. Most
writers would reserve this project for after their
death; I prefer to enjoy the show while alive, even
at the risk of being called an egomaniac.

It's this. In the letter files at U.C.L.A. Library are
thousands of letters from my fans—a loose term. I
feel that the reading public is missing something in
not reading some of them. They go hand in hand
with my books. I am thinking only of letters to me,
not of my own to others.

Naturally, they cover every subject under the sun.
Many are about the readers' reactions to the banned

books, and they are good, healthy reactions, which would put to shame the "opinions" of American judges in the court trials. Many are about New Directions publications, some of the most remarkable ones being about the *Colossus,* the *Books in My Life,* the *Nightmare,* the *Wisdom of the Heart.* . . .

My thought is to get out one good-sized volume, of possibly 400 to 500 pages (including photographic copies of certain pages of the letters) and, if it proved successful, follow it up with others. I rather think that the first volume should be from readers of the banned books. Now some of these are in French, German, and perhaps other languages too. Question: should we publish in original language, or in English, or in both?

Well,   enough   to   give   you   the   general thought⟨. . .⟩

I enclose a letter I got from Covici the other day, and which I have not answered, as I am waiting to hear from Malcolm Cowley and from you first. This idea of a "Henry Miller Reader" is what Lawrence Durrell has long had in mind, and in fact, wrote Jay about some years ago. He's been busy with the idea again recently, hoping, I suppose, to induce some British publisher to go for it. He is also just beginning a deliberate correspondence with Perlès about me, or rather about my work, which he hopes to turn into a book. The idea being that Perlès gave a good picture of the man but not of my work.

We're still blocked off by the slide, but all's well.

HENRY

/ • /

Covici: Pascal Covici, an editor at Viking Press.

Malcolm Cowley: Longtime editor at Viking. He had proposed a volume devoted to HM in the Viking Portable Library.

123. CC-2   April 24, 1958
                                               [New York]

DEAR HENRY:

   . . . Thank you so much for the copy of your letter to Malcolm Cowley about the proposal for a
"Henry Miller Reader." I ran into Malcolm on the
train from the country last week and we had a most
interesting and pleasant conversation. I respect his
judgement greatly and am so pleased, as are you,
that he has taken an interest.

   However, as I told Malcolm on the train, it would
be very hard for Bob and myself, for a great many
reasons, to turn over the cream of your writing to
another publisher. As you know, we have long had
in mind this very same idea, or something close to
it, and it seems to me that the moment is now propi-
tious for us to go forward with it, especially if Durrell wishes to work on it again.

   I think that the position which you take on inclusion of material from the "banned" books is a very
reasonable one. I think too that recent experience
shows that it is possible to do in a high-priced volume things that one cannot do in a paperback that is
available in drug stores to school children. One
point that should be studied, I think, is the question
of what is known, I believe, as "artistic wholeness."
I have not read Judge Woolsey's famous decision on
the *Ulysses* case for some years, but my recollection
of it—and it remains, I think, one of the major precedents to which jurists look in this field—is that he
made the point that the last chapter of *Ulysses,*
which is so sexy, was justified because it was part of
a whole work which covered the whole span of
human living. From this point of view, it would not
be advisable to pick out isolated passages from the

"banned" books which would stand out specifically for their freedom of expression, without, at the same time, showing that they were part of a whole, coherent, carefully planned artistic structure.

The solution might be to plan a rather large book, which might sell for as much as seven dollars and a half, which might include *Cancer* entire.

If this were presented along with a dozen or so of your more serious philosophical essays, so that the whole collection presented you [as] what you truly are—an important thinker as well as a brilliant writer of fiction—I think that, in the present climate which has been influenced by recent liberal decisions, it might be possible to sustain the book in the courts. Obviously, a good introduction from a man of the almost sanctified standing of Van Wyck Brooks would be most helpful. . . .

> With very best wishes to you both,
> JAMES LAUGHLIN

/ • /

Judge Woolsey's famous decision: In 1933, U.S. District Court Judge John M. Woolsey ruled that James Joyce's *Ulysses* was not obscene and should therefore not be banned in the United States.

Van Wyck Brooks: (1886–1963), the dean of American literary and cultural historians.

124. TLS-3   5/5/58
                                                Big Sur

DEAR JAY L.:

Regarding your letter of recent date with regard to a H.M. Reader, here are my thoughts on it, pro

tem. First of all I must tell you that Durrell has not
shown me as yet a table of contents for such a project. I rather think that he, you, Cowley and myself
would have varying ideas on the subject. And right
here I am inclined to say that, provided certain basic
considerations can be agreed upon between publisher and author, that it might be wiser to let two
men like Durrell and Cowley decide upon the contents rather than you and me. (Of course it would
have to be seen whether these two would care to
cooperate. Certainly we couldn't ask for two better
editors.)

Off-hand I must also say immediately that I think
Viking Press could do a better, bigger and more
efficient job than New Directions. They would, for
one thing, reach a wider and a different public than
you would, I should think. And the question of
expense, for it would be an expensive undertaking,
would not be such a great consideration with them.
Here is how my practical mind sees it. If they do the
job you derive an income from the books, you have
no worries, and your publications get increased free
publicity, from a reputable house.

But regardless of who does the job, here are my
thoughts about the contents of the book. Representative excerpts should be taken from virtually everything I have written, that is, everything published in
book, pamphlet or brochure form. . . .

The snag in the aforementioned, for me at least,
is this matter of including material from the banned
books. Cowley and Durrell, I know, will urge that
if this be done it should be with *uncensorable* fragments only. I see the point of this all right, but at the
same time I feel rebellious about it. I have a double
attitude about this matter. One is a desire not to
deceive the reader or let him down, knowing as I do
that when he learns that fragments of the banned

books will be included he will be prepared for "the real stuff" of which he has been so long deprived. Secondly, in view of the fact that England and America will not permit the publication of these books, and also since I more than any writer in the English language have not only championed freedom of expression but paid the price for it—I mean by permitting myself to be cut off from the main body of my reading public—I feel loath to make any compromise whatever, and certainly not a compromise which would make it look as though, towards the end of my life, I had grown weary of the struggle and for the sake of a few shekels had decided to give in. For me to lower my standards, after all these years—it will be 25 years next year since the *Tropic of Cancer* came out!—would be treason.

You raise a question of precedents, the Woolsey decision on the *Ulysses* case and the more recent decisions in the San Francisco trials. It is my belief, based on the talks and the correspondence I have had with legal minds, that no previous decisions, favorable or unfavorable, can be relied on in predicting the results of a court case with respect to my banned books. Whatever the law reads at any given time is only a starting point. Everything depends on the interpretation of the law, and particularly who interprets it and at what moment in time. I would hazard the opinion that my work would be the very last to be recognized as publishable by our courts. As to whether, in an omnibus edition, where the intent is clearly to present every facet of the writer and not a work of pornography, the situation ⟨be⟩ different, or could be viewed differently, I am unable to say. (I can envisage the possibility of a biased judge viewing such a work as a cloak to permit the entry of salacious material.) The point is that we never

know and have no way of telling how the minds
of judges work or will work. However, one might
sound out in advance such people as Huntington
Cairns, Judge Horn (of the *Howl* case) and such like.
From past experience, however, I am almost certain
that they will refuse to commit themselves.

But to answer a point you raised in your let-
ter⟨. . .⟩No, I would never dream of permitting the
Tropic of Cancer to be included in toto in such a
book. Nor would I even consent to a trial publication of it on its own—or any of the banned books—
unless I was certain in advance that it would not be
subject to seizure and suppression. I don't believe in
fighting lost battles. And I refuse to be a scapegoat.
I am quite content that these banned books continue
to be republished (in English) abroad and in translation. They are all as much alive and sought after
now as the first day they were published.

And here I shall answer obliquely a point which
my good friend Durrell is forever bringing up and
which, it appears, is the reason for his renewed
interest in doing something about H.M. Durrell has
the impression, correct enough, that the British
public, for example, in being denied access to my
major work, have formed a distorted image of the
man and his work. Aside from an H.M. Reader he
now has in mind writing a book with Perlès which
seeks to evaluate my work. In the back of his head,
I fancy, is the hope that by giving the British public
a full picture of H.M. the man and author, pressure
might be exerted on the authorities whereby these
works now prohibited might be openly published
and circulated there. If he does entertain such a hope
I think it is an utterly forlorn one. And I would say
the same for our own public. To my mind, the fact
that they are sold in increasing numbers abroad,

both to English speaking peoples and to foreigners through translations, accomplishes much more in this direction. The image which the public and the critics and the authorities form of an author such as myself—and I am in the tradition, so to speak—is hardly likely to be influenced by a full, truthful and generous portrait (or evaluation of the work) given by a compatriot. There are certain artists who, once broadly condemned, remain so for their lifetime. It pleases the public, if I may put it that way, to hold fast to such an image, even though at heart they may admit it to be wrong. If you ask me why I can only say—through natural human perversity. And perhaps, all unconsciously, the public chooses this attitude in order to make it possible for the succeeding generation to right the picture and give the author his due. We are none of us sufficiently aware, it seems to me, how great a part the "wrong-doers" play in manifesting the right, or in abetting the right. That fecundating element called time, on which we finally rely when all else fails, is the catalytic agent which takes into account *all* the elements of a problem and not merely the ones which we think are important. Something—"it," if you like— knews better than us. And "it" takes its own time, regardless of justice or injustice, right or wrong.

So where are we? There are two courses open, as I see it. One is to do the big thing and the brave thing, heedless of opinion, reckless of consequences, or carry on as heretofore within the limits prescribed. To try to accomplish our purpose by half- way, sensible, cautious methods seems useless to me. I hate muddling and compromise. The whole question is, is the moment opportune or not? If it is not, your bravery will get you nowhere. A man should *know* that he is going to win before he begins fighting; if he doesn't, if he's the least unsure of himself, he had better run and fight another day. . . .

All the best meanwhile.
HENRY

/ • /

Judge Horn: In 1957, Judge Clayton W. Horn of the San Francisco Municipal Court ruled in the obscenity case against Allen Ginsberg's *Howl* that a work must present "a clear and present danger of inciting to anti-social or immoral action" before it can be judged obscene.

125. TLS-1   5/12/58
                                                      Big Sur

DEAR JAY L.,

. . . If you get to the World's Fair, Brussels, look up a film called *Once Upon a Sunday* given at the Festival. It was made at Point Lobos by Nick Cominos, a documentary of that place. Eve, myself, Doner, Hugh O'Neill appear in it—briefly. So does Robinson Jeffers, at the end, and I find him wonderful to look at. He has the look of rock—and of the hawk too, of course. And very sad, sombre, almost inhuman. At this film festival I am told there is also a Swedish documentary being shown on prison life there, and in it they show a prisoner masturbating before his wall of pin-up girls, to the accompaniment (sic) of a reading, in Swedish fortunately, from my *Sexus*. How do they get away with it, I wonder?

All the best,
HENRY

/ • /

Doner: HM devoted a chapter to the artist Ephraim Doner in *My Bike and Other Friends.* Doner's tile mosaics decorated HM's studio.

Hugh O'Neill: Poet who lived at Anderson Creek. He and Doner are portrayed in *Big Sur and the Oranges of Hieronymus Bosch.*

126. CC-1   July 19, 1958
                                          [Snake River Ranch]
                                          [Wilson, Wyoming]

DEAR HENRY—

. . . I think you are far too generous in wanting to offer Durrell *half* of the royalties from the *Reader.* I know how you are about money—always giving it away with no thought for the morrow⟨. . .⟩and, objectively, I admire you very much for being that way⟨. . .⟩but may I respectively suggest that you have wife and children to think about, and that this is a book which should be selling well for a great many years. I think that if LD gets the 2¹/₂[%] royalty that I suggested this will add up to quite a bit for him, over the years.

I've written to Cowley to find out how much wordage could fit in a Viking Portable—if it can be worked out for that—and will write to Durrell as soon as I hear back.

Yes, this Jackson Hole country is physically superb. The Grand Teton looks like the Dolomites, and the Snake River Valley is broad and lush. But the local culture is centered on the cow and the dude or tourist, and this does not produce a very rarefied sensibility, though there are a few rather charming eccentrics about, including one, age 90, who got knocked a bit goofy when on the Harvard boxing team, and still writes letters of protest to the President of Harvard about the Harvard "toughs."

> Best wishes, as ever,
> J . L .

/ · /

royalties: Lawrence Durrell refused to accept any royalties for editing *The Henry Miller Reader*.

127. TLS-2   August 13, 1958
                               New York

DEAR HENRY,

. . . I have been running around town to try to find something drawn by you that we could use in *Smile at the Foot of the Ladder,* and still keep it illustrated by you. . . .

Did you know that that mock-up, as you call it, by Léger may be very valuable? It arrived before your letter telling about it, and I took for granted that maybe this was something by you in a new style. I thought it very attractive, but didn't feel that it went with the other drawing which we are planning to use. I'll hold onto it, until we have all our plans finally set, and then return it to you insured. It's also insured while it's in our care, by the way. If you found the proper buyer, I'm told that something like this could perhaps bring $1000. Do please put it behind glass and take good care of it, when you get it back. Oh, the trials of possessions!

I spent some time with Frances Steloff, looking at her "Henry Miller Exhibition," copies of rare books

which she has, and which she allows people like me
to see. It did occur to me that there were a couple of
parts of paintings reproduced in *Semblance of a
Devoted Past* that could be decorations at the beginning or end. . . .

> Yours ever,
> BOB

/ • /

Léger: Fernand Léger (1881–1955), French painter. As HM explains in
the Epilogue, *The Smile at the Foot of the Ladder* "was written expressly
for Fernand Léger, to accompany a set of forty illustrations on clowns
and circuses."

128. ALS-1

> 8/16/58
> Big Sur

DEAR BOB—

. . . Thanks for tip about Léger maquette. I have
two more on same order. Have you any idea where
to unload them? I'd sell in a minute for a sum like
that. . . .

> More anon!
> HENRY

129. TLS-2

> September 5, 1958
> New York

DEAR HENRY,

. . . I spoke to Ann Laughlin about your Légers,
and she suggests that you send the other two to me

(insured, please) and she will take them to the Parke-
Bernet Gallery (Auctioneers), to Pierre Matisse, etc.
I told her that you had written Sidney Janis, and she
thought that was a good idea, too, because it's
important to get some comparative offers. She also
thought that perhaps the best thing would be a
woman who has sold quite a few of her mother's
pictures she wanted to get rid of, all paintings by big
name moderns. . . . Ann Laughlin knows this girl
very well, through her mother, who was one of the
early collectors of modern art, and has long been a
trustee of the Museum of Modern Art, as you
know.

Your letter to Lawrence Durrell is great. Maybe
we'll have to publish *A Correspondence Reader to the
Henry Miller Reader!* . . .

Yours,
B o b

. . . Oh, Ann Laughlin asked if by any chance you
have any of the correspondence between you and
Léger. Letters would evidently add to the material's
value and bring you a better price. . . .

The art collecting world sounds as screwy as the
manuscript and first edition one! . . .

/ • /

Ann Laughlin: JL's wife had been collaborating with RM on the pro-
jected portfolio of Abraham Rattner's drawings.
Sidney Janis: New York art dealer whose gallery specialized in modern
French art.

130. ALS-2   9/10/58
                                                     Big Sur

DEAR BOB—

   Just got yours of 9/5/58. Here are the other two
Léger maquettes. Writing U.C.L.A. Library to send
me Léger's letter(s) regarding these sketches. Think
they have them. Very good of Ann Laughlin to do
this for me. Is she Jay's wife—or daughter (grown
up)? . . .
   You know, I gave the Library all of Durrell's letters to me over the years. Larry Powell, director, is
crazy about Durrell's work. But can't get him to
bring out (yet) a book of our correspondence. *His*
letters (D's) are gems! Always "landscapes"—and
from wonderful places. . . .

                                                    HENRY

(I may dig up another one or two of the Légers.
Think I had more—but may have given them
away.)

                        / • /

a book of our correspondence: Lawrence Clark Powell, now head librarian
at UCLA, hoped to edit the Miller-Durrell letters himself but could
never find time to do so. He subsequently commissioned GW to edit
the letters, and *A Private Correspondence* was published by E. P. Dutton
(Durrell's American publisher) in 1963. The correspondence continued
after that date, and a fuller edition, *The Durrell-Miller Letters, 1935–
1980,* edited by Ian S. MacNiven, was published by ND in 1988.

131. ALS-1   9/20/58
                                [Big Sur]

DEAR BOB—

Here are the Léger letters re the drawings and plan
for the book—12 of them! Ouf! Haven't reread them
And they may be out of order, chronologically. But
any one wanting to buy has enough proof here!

                              Good luck!
                              HENRY MILLER

132. TLS-1   Nov. 27th, 1958
                                Big Sur

DEAR BOB:

As I'm never certain whether Jay is in town or
traveling, I address this to you with request you
contact him about it. Hoffman is holding for me the
sum of 540,000 francs (roughly $1200 to $1300)
received from Rowohlt for German editions printed
in Paris. Because of the nature of the deal, this
money cannot be transferred to me in the usual way.
I can get it only by having some one accept francs to
be used over there, in exchange for dollars here. I
thought that Jay perhaps might be able to use such a
sum, either in traveling or in business deals with
French authors or publishers. Would you ask him,
please? If he says, yes, then tell him to write airmail immediately to Hoffman, who could arrange
the exchange.

I am writing at the same time, in the same fashion, Pierre Matisse and Abe Rattner. (Rattner's letter I enclose for you to forward, as I don't know his

Paris address.) Whoever writes Hoffman first will get the money, of course.

The reason for making this request is that I now have a chance to buy out my ex-wife's interest in this home here; she has half ownership (unjustly) by terms of our divorce. Now she needs money—got divorced again and is buying a new home—and I am quite certain she will agree to my proposition. She needs the dough quickly, hence all this dispatch. . . .

One other question . . . Dennis Murphy, author and neighbor, suggested to me last night that I sell *Playboy* (mag) the story called "Astrological Fricassee," which you published and Signet too. He seems to think that wouldn't matter with them. If it is possible to do that, I would take the matter up with them. (I shall probably also submit a chapter from *Nexus* to them.) They pay damned well, as you know, and have written me several times asking if I couldn't send them something. Now then, if they took the "Fricassee"—or any other story already published in N.D. books—could we do this, for a change: could I ask them to pay me and then I pay you your share—is it half—on receipt of their check? This means you would have to make a slight concession—and trust me. Can you?

It's not easy to raise $3500.00 overnight, even if your name happens to be

HENRY MILLER

P.S. What about the Léger maquettes? Now would be the time to sell them, if they are saleable.

/ • /

"Astrological Fricassee": A spoof on astrology first published in *Remember to Remember* (ND, 1947).

133. TLS-2   December 10, 1958
                                      New York

DEAR HENRY,

This is of course the kind of situation in which we wish we could phone you!

Ann Laughlin is back from Alta, Utah, and her first act yesterday was to see her friend and advisor about modern art, Miss Weidler. (I think I told you about her before; she works for the Carnegie International and had been in Europe, picking pictures for their next great exhibition in Pittsburgh.) Mrs. Laughlin hesitated going very far with your Léger maquette without Miss Weidler's advice, because she really didn't know how much to ask.

Miss Weidler saw the pictures yesterday afternoon and she thought that it might be possible to get up to $3500 for the three. This would be $1000 apiece, with $500 extra for the one that has a drawing on both sides. You will remember that was the first one you sent me.

However, this morning Mrs. Laughlin has been out seeing the galleries and individuals and she went again to Pierre Matisse, who had seen the drawings before. It seems that right now is a very good time to sell them, because just before Christmas there are people looking for unusual Christmas gifts, and the gallery people see the possibility of a quick re-sale.

Pierre Matisse offered her $3500 in cash, but he would like to take possession of the drawings within the next few days, if his offer is to hold firm. (Matisse may double the price, but that's what one has to expect.)

. . . If Miss Weidler should sell the drawings, she would expect a commission, but if Mrs. Laughlin sells them herself as to Pierre Matisse, there will be

no commission and you will get the full amount.
She, of course, would do it for love of New Directions and of you and our great desire to help an
author out ⟨, particularly when that author is Henry
Miller.⟩ . . .

I'd suggest, Henry, that you let me know by the
fastest means.

Yours,
BOB

134. TLS-2   December 15, 1958
                                New York

DEAR HENRY,

. . . Here is the situation in regard to the fragments from your banned books. I guess technically
any parts that were published by New Directions
are controlled by New Directions and should be
arranged with us. In other words, there is a split.
Why don't you send parts that were not in the New
Directions books? Or why don't you first see if
Playboy or *Esquire* will really take these fragments?
They are throwing their money around like fools, as
you say, but like fools they pick and choose
according to their own foolish criteria. At least
Esquire, with whom we have a good many dealings,
is very unpredictable.

Ann Laughlin will hold up on any closing as far
as the Léger maquettes, but has good reason to
believe that the offer from Pierre Matisse for $3,500.
will not last beyond this week. . . .

My very best to you and Eve.

Yours ever,
BOB

135. TLS-1   December 19, 1958
                                      New York

DEAR HENRY,

Have just telegraphed you as follows:

AM AIR MAILING MATISSE CHECK FOR $3500. HURRAY!
NEED SECOND SET PHOTOSTATS. AM WRITING YOU AND
POWELL.

Hope it came through all right.

And here is the check.

Needless to say, publishers don't usually go in for
this sort of thing, but Ann and J and I are delighted
that we were able to do this for you at this crucial
time. Pierre Matisse is delighted, too, I know. . . .

Hope you will have title to the house by the time
we hear from you again.

                                      Yours,
                                      BOB

136. TLS-1   Dec. 22, 1958
                                      Big Sur

DEAR BOB:

Got your wire a couple of days ago and nearly fell
over. Still don't believe it till I see the check! Since
this windfall is entirely due to your astuteness, I
hope you will let me offer you a little token of grati-
tude. I would like to send you $250.00 right after
the first of the year. Can't do it before, as I will need
every cent of Matisse's check to bargain with my
wife. Indeed, I may need more, and I am now wir-
ing back and forth—Paris–Matisse–Big Sur—to see
if Matisse will exchange those francs (more than I

originally expected) for dollars. I rather think he will. He's a brick, in any case.

And Bob, please convey my warmest thanks to Ann Laughlin, will you, for all her valiant efforts. I would like to give her something too—money I know she doesn't need. Can you suggest something?

I still have Léger's *Le Cirque,* inscribed to me with his "locomotive" signature; copy "hors commerce." If you know of any one interested in acquiring it, do let me know, eh?

As I said to Pierre, there is indeed a Santa Claus!

Merry X'mas!
HENRY

---

137. TLS-1   December 30, 1958
                                 New York

DEAR HENRY,

I have just finished reading the proposed *Henry Miller Reader* from beginning to end. I am in a daze; my head swirls; I am elated. I feel as if I'd been talking to you for days on end and as if we'd grown up together and never been separated.

Durrell has obviously done an incredible job, for without effort or formalization the meat all seems to be there. There are few living writers who could hope for so intelligent, perceptive and self-effacive an editor.

I do miss some of the strong stories left out because New American Library had used them in the first volume or expect to in the new one. I know I'm the one who brought this matter up—and it is because of my big foot that Durrell left them out. I

wonder if at least two or three shouldn't be rein-
serted, to complete the picture. I'd be willing to sacrifice Mona for instance for the sake of getting
Moricand in, although she does stretch her legs and
her soul into areas he never knew. Maybe it would
be better to get in "Mademoiselle Claude" by snip-
ping out something less pervasive and persuasive.
Anyway when you're reading would you keep this
in mind.

Saw Malcolm and Muriel Cowley last night at a
party. They're leaving tomorrow for California and
I was trying to insist that they drive into the Big Sur
world and see you.

Now I'm too dead to hit the keys straight, so I'll
wish you the very best, for 1959 and always.

                                            Bob

/ • /

New American Library: NAL published six HM narratives in *Nights of
Love and Laughter* (1955) and was soon to publish another selection in
The Intimate Henry Miller (1959).

Mona: The femme fatale of *Tropic of Capricorn,* based on HM's second
wife, June Mansfield. Lawrence Durrell's reaction was that he felt
"rather like someone asked to do an anthology of Dante which made
no mention of Beatrice!"

"Mademoiselle Claude": Story of a Paris prostitute originally published
in Samuel Putnam's *New Review* in 1931.

138. ALS-1   1/28/59
                                                [Big Sur]

DEAR BOB—

    . . . Got notice (from you) of my earnings for
1958. Hope you will be able to get what's due me to

me by end of March. We plan to go to France April
14th & stay till mid-August—with the kids, and by
jet from N.Y. Paris & back. I just got what Hoffman had for me in francs, thru Matisse.

It was damned good of you to refuse the check I
sent you. *But*—I hope it wasn't because of the
amount! (I didn't insult you, did I?)

Will wait to have your full ideas on Intro. to Portable. More work. Oof! And I have yet to do the
complete Bibliog. & Chronology for you!

> Ta ta!
> HENRY

139. TLS-2
February 5, 1959
New York

DEAR HENRY,

I like the story, "Berthe," very much. I was a little
afraid it was going to go over into the sentimental
at one point (romantic sentimentality for whores has
spoiled many a writer, I think!) but very soon that
suggestion had gone and she seems very real and
your attitude toward her seems real. Or should I say
the narrator's attitude? Indeed, I think it should be
included as one of the stories in the *Henry Miller
Reader.*

. . . Did you ever look at the introductions in the
sample Portable (I think it was the *James Joyce,*
edited by Harry Levin) that we sent you? That's
why it went off to you, so that you could see what
they require. Viking wants these introductions very
much and feels that they are an essential part of the
whole formula of the Viking Portables. Even if we
didn't work things out whereby Viking would do

the paperbound edition as planned, I think they would be very important. Take a look at the one that precedes *Dubliners*. It is only two pages but it covers all the ground.

Now somebody else could perhaps do this but not in any way as well as you. Joyce could have done it much better than Harry Levin, but he wasn't around when the *Portable* was put together. Your book, of course, is not chronological, so that you couldn't follow exactly the same formula, but take the story section. Why not give a paragraph on each and how they were written and when and what you can remember of your mood at the time. Then you could do the same thing for the literary essays, and finally, the portraits. A short introduction of 5 or 6 or 4 paragraphs to each section is all that is needed.

Why don't you try one; begin with the one on "Places," if that seems the more easily palpable. I have a feeling that once you get into this, and it shouldn't take much time, you would find it a very pleasurable exercise in memory. . . .

Yours,
Bob

/ · /

"Berthe": RM added a marginal note to JL on the carbon copy: "Henry says it has never been published, except in a reworked form in *Quiet Days in Clichy.*"

140. ALS-1

2/6/59
[Big Sur]

DEAR BOB—

I told the "opera" trio that I could not do the libretto, but that when they had finished it I would read and make suggestions. I don't like to extract further monies from them for my poor efforts. Don't much mind exacting tribute from big publishers, *Playboy,* et alia, but not from poor artists— especially foreign ones.

Enclose letter from Durrell regarding the *Reader.* I still prefer Cendrars to Balzac. Balzac is long dead and had all acclaim. Cendrars is now about to die— and is virtually unknown to Anglo-Saxon readers— a crime! He means more to me than Balzac ever will. And I still think the excisions I recommended should stand. Don't want any banned books chopped up.

HENRY

/ • /

the "opera" trio: Two months earlier HM had written that an Italian composer, Antonio Bibalo, and his two Norwegian colleagues wanted to use *The Smile at the Foot of the Ladder* as the libretto for an opera to be entered in a competition.

141. CC-2

February 17, 1959
[New York]

DEAR HENRY,

. . . About the opera trio in Sweden, I think it's wonderful of you to be genero[us] to them, but nothing has been earned or won this prize as yet, and they are, after all, going to the prize with your libretto or with the story based on your writings, and, if they win the prize, it will be partially because of your story. If I may say so, Henry, I think you owe it to your children and your wife to accept 50% which is usually the amount in these cases and whic[h] is what these boys expect. Anyway, I'm sending it all to Hoffman and takin[g] the liberty of suggesting a 50-50 split in royalties, as well as prize money. After all, nothing has been earned yet and nothing may be. They're nice boys obviously, but no one you know, and how do you know they aren't making more money than you anyway. In any case, by giving them 50%, you are being generous; it's very generous of you to let them use your story.

I'm making a photocopy of Durrell's letter regarding the *Reader* and returning it to you.

I fear I agree with him in regard to the Cendrars-Balzac choice. I think the thing to face here is that *The Henry Miller Reader* is primarily to present you, and not Cendrars or other people that you admire, and your writing comes over better in the Balzac than in the Cendrars. Maybe you cared too much for Cendrars, or tried too hard; at least I always felt, Henry, that this was not one of the passages in *Books in My Life* that communicated, to me, at any rate, what you obviously felt. Of course, as Durrell says, you should have the final choice. But do listen, please, to Durrell or someone else who is able to see your writing from afar. . . .

Yours,

ROBERT M. MACGREGOR

/ • /

the Cendrars-Balzac choice: "Against the advice of editor and publisher," HM wrote in his preface to the essay on Blaise Cendrars in *The Henry Miller Reader,* "I have insisted on the inclusion of this piece—as a substitution for passages on 'Mona' in the *Tropics.*"

142. PCS   [March 19, 1959]
                                                [Tokyo, Japan]

DEAR HENRY & EVE—

. . . Japan is wonder filled—and I must admit I like the extremes of beauty and barbarism. Have just been in Nara—the capital in the 8th Century— seeing rites 1100 years old of wonderful mystery. You *must* come—besides you're almost a national hero here!

Best affection to you both
BOB MACGREGOR

143. TLS-1   March 29, 1959
                                                Alta, via Sandy, Utah

DEAR HENRY—

I think that the little commentaries that you have done for the pieces in the *Reader* are very good⟨. . .⟩fascinating, in fact. They will help to personalize the book, and to carry the reader along through your life story. The one suggestion I would make is that you add dates to each one—the year when that piece was composed, as close as you can remember. This would then tie the commentary in to the Chronology of your life, which should go, I think, at the front of the book, not the back. . . .

One small point: in your introduction to the commentaries—which is nice—do you want to make any mention of the recent slight change in the import regulations on the *Tropic* books? I think I sent you the clipping from the *Times* about it: that qualified scholars may now get the books through? I see this as a milestone, and think it should be recorded. It also gives us basis, I think, for being a bit more aggressive in promoting the inclusion of the Paris books material. . . .

Best to you all,
JL

144. TLS-1   4/4/59
                                Big Sur

DEAR JAY L.:

. . . No, I don't think I would mention anything about that *Cancer* release recently. Let others do the fluttering! I've heard from Clark Foreman and, as you will see from the enclosed telegram, reverberations have begun. I wrote Barney Rosset that you had first option on any American publications, also that I thought he was somewhat premature. You see, even if the ban were lifted on my books (which is not yet the case), no one can predict what would happen when publication of them began here. My feeling is that the time is not ripe yet. I would want to have inside information, first, on the attitude of the Postmaster General, for one thing, and more definite favorable information about recent court rulings (on other books). Huntington Cairns, who is a friend of Foreman, is a man you might sound out for an opinion. I know that *Lady Chatterley* (unexpurgated) has just come out, by the Grove Press, but that again means nothing where my books are concerned. I am not going to be made a scapegoat. And I am very leery of all American publishers—how far they will go, what they will do at the last minute, when threatened with bankruptcy, fines, imprisonment, etc. I can picture them leaving me to hold the bag. . . .

All the best now!
HENRY

/ · /

Clark Foreman: A sociologist active in civil liberties causes, who brought a copy of *Tropic of Cancer* into the country and challenged its seizure by the Customs Bureau, eventually obtaining a ruling that the book could be imported for literary and scholarly purposes.

Barney Rosset: Founder, publisher, and editor of Grove Press. He had sent HM a telegram asking: WOULD YOU CONSIDER TEN THOUSAND DOLLARS ADVANCE FOR UNITED STATES RIGHTS TROPICS CANCER CAPRICORN.

Lady Chatterley (unexpurgated): In 1928, D. H. Lawrence published an unexpurgated version of, *Lady Chatterley's Lover* in Italy, but only a bowdlerized version, published in 1932, could be sold openly in the United States. In 1959, Barney Rosset decided to challenge the interdict by publishing the unexpurgated version.

145. TLS-2   April 9, 1959
                                           [New York]

DEAR HENRY:

. . . Needless to say, I was fascinated by Barney Rosset's offer to you for American editions of the two *Tropic* books, unexpurgated. He is a good, and an aggressive, publisher, and it will be interesting to see whether he gets away with the unexpurgated edition of *Lady Chatterley* which he has just issued.

Naturally I was very pleased by your telling him that New Directions has first call on these books if you ever decide that you want to try to have them published in this country.

I think, however, that your decision to hold off on them here is the wise one. There is a great deal of difference between the decision of the U.S. Customs to allow qualified specialists to import single copies, and what might happen in some court in one of the less sophisticated regions of our great country if a bookseller were arrested for selling the *Tropic* books here. I believe that despite the general relaxation in censorship matters which has been taking place in this country, that success on the *Tropic* books would depend entirely on whether the case came before a very liberal-minded judge, and there is no way at all to control that. We know already from the California case what the result would be if the judge were a typical one. I sympathize with your reluctance to be made the goat in a proceeding for which there would be little hope of a favorable outcome.

Speaking of the *Tropic* books, I picked up a bit of curious information yesterday which you may wish to follow down. I was discussing censorship matters with Phillip Wittenberg, our lawyer, whom I believe you know, and he told me that a New York publisher for whom he also works, has been contemplating a pirated, expurgated edition of the books, based on the fact that in terms of American copyright, they are in the public domain. Have you heard anything about this plan? Wittenberg declined to tell me who the publisher involved was, but he said it was a successful firm here in this city. He said that the editors of this firm had been going through the volumes trying to decide how much would have to be cut out. I find it hard to believe that any reputable publisher here would attempt to pirate right under your nose, but I think we should try to develop more information about this. . . .

As ever,
J L

146. ALS-1   5/28/59
                                           Paris [France]

DEAR J. L. —

Am leaving for the country to-morrow and won't be back here till mid-August. Mail c/o Hoffman, Paris, will be forwarded. This to tell you I had a long luncheon the other day with Barney Rosset and Girodias—they are good friends and cooperate somewhat as publishers.

Rosset is very eager to publish *Cancer*—as soon as possible—possibly an expensive de luxe limited edition which would probably be sold out (in advance) before any action could be taken. Thinks Girodias could bring out same here—as a sort of 25th anniversary of *Cancer*'s publication here. All dependent, of course, on outcome of *Lady Chatterley* trial now pending. He thinks copyright in America has lapsed—Hoffman thinks by a new international agreement, it's still in force, everywhere.

Anyway, you have first choice, if you think you want to take the book—and all the consequences. Think it over and let me know how you feel. Should add this—Rosset is willing to share the publication with you, if you prefer. He realizes you deserve first consideration. He doesn't seem to care about money. Offers same huge advance as before and will sacrifice it if he failed to go thru with publication. He returns to N.Y. next week, I believe.

You could talk to him there—and by then know more about P. O. reaction to *Chatterley,* etc. etc. This in haste—but I think clear enough. I have not yet decided what I want to do about publication—only trying to get your position.

Cheerio!
HENRY

/ • /

Lady Chatterley trial: As Barney Rosset anticipated, the Post Office promptly seized copies of the unexpurgated edition of *Lady Chatterley's Lover,* whereupon he took the issue to court, and on July 21 the unexpurgated version was declared not obscene.

147. CC-1   June 24, 1959
                                                   [New York]

DEAR HENRY,

. . . I have delayed in writing you my thoughts about Barney Rosset's proposition for publishing the *Tropic* books here, until Barney got back from Europe and we had a chance to find out what was in his mind. Bob has now seen him—I have been up in the country—and given a very full report.

From this I gather that Rosset does not feel he would be able to go ahead, in any case, until there had been a final judicial ruling on *Lady Chatterley.* As you have doubtless heard, the Postmaster General ruled against the book, as was to be expected, and now they will be taking it into Federal court to try to get a reversal.

So we have time to think about this, and perhaps the situation will clarify somewhat when the decision on *Lady Chatterley* comes through.

All in all, it strikes me that this is something you have got to decide yourself. And there are a great many angles on it. First of all, you would get a handsome piece of money out of the publication, and that is certainly not to be sneezed at. On the other hand, the nervous strain of the legal action might take more out of you than the money would be worth. As it now is, the books do get a pretty good circulation, and you derive some income from them and the very fact that they are not easily available produces a very special and valuable kind of promotion and advertising. It is just human nature that people always want very much what they can't easily get.

As far as New Directions is concerned, I think that we would be interested in making the attempt, or at least participating with Grove in it, if we felt that we had a really strong chance to win out. Up till now, I have never discussed the books with any really first class literary lawyer who felt that they had a chance of being approved by the courts here. There is, of course, the kind of lawyer who will take any case, just to get the business. I wouldn't want to get us, or you, into that sort of situation.

Summing it all up, I think that we ought to wait until we see how *Lady Chatterley* comes out, and then ask Wittenberg, or someone equally eminent, to study the books carefully again and give us an objective opinion on what the chances might be. . . .

With best wishes, as ever,
JAMES LAUGHLIN

148. ALS-2   6/28/59
                    Sommières (Gard) France

DEAR BOB—

Enclosed find two letters from Pollinger re the
Hamlet book. Do let me know soon if you care to
reconsider publication. I have no rights, as you see,
and if you contract for it, it will be with D.M.G.
(Fraenkel's widow—tho' unmarried). I believe I
haven't had a cent of royalties on the French edition,
for my part of the book, as yet. . . . *But,* I am keen
to see the book republished, properly, whether I
collect a cent on it or not. It's an important part of
my whole work—and positively unknown, except
to a handful.

The reference to B. Rosset in P's letter please keep
to yourself. I'll be writing him shortly about the
Cancer biz. As I wrote Hoffman to-day, I am less
and less interested in the project. The attendant publicity involved is not worth the small fortune anticipated. I wanted word, however, from you or Jay, in
order to answer Rosset—also out of curiosity, I
must say, to see what your attitude would be.

The P.O. and the Court's attitude on *Chatterley*
confirms my opinion—that America is utterly hopeless. I don't expect miracles of the Supreme Court
or near miracles of the idiots in Congress. We're
fucked—that's the long and short of it. Cowley's little piece in the *Times* is so tame. It's like shooting a
water pistol at a rhinoceros! Pooah!

Off now to the bullfight in Nîmes. We oscillate
between Montpellier, Nîmes, Aigues-Mortes, Stes.
Maries, Arles, Uzès and Sommières. Our Fiat is a
gem of a car—beats any American make I've ridden
in.

Still eating, drinking too much, too often. And

talk, talk, talk. Richard Aldington's daughter Kathryn is taking Val riding—both good horsewomen. Tony talks French to his pals, treats them to cokes and ice cream, *and* listens to Durrell (who is a story teller) as if enchanted. I go to see an old Monterey friend soon in the Vaucluse—he bought a chateau (for a song) belonging to the Marquis de Sade. Could have bought a good (chateau) myself the other day for $12,000.00. Worth in the States about $50,000.00.

Alors, amusez-vous bien. Amitiés à tout le monde. Vacation (for 40,000,000 Frenchmen) begins to-morrow!

⊣Henry

/ · /

Pollinger: Laurence Pollinger, HM's literary agent in London.

D.M.G.: Daphne Moschos Gillam. Michael Fraenkel, with whom HM had had a falling out, owned the rights to his *Hamlet* correspondence with HM and passed them on to her. She proved to be completely uncooperative.

Cancer biz: On July 3, 1959, HM wrote again: "Just got Jay's letter of 6/24/59—which crossed mine, anent the *Tropics,* Rosset, etc. I note we are d'accord! Bon!" Two months later, writing from Big Sur on September 3, 1959, he expressed similar sentiments: "I wrote Rosset, several times, from Sommières, that I would make no decision yet about his offer. And I doubt very much I ever will. Don't think (now) I ever want to see any of the banned books published here, whether I could win in court or not."

Aldington: Richard Aldington (1892–1962), English writer, had settled in Montpellier and made friends with Lawrence Durrell.

149. TLS-4

October 2, 1959
New York

DEAR HENRY,

. . . I don't think I told you how really very impressed the editors of the various book clubs, who have seen galleys [of *The Henry Miller Reader*], were. . . . The new Readers Subscription made the largest bid, cash-wise, or should I say single bid. They offered an $8100. guarantee, but wanted it exclusively. Since both Jacques Barzun and Lionel Trilling, who are important names in the intellectual world today, were enormously enthusiastic about the book after reading it, and since their new book club does certain other things that are advantageous to the author and to the book, and since I thought their imprimatur would have a special effect of bringing you and the book to a broad world in the highest standing, I thought it was best for you to have their Mid-Century Book Club do the first book club presentation. They are new and can't guarantee such large amounts, particularly for a January selection, which is what the *Reader* would be. Marboro had originally offered a guarantee of $7500. Originally they wanted to cut their guarantee in half on the basis of a delayed selection of the kind we worked out, but I got them to come back up to $5500., making the total guarantee $9500., or $1400. over. You will thus get $4750. in all, and you can have it as soon as we get it, if you want, in addition to what will be earned by our edition and paperback reprints, which I think will be considerable. . . .

Yours ever,
BOB

/ • /

Jacques Barzun and Lionel Trilling: Professors at Columbia University
and prominent New York intellectuals who together with the poet W.
H. Auden made up the editorial board of the highbrow Mid-Century
Book Society.

150. TLS-1

October 9, 1959
New York

DEAR HENRY,

It seems that even with the "Automotive Passacaglia" we haven't gotten the *Henry Miller Reader* up
to full strength, as they used to say in the army, to
fill the place of the dropped selections from *Hamlet*.
This means either having a lot of blank pages at the
end or cutting some off and just throwing the
paper away.

It occurred to Griselda and me that what we
might do, which would in fact add to the book
very greatly, is reprint from the *Evergreen Review*
the letter you wrote to the Attorney General of
Norway together with the statement of Trygve
Hirsch, the barrister. This would be an appendix, and you wouldn't have to write anything
further to go with it. ("Defense of the Freedom to
Read.")

Since time is so short, I am sending it to the
printer, and will only pull it out if there are loud
squawks from you.

Is the text as it appeared in the *Evergreen Review*
the way you want it? We will mail you proof in any
case. It's a wonderful statement and pertinent to
your whole career as a writer, and particularly pertinent thus to this book.

Don't you think I should let Durrell know about
the changes in the book he edited, or have you?

My best to you and Eve.

Yours, in haste,

BOB

/ • /

"*Automotive Passacaglia*": This chapter from *The Air-Conditioned Nightmare* (ND, 1945) had to be added to *The Henry Miller Reader* when
Michael Fraenkel's widow refused permission to include an excerpt
from the *Hamlet* correspondence.

Griselda: Griselda Jackson Ohannessian, member of the ND staff in
New York since 1956, in charge of publicity and production at this
time.

Evergreen Review: Literary magazine founded by Barney Rosset in 1957
as a showcase for Grove Press authors.

Trygve Hirsch: Norwegian attorney who defended HM's *Sexus* against
charges of obscenity before the Supreme Court of Norway. His statement and HM's letter to him both appeared in the *Evergreen Review*
(Summer 1959) and were reprinted in *The Henry Miller Reader*.

151. TLS-2   December 1, 1959
                                                 New York

DEAR EVE AND HENRY,

   . . . Thinking of artists, I am very sorry indeed to
report that our project for the Miller-Rattner book
seems to be getting on the rocks. It's a long, and
very complicated, and rather tiresome story, with
which I won't bore you, but the gist of it is that
Esther is so ambitious for Abe that she wants a production far more elaborate and expensive than we
had ever intended. We sympathize with her desire
to push her husband's career, but she has gone so far

with it, insisting on more and more illustrations, and the most expensive possible reproduction process, so that the thing now lines up as a portfolio, which would have to sell at a very very high price, rather than a book, and we just feel we have to bow out of the picture and let her find another publisher.

I do hope you will understand the situation. We are all of us enormously fond of Abe, and we like your text a great deal, and really wanted to do this book⟨. . .⟩but, somehow, the original rather modest idea has been expanded to a scale where it is quite beyond our scope. It looks now as if it will end up as a portfolio to be sold to wealthy art collectors, rather than a book collaboration between a writer and an artist for ordinary book readers. . . .

> With best to you both, as ever,
> JL

152. TLS-1

DEAR BOB:

I enclose a letter from Barney Rosset who paid me a visit the other day. ⟨*Please treat confidentially!*⟩ I'm beginning to wonder if I shouldn't think seriously about his offer. In your contract for the *Reader* I noticed, but said nothing, that you had included an option on the next two (publishable) books from my hand. Rather strange, I thought, since you automatically receive first choice of all I do that is publishable. It occurred to me that you probably had the publication of the *Tropics* in mind.

Now I'd like to know your attitude. Are you

ready to let me accept Rosset's offer, if I decide to
do so? . . .

All the best meanwhile.
HENRY MILLER

/ • /

letter from Barney Rosset: For permission to publish the *Tropics,* Rosset
wrote HM: "We not only are still willing to pay $10,000 for an option
on the books, but we would also like to offer a guarantee of $50,000.
Specifically, we would pay $10,000 out of the proposed $50,000 upon
signature of an option; the balance to be paid when the option would
be turned into a contract, and you would yourself decide when the
contract should be signed, and when the books should appear—
whether it be in six months or ten years."

153. TLS-2   January 27, 1960
[New York]

DEAR HENRY,

Bob and I have just been discussing your letter
of January 20th, with which you enclosed Barney
Rosset's letter to you, offering a guarantee of fifty
thousand for the *Tropic* books.

Well, as you know, we had always hoped that if
we were convinced that the books could be done
here, without expurgations, that we would be able
to bring them out for you. (However,) we both feel
that Rosset's offer is so stupendous for you that we
should not take anything but a favorable attitude
toward it, provided that you yourself are satisfied
that you want to go ahead with it. It's a decision, we
think, that no one except you yourself can make,
but certainly Rosset's terms are very fine. Unless

there were an attempt at piracy here, the ultimate decision would still be entirely in your hands, and yet you could draw on the ten thousand option money now, which certainly ought to be useful.

Barney's lawyers must be very confident that they can get a favorable court decision. No doubt they think this because of their success with the Lawrence book. But I feel there are certain basic differences which might cause many judges to rule against the *Tropic* books. After all, *Lady Chatterley,* except for the four-letter words, is a rather "sweet," even a conventional book. Whereas the *Tropics* are "anarchic" (I use the word in the good sense), and I think that some judges, and even more so a typical jury, would feel that they were an attack on the bourgeois order and react accordingly. Of course, that is part of their greatness, ⟨yet⟩ the last thing which the kind of mind which puts up with the social system as it is can accept. However, you are the one who should decide. . . .

> With best wishes to you all, as ever,
> J L

154. TLS-1

DEAR BOB:

Got your several letters along with Jay's recently. Just getting round to answer.

Regarding release on the two *Tropics.* Are you limiting it to these two—or to all the banned books? As I told Jay, I have not yet made up my mind about Rosset's offer, but will in a few days. Hard nut to crack—for me. . . .

Ah, Japan! Wish I were there now! Expect to begin a brand new life there. This one is about closed out—from every standpoint. . . . I may take it into my head to stay longer than 3 or 4 months— or I may decide to go to Europe after leaving Japan. Want to keep fluid, free, flexible. (If this means any- thing to you—just had word from my astrologer friends—always accurate and reliable—that this will be the biggest year of my life, in every way, but especially from a material standpoint—should add, for me, a more important one, also assured, is in the fulfillment and realization of all my hopes, dreams, plans, etc. Almost too much for me to believe.)

Well, stay well and work less! It's pouring cats and dogs here, has been for days, and will continue for five more. Don't know when I'll get down to the mail box with this. New slides looming up on all sides. Well, fuck a duck, eh!

All the best, ever.
HENRY

/ • /

Rosset's offer: HM also wrote to JL on the same day, again expressing his uncertainty and perhaps his trepidation when he said: "Rosset *should* realize that if the case goes against him he will lose his shirt—and per- haps even go to prison—in good company." JL wrote back: "I can well understand how hard it is to make the decision about Rosset's offer. I certainly do admire him for the guts he has to charge in like the Light Brigade."

Japan: HM had been considering a trip to Japan for some time and had asked RM for advice on the best time of year to go. But in September he wrote that he had postponed the trip till the following year. Actu- ally, though he had long dreamed of traveling to "the Orient," he was never to go.

155. TLS-1   March 1st, 1960
                                         Big Sur

DEAR BOB:

. . . Enclosed is my answer to Barney Rosset. I have informed Hoffman likewise. Entre nous, I have very good reason to believe that neither the *Tropics* nor any of the other banned books will ever see the light of day in this country. . . .

Oh, the most important thing⟨. . .⟩since last writing you I've had an exchange of cablegrams with the Film Festival people at Cannes. They asked me to be a member of the jury May 4 or 5th. I said yes if they would pay expenses. They agreed. Now I await a letter giving full details. So, it is likely I will go to France first, travel around a bit in Europe—Italy, Germany, England, Greece maybe—and then go to Japan. Or I may come back home for a month and leave from this end. . . .

Best to Jay, wherever he is.
HENRY

156. TLS-1   March 20th '60
                                         Big Sur

DEAR JAY,

. . . It's wonderful the way you go on producing children. I wish I had a flock of them. As one gets older they mean more. At seventy or eighty it's ducky to hold a new-born in one's arms. I still have hopes⟨. . . .⟩

All the best to you and Ann. My stay in N.Y. will be brief, but I hope to see you—doubt, though, that

I can make a dinner date this time, as I explained to Bob.

HENRY

P.S. I do want to see Italy this trip. With all those publishers I have there now, I ought to get around, what! Would love to see the Etruscan tombs—and the Assisi Francis knew.

P.P.S. Georges Simenon writes he hopes to meet me in Cannes, perhaps with Chaplin. He's been made one of the judges also. Wonder who else?

/ · /

children: On March 15, JL had written: "I think Bob wrote you that we now have a little Henry of our own. A month old this week, and going strong. He has already distinguished himself by letting fly a good stream on a copy of Pound's *Cantos* that happened to be near the table where he was being changed the other day. This seems auspicious."

Georges Simenon: (1903–1989), Belgian writer of detective fiction. HM stayed with him in Switzerland the following year and met Charlie Chaplin there.

157. ALS-1   May 10th [1960]
                                                  Cannes [France]

DEAR BOB—

. . . Lunch to-day with Michel Simon. Tomorrow Picasso. Next day *Simenon* (we're great friends). First day with the "Begum" (Aga Khan). So it goes. Wow! And radio & television. Ouf!

Cheers!
HENRY

/ · /

Michel Simon: (1895–1975), French actor. In 1953, HM had been his
guest for a month in the South of France.

158. ALS-2   Dec. 5th 1960
                                 Reinbek/Hamburg [Germany]

DEAR BOB—

. . . Am enjoying my stay here. Despite bad food,
bad (rainy but mild) weather. Meet loads of interesting people here at the Verlag. (What a place!
America has no pub. offices like this!)

By the way, Ernst Rowohlt, father of Ledig-
Rowohlt, died a few days ago. Don't know if you
read of it in the papers.

May go to Berlin for a few days, around X'mas.
Will see Hildegard Knef (stage & film actress) if I
do. Ever see film *Subway in the Sky?* She's in it—
with two feet. *Good!* Don't want to bother Jay—
not too important—but Rowohlt is now preparing
a book about me for their Series of great men (writers, musicians, etc.)—most of them dead. They
want all the documentary material possible—interesting photos, calligraphic abracabra [sic], and such
like. Eve has sent a slew of stuff, but they can use
more. Should Jay happen to run across anything he
might think pertinent, why send it on to Herr
Ledig-Rowohlt, please.

You might also ask Jay this—if he had to choose
a second home, in Europe, where would he go—
what is best from standpoint of climate, landscape,
people, etc.? (Big question.) I have the car and will
travel thru France in January, keeping eyes and ears

open. Prefer France, of course, but one never knows.

> All the best to you both.
> "In love again."
> HENRY

P.S. When new paperback edition of *Wisdom of Heart* comes out, please send complimentary copy to—
Frau Renate Gerhardt
Schaumanns Kamp 28,
Reinbek-bei-Hamburg
Germany

/ · /

the Verlag: Rowohlt Verlag, the German publishing house founded in 1909 by Ernst Rowohlt, introduced many American authors to the German reading public and brought out most of HM's works.

"In love again": HM's new love, Renate Gerhardt, was a translator for Rowohlt, then at work on HM's *Nexus*. He hoped to find a place to live with her in Europe.

159. CC-1   December 16, 1960
                               [New York]

DEAR HENRY,

Bob showed me your letter to him of December 5th, and I am so pleased to hear that you are having a grand time over there. Do give my best regards to Ledig. I had read in the paper here of the death of his father, and thought of writing him a word of condolence, which perhaps you will pass on to him for me.

That's fine that Ledig is going ahead with the pic-

torial-documentary book about you. I wish that we
could publish it here, but I have the impression that
he has some kind of permanent tie-up on this series
with Grove. You might just tell him that if anything
falls through on that arrangement, we would be
much interested.

This weekend, when I get up to the country, I'll
go through my folders and see if I can turn up anything interesting for him along the line of snapshots
or other material.

You ask about where I would settle in Europe if I
had the chance. Actually, I think I would want to
move around a bit by the seasons. I can't really think
of any place that has good weather all the year
around, at least where you would want to live, from
the point of view of interesting people and sur-
roundings. I love the Dordogne in summer, but it's
terrible there in winter. And I've always felt very
much at home in all parts of Italy, but it's getting
so terribly over-run there now with tourists from
everywhere in certain seasons. Then there is Aus-
tria, where the people are so nice, the living inexpensive, and the countryside beautiful, but there
isn't too much intellectual stimulation, you might
say. Spain, I'm afraid, is out, because of the climate
that you feel from the political situation there. But,
although I've never been there, I have heard many
fine reports about Mallorca. Italian friends have also
reported favorably on parts of Sardinia.

If you do get down to the Dordogne on your car
trip, and feel like it, I think you would enjoy my
old friend the sculptor Henri Henghes. He is a most
delightful character, and married to a lovely English
girl, who once was a ballet dancer. They live on a
little hillside farm called La Peyrière, in a village
named Tursac, which is close to Les Eyzies. They
make occasional trips away when he has an exhibi-

tion somewhere, or a commission to do a piece of sculpture for someone, but most of the time they are there, and you could write ahead to find out. He knows all about the cave paintings and the interesting sights in the region. . . .

As ever, and Merry Christmas!
JAMES LAUGHLIN

/ • /

Ledig: H. M. Ledig-Rowohlt, illegitimate son of Ernst Rowohlt and his successor as publisher of Rowohlt Verlag.

Henri Henghes: Pseudonym of Heinz Winterfeld Klussmann, German Jewish sculptor. JL had met him in the 1930s when Henghes hitchhiked or walked from Hamburg to Rapallo. Pound took him in and provided materials, from which Henghes carved a stone centaur that became the model for the ND colophon. (See JL, *Pound as Wuz* [Graywolf Press, 1987], p. 13, and *The Man in the Wall* [ND, 1993], p. 66.)

160. TLS-2   Jan. 9th, 1961
                                          Reinbek/Hamburg

DEAR BOB:

. . . Haven't heard any more from you about the new book of Selections from my writings; are you still working on it? Among the Mss. I furnished for this project was one called "Stand Still Like the Humming Bird," which I had once sent to the *Noonday Review* and which they returned, saying the mag had folded, or something like that . . . can you think of any American or English mag. which might take this script—*and pay for it?* I get many requests for texts, but seldom any suggestion about real money. The paying ones usually want nothing to do with me, or else don't like what I offer. Have a look-see,

if you can find time for it. If you could make *readable*
photocopies of it, I would love to have two copies—
for foreign editors⟨. . .⟩here in Europe they take
what I offer and no bones about it.

And now for the big news⟨. . . .⟩I've just written
a play⟨. . .⟩my first. I wrote it without thinking,
you might say, in three days. Now I am revising,
inserting, and retyping—more slowly and think-
ingly(!) It's a mixture of farce, melodrama, bur-
lesque⟨. . .⟩with musical numbers—largely over the
juke box, but in last act, which is supposed to be a
riot, real musicians perform several numbers—hilar-
iously—but must be good players. Three acts, with
a short in-between scene—like an oleo. I don't know
what to make of it, naturally. Am rather surprised it
came out of me—after all these years of not writing
plays. But am delighted that I broke through—and
no longer fear the medium, as I once did. (In fact,
I'm already thinking if I may not try another soon.)

It'll take a few weeks, no doubt, to get good copies made. Meanwhile perhaps you could suggest
whom to show it to—for stage production. And, if
you take it for book publication, I presume that does
not mean that you also come in on royalties from
theatre productions. Or how do we stand on this
business contract wise? . . .

In a few days I'm off to Berlin to see Hildegard,
who just opened in a new play there. Then back here
for a few more weeks, I expect. By the way, Joan
Miró has just said he will do cover and illustrations
for Rowohlt's coming new edition of *The Smile*.
Good news. Both Rowohlt and Feltrinelli are going
to bring out *To Paint Is to Love Again*—better for-
mat, more reproductions. The big album (Dumont-
Schauberg, Cologne) comes out in April.

> *Enuf.* Good cheer!
> HENRY

/ • /

the new book of Selections: Published in due course as *Stand Still Like the Hummingbird* (ND, 1962).

a play: Just Wild About Harry: A Melo-Melo in Seven Scenes (ND, 1963).

Joan Miró: (1893–1983), Spanish artist, one of several painters HM acknowledged as an influence on *The Smile at the Foot of the Ladder*.

To Paint Is to Love Again: HM essay on the role of painting in his life published as a brochure with HM watercolors as illustrations (Cambria Books, 1960).

The big album: This publication included reproductions of HM watercolors, together with the German translation of "The Angel Is My Watermark," his essay on writing and painting from *Black Spring*.

161. TLS-1   January 13, 1961

                                            New York

DEAR HENRY,

Thank you so much for sending us the autographed copy of the beautiful little "Christmas Eve at the Villa Seurat" which you have gotten out with Rowohlt. It is a most attractive booklet to add to the ever-growing collection of your works, and the tribute to the elder Rowohlt is very touching.

Bob has just shown me your letter to him of January 9th, and that's most exciting news about the play which you have written. More power to you! We can all hardly wait to see what you have done in this new field. Bob will be writing you soon, I know, about the questions you raise in regard to publication and production. Generally speaking, book publication does not carry with it any participation in the stage rights. However, if you decided that you wanted to have us act as an agent for stimulating productions in this country, that could be arranged separately. Bob has done this for a number of dramatic authors; because he is very modest, I should perhaps tell you that he has done a crashing job of it for the Lorca family and several others. Through his Theatre Arts Books work he has numberless valuable connections [in] the theater world all over the country.

We definitely do want very much to go ahead with another volume of selected pieces, and I know that Bob has been doing a great deal of work in getting the material which might be included collected and lined up.

That's fine news, too, about the various editions of the painting book. All in all, it sounds as though you are having a marvelous time over there, and exerting a very stimulating effect on the European literary scene.

As ever,

J

/ · /

Theatre Arts Books: Before coming to ND, RM was directly involved with the theatre world through his work as director of Theatre Arts Books.

162. TL-1   January 31, 1961
                                                                     [Norfolk]

DEAR HENRY,

At the request of some good friends in India, I am forwarding on to you under separate cover, care of Rowohlt, a French novel called *L'Orpailleur,* written, apparently by a Frenchman who has become a Hindu, has taken the name "Satprem" and is now connected with the Sri Aurobindo Ashram in Pon-

dichéry. You will notice that he has enclosed a dedi-
cation to you in the book, and I guess he is one of
your many fans throughout the world.

I am so swamped with other work that I haven't
had a chance to read it, but it looks interesting. It
was sent to me by a most interesting couple, a
French count who abandoned his wife and children
in France to marry a beautiful young Indian girl
from the Malabar coast, and they now inhabit the
garden villa of the favorite of a former Nizam in
Hyderabad. When you make your long-planned trip
out to India, you certainly ought to meet them.

I hope you are having as fine a time as ever over
there in Germany. Here in Connecticut we have
been having a real winter—several feet of snow and
really cold!

As ever,
JAMES LAUGHLIN

163. TLS-1   Feb. 27th [1961]
                                          Reinbek

DEAR BOB:

. . . (Incidentally I signed up with Rosset for the
two *Tropics;* he and Hoffman came to Hamburg last
week for that purpose.) But keep this under your
hat for the time being, yes? (I was obliged to do this
for reasons I'll explain another time. No
choice.) . . .

I think you're too concerned about the selection
for that anthology of stories and essays. Close your
eyes and pick a dozen—like that. Nothing to fret
about. . . .

And now a word about my play. I am on final

rewrite. In the middle to-day. Completely new scenes in beginning—scrapped my first ones. Much better, livelier. Have it in hand, and will finish definitely in next three days. . . . Once you have it in your hands, can I know in ten days or so if some one (first one you show it to) is interested or not? I don't want to wait months to get a verdict from America. If they don't jump for it, the hell with them! I'll be satisfied with European productions. Hoffman, of course, will handle it for Europe and England. You for America—unless you feel it's no good, not worth handling. Let me know frankly. I understand better, since talking to Rosset, what means Broadway and Off Broadway—not a hell of a lot of difference, it seems. Says Barney—there's a dearth of material (plays) at present, but good actors, directors, etc. . . .

Many thanks for all your valiant efforts. And my best to Thomas Merton (a sort of "Father Brown"). I got the book by the French author (now Hindu) yes.

All the best to you and Jay.
HENRY

/ · /

Broadway and Off Broadway: In response to HM's letter of January 9, RM had written that the Off Broadway theatre was producing some wonderful non-traditional works. HM had replied: "You speak of 'off-B'way' theatres. I was hoping mine might make Broadway. I don't think it's avant-garde stuff."

Thomas Merton: (1915–1969), American poet, Trappist monk, and ND author. He and JL became close friends. HM likens Merton to Father Brown, the priest-detective in a number of novels by G. K. Chesterton.

164. CC-1   March 3, 1961
                                               [New York]

DEAR HENRY:

. . . Both J. and I understand about Rosset and the
Tropics. Only hope you got a very good price. . . .

About the play. Shoot it on just as quickly as you
can. No, it does not have to be printed, although
when a big play agent goes out with a script, he has
it mimeographed. I don't think we want that at this
point, but we should have several copies, if only
because a producer usually wants more than one if
he is at all interested. If it is all right by you, just as
soon as we get the script, we'll have a typist start
working on it, and produce about five or six copies
which can be of course clearly done on an electric
typewriter today. It all sounds most exciting, and
I've already spoken to the boys at the Circle at the
Square, which of course is the best and most successful consistently of off-Broadway theatres. Trouble there is that they've been so successful that
they're booked up for a year or so, and Jose
Quintero, who is their genius director, is now off
making films in Rome. Circle in the Square, of
course, is where the Genet *Balcony* has been running
for some months.

                          Yours in haste,
                          ROBERT M. MACGREGOR

                          / · /

Genet: Jean Genet (1910–1986), French playwright.

165. CC-2   March 31, 1961
                                               [New York]

DEAR HENRY:

. . . *Wild About Harry* came while I was away, but
has now been typed up—despite the fact that most
of the typists we use seem to be typing dissertations
at New York University; this must be the high-pro-
duction period for that factory! We have ten copies
of *Wild About Harry,* and one was mailed right away
to Michael Hoffman. Perhaps you have it.

Another was given to Ted Mann of Circle in the
Square who said he'd have a report back to me by
Wednesday. However, their production of *Under
Milk Wood* by Dylan Thomas opened Wednesday
night, and I thought I'd wait until tomorrow at least
before I start bothering him. *Under Milk Wood*
received a very good review in *The Times* yesterday
morning. I saw a preview of it last Sunday and was
greatly impressed with the simplicity with which
they treated this remarkable work which of course
isn't a play and isn't a poem. It is something in
between. As I told Hoffman I am "wild about
Harry" myself. I think it is wonderful, and I love
the clown characters that keep coming in and out. I
also think you have developed the main characters
very well and the whole gives a quite wonderful
feeling of the abortiveness of city life, ⟨while⟩ the
ending is magnificent. It is the characters I keep
thinking back on, and as the typist said, "They are
fabulous American creatures!"

Should we plan to start book production right
away, regardless of a play production? As you may
know, the theater in this country is a chaotic mess.
Hopes are raised and lowered, and one never knows
really which set of plans is going to materialize. (I've

just gotten through talking with an off-Broadway producer who has paid quite a large amount of money to have an option on a Lorca play that has never been done in New York, and who is going to let this money go—it is non-returnable—because he and his director would rather do *The Blacks* by Genet which they must do right away in order to hold their option on that. But even for that they can't find a theater and may lose out!) . . .

All the best, to Vince and you.

Yours,
ROBERT M. MACGREGOR

/ • /

Dylan Thomas: (1914–1953), Welsh poet. ND published a number of his works, including his play, *Under Milk Wood* (ND, 1954).

Vince: Vincent Birge, HM's driver and companion as he traveled around Europe. A chapter devoted to "good old Vincent" in *My Bike and Other Friends* (Capra, 1978) gives an account of HM's wanderings around Europe at this time.

166. TLS-1   April 12, 1961
                                         Montpellier, France

DEAR BOB:

. . . Sounds awfully limited, chances of getting anything produced on or off Broadway. And so many theatres! Patience! But remember what I said before—if *Cancer* goes over, or even if not! that's so much publicity for my play—in advance. One shouldn't wait too long, or the effectiveness is lost. (I still have to send you dope on records, singers, etc.—not very much—but am in a low mood, have been, for weeks. Can't seem to find the spot to settle

in. Europe in general seems run-down to me—lacks
the old spirit. Or else I'm off, worn down myself.)

I suppose the Rimbaud copy arrived but haven't
got it yet. Am checking with Rowohlt now. Started
translating from the French but gave up because of
low spirits. Will tackle again, however. This is my
own "Season in Hell," it seems. . . .

Funny item: two of my good astrologer friends
predict that no matter what the seeming obstacles
the play will be taken and prove a success—because
of the period during which it was written. Put that
in your pipe for the time being. It's your trump
card. Rowohlt turned it down, as you may know,
but that doesn't bother me—there will be others in
Germany ready to pounce on it. Personally, or
frankly rather, I don't give a damn now what happens to it. If I write another, as I probably will, it
will be entirely different—more like a bomb than a
play, I think.

Write me care of Hoffman as usual, eh? All the
best meanwhile.

Maybe I should have gone to Japan, what!

H E N R Y

167. CC-1   April 27, 1961

D E A R H E N R Y ,

I hope that this will find you in good health and
spirits, enjoying some lovely part of Europe in the
full bloom of spring. After much cold and wet, it
has finally turned warm here, and we are all reviving
after the hard winter.

I wanted to tell you how much I enjoyed reading
your play. That Harry of yours is quite a character,

and the whole thing has a wonderful verve and rol-
licking dash. I hope we will see it on the boards here
soon, which I believe Bob is working on, and, of
course it should be published, too.

Barney seems to be going full blast, with his usual
wonderful energy, on the *Tropics,* and I believe Bob
has sent you the story that was in the *New York
Times* this week. We certainly wish him luck, and
will help him all we can, and hope it turns out to
your satisfaction.

We have already started with plans to put *The
Cosmological Eye, Remember to Remember* and *The
Sunday After the War* back into print. As you will
recall, we held back on the reprint of these titles for
a time in order to focus attention on the *Reader,* but
now I think they should all be available again. And
I believe we should do them both as hardbounds,
and as paperbacks. Simultaneously. . . .

We'll want to be following along soon, too, with
a new printing of the *Rimbaud,* unless you decide
that you want to hold this up for the new translation
of him that you are doing, but I think these other
big representative volumes are more urgent to
tackle first.

A new printing of the *Reader* is just coming off the
press this week, so we'll be well supplied with that.

> With best wishes, as ever,
> JAMES LAUGHLIN

168. TLS-2   May 1st. [1961]
                                 Lausanne (Suisse)

DEAR JAY,

Just got your letter here, where I am fishing
around for a place to rent, for the Summer at least.

Am getting weary of traveling and looking. Got out
of France because of Algerian trouble—things look
bad still, to me, in France. If nothing good here I
may try Portugal. Do you know it at all? . . .

Tell Bob I'm grateful for what he did with
Esquire—on the "Humming Bird." Good work.

(Apparently the *H.M. Reader* is doing well—to
my surprise. Must be Durrell's preface and selection
that is doing the trick.)

I haven't heard any more from Bob about my
play. Wonder what's happening! Was surprised that
you both liked it so much, though glad to know it.
I have a hunch I'll do another, once I settle down
somewhere. . . .

I have many reasons now to believe that the *Tropics* (Rosset) will come off successfully—trium-
phantly, in fact. Will give you my reasons later,
when this becomes a fact. It will interest you to
know how I know. . . .

All the best!
HENRY

/ • /

"*Humming Bird*": RM had succeeded in selling HM's essay "Stand Still
Like the Hummingbird" to *Esquire* for $500.

169. CC-2   May 19, 1961
                                              [New York]

DEAR HENRY:

. . . I expect that Michael [Hoffman] has been telling you of the various excitements in regard to
Tropic of Cancer. Grove Press sent a couple of copies

over to us last Friday—evidently because they didn't get in touch with us early enough to get permission for the quotations from your other books included in Karl Shapiro's essay which they are using. At first the bookshops even in the Village were afraid to put the books on sale, as you may have heard, but I believe that following the acceptance by *The New York Times* of an ad for Grove Press they have the book available. I haven't been able to check the uptown shops yet to see what is happening there. Some of the very small shops, who may not have so much to lose, have it in their window at least around here. We are cheering them all on as you know. . . .

The fellow at Circle-in-the-Square wants to get a couple of more readings of your play. He however has said that I could also show it to Julian Beck and his wife of The Living Theatre since they are going abroad at the end of next week, taking the William Carlos Williams play, *The Connection,* and one other to The Theatre of Nations in Paris where they have been invited as perhaps you know. I want them to have a chance to read it right off. . . .

Yours,
ROBERT M. MACGREGOR

/ · /

Karl Shapiro's essay: "The Greatest Living Author," reprinted as a preface to the Grove Press *Tropic of Cancer.*

170. CC-2   May 26, 1961
                                               [New York]

DEAR HENRY:

. . . I am enclosing a proposed table of contents which makes a solid-sized book. It has some of your very best writing I feel, and it's also broad and comprehensive. Included are portraits, stories, pieces that are angry and quite wistful. It has views that are hard hitting and views that are close to ecstasy. There is also philosophy and something akin to religion. It touches on censorship and the joy of living, loving and painting. . . .

Oh, one other thing about the table of contents: it turns out that the reason J.L. didn't want to do *Aller Retour New York* when you originally brought it to him was that there were certain things in it that could be interpreted as anti-Semitic. We all know very well that you aren't now and never were. He is rereading it from this point of view, and either he or I will write you about small points. I expect you would want them changed if we republished.

Enclosed is a copy of an ad Rosset had in this week's *Village Voice*. Also a photocopy of a note he and we had in this week's *Publishers Weekly*. I will also enclose anything else that seems at hand that I know will be of interest to you.

I ran into Barney on the street yesterday morning while I was walking the little Corgi. He seemed very happy about everything, possibly a little disappointed that there hasn't been more to buck on *Tropic of Cancer*. He told me quite a bit about the jury choice on Mallorca of Jorge Luis Borges who shared the prize that Barney thought should have come to you. We are of course interested because we are publishing the first volume of Borges' works in

English early in the fall, and so far hadn't even been able to get an English publisher to nibble on the idea. Congratulations on your special citation from that jury meeting.

My best to Vincent.

Yours,

ROBERT M. MACGREGOR

/ • /

table of contents: For *Stand Still Like the Hummingbird*.

the prize: The Formentor Prize, awarded to Borges and Samuel Beckett in 1961.

171. CC-2   Transcribed July 10, 1961

[San Francisco]

DEAR HENRY:

This letter will come to you from the New York office, but actually I am dictating it out in San Francisco, where I am visiting with Rexroth in his wonderful house on Scott Street, and also hope to see something of various of the other writers in this part of the world. . . .

There is a very interesting group of young poets and writers centered around Ferlinghetti. They are now planning to get out a new magazine, or rather an anthology, which will be sort of a "protest" statement. Ferlinghetti hopes very much that you will be able to send him something for this. I have only seen some of the material, but the general idea seems to be that writers should express their dissatisfaction with the way the "system" is conducting our affairs in this sad world. Of course, your whole oeuvre has been a protest of this kind—and perhaps the most eloquent of our time—I hope that you will still find something that you will want to add to this young group of Ferlinghetti's friends.

It is a big disappointment that you aren't down there in Big Sur. But perhaps I'll be able to stop by and say hello to Eve and the children if they are still there, if I drive down that way.

Ferlinghetti is selling the *Tropic of Cancer* quite openly in his store, and he tells me that all of your books are doing extremely well. He does not seem at all worried about eventuality, and, in fact, I think he would welcome the opportunity to go to bat again. I haven't seen the book in any other store windows around town, but I haven't as yet made a very thorough search. I'll let you know of anything I hear, but I daresay Bob is more in touch with developments back there in New York. . . .

With best wishes,

As ever,
JAMES LAUGHLIN

/ • /

Ferlinghetti: Lawrence Ferlinghetti (1920–), San Francisco poet whose City Lights Bookstore was the headquarters of the Beat Generation in the 1950s. ND published a number of his books, including *A Coney Island of the Mind* (1958), which sold over 700,000 copies. The title is taken from HM's *Black Spring*.

172. ALS-1   10/5/61
                      Pac[ific] Pal[isades, California]

DEAR BOB—

   . . . I found that "duologue" between Merton and
Suzuki very, very exciting. What Merton has to say
about Paradise and Heaven—most interesting. Do
send me the finished product, when out. If you have
published Merton, send me one, won't you, that
you think I'd like. Not a novel—the metaphysics. I
like his thinking. Give him greetings from me some
time. Never read a line of his before. . . .
   All the best—to you, Jay, Anne and all those
lovely colored people in your office. More power
to them!

                                    HENRY

                      / • /

duologue: "Wisdom in Emptiness: A Dialogue by Daisetz T. Suzuki
and Thomas Merton" was to appear in *ND 17.*

173. TLS-1   Nov. 13, 1961
                                  Pacific Palisades

DEAR BOB:

   . . . Was happy to get the new annual with Merton's fragment on the Desert Fathers. Do give him
warm greetings from me whenever you write him.
I feel closer to him, his way of thinking, than any
other American writer I know of. By the way, the
man he ought to read, is Erich Gutkind. Author of
The Absolute Collective (one of my very great favor-

ites, along with Berdyaev's work) and *Choose Life*. Merton might find Gutkind as enthralling to grapple with as Suzuki. Of course he is thoroughly anti-Christian, but in another sense closer to Merton than the so-called Christian apologists.

Enuf!
HENRY

174. TL-1   December 12, 1961

DEAR HENRY,

Not long ago I passed on to Thomas Merton, down there in his monastery in Kentucky, what you had written about him and his work in a letter to Bob, and now I have heard back from Tom about you, and I thought you would be interested in what he says. Here it is.

"Thanks for the quote from Henry Miller. Well, that is a testimonial. I am really warmed by it. To me that is an indication that I am perhaps after all a Christian. I believe that this element of inner recognition that cuts right through apparent external barriers and divisions is of crucial importance today. It is in this kind of recognition that Christ is present in the world, and not just in the erection and definition of barriers that say where He is and where He isn't. *There are no such barriers*. Those who imagine them too literally are in illusion. Not that the Church isn't visible, but there is that little man in Boston who says that only the ones who are members and Catholics are really saved: and he is excommunicated for saying it."

Isn't that fine? You and Tom have so much in common and your wonderful spirit of understanding humanity, that I hope some time the two of you can get together. If you are ever down there in Ken-

tucky, you ought to go see him. I suppose that
Father Abbot would bar the door if there were too
much advance publicity on your visit, at least if he
has been reading the newspapers, but I think if you
just turned up there would be no trouble about
seeing Tom and that you would enjoy him greatly.

Tom is much interested in the Gutkind books that
you suggested, and I'm going to round them up for
him.

I hope that you will have the kids with you for
Christmas and that you will all have a very merry
and happy time.

As ever,
JAMES LAUGHLIN

/ • /

Thomas Merton: The Trappist monk would seem to have little in common with the author of the *Tropics,* but after JL quoted each to the
other, they entered into correspondence, read each other's writings,
and found much common ground. JL, who often visited Merton,
smuggled some of HM's books to him. (See "Thomas Merton and His
Poetry" in JL's *Random Essays.* See also "Thomas Merton/Henry
Miller: An Exchange of Letters," ed. David Cooper, *Helix,* 19/20
[1984], 15–28. David Cooper is editing the correspondence between JL
and Merton.)

175. TLS-1   Jan. 17, 1962
[Pacific Palisades]

copy for Bob Mac Gregor (in case Jay is away)
DEAR JAY:

I've been having some correspondence lately with
Patchen following upon his last operation which
was again an ordeal and somewhat of a mess. He

says that he can no longer take any pain-killing drugs—only aspirin, which is utterly inadequate—and is in constant, great pain.

It started with his writing me from the hospital. Wanted to know if I would find him a publisher for his collected poems and drawings. Thought if he got published—his collected work—then he might stand a chance of receiving money from some Foundation.

In a more recent letter he reminded me of the fact that he had suggested to you to bring out the collected work in two volumes, instead of one, one one year, the other the next, in order to reduce the sales price and make the book more available to the general public. And then he adds—but I never had a response to my letter. Written evidently months ago. Thought I might take it up with you, and if you would do something, perhaps I could write a Foreword for it.

He also suggested that an Open Letter to mags, newspapers, etc. by me might help some. I had had the same idea myself, but was turning over the construction of it in my mind. At the same time I received a little mag or sheet called "The Paper," from my attorney in Chicago (working on the *Cancer* case there), in which I see that in 1959 an appeal had been made—over 1500 letters sent out—by the group writing for this little sheet. In it was Rexroth's wonderful tribute to Patchen. But then, what has been the result? I know some money was raised—I remember asking Eve to send him something for me—but how much and to what end? Sometimes I think it is well-nigh impossible to help Patchen; he seems to live under a black star. His is certainly the most tragic case among all our writers to-day. And I doubt if even a millionaire could solve his financial problems. To say nothing of his chronic illness. It makes me despair. I keep looking at it from every angle and can't seem to arrive at a solution.

You know as much or more about all this. I write merely to see if it is hopeless in your mind to bring out the two volumes as he suggests. Naturally he wants them done in de luxe style—and I can't blame him for that. It must be done superbly or not at all.

Do let me hear from you, or write him direct, if you like. I will probably go to Big Sur next week for a few days only, then back here. I am just getting over a bad attack of the flu—hence my silence. It was nice to get Thomas Merton's note about me, but I doubt if I'll ever get to his neck of the woods. I must go to Berlin soon, to attend rehearsal of my play and after that (April–May) to Mallorca as member of the jury awarding the Formentor Prize. Meanwhile I am working on *Nexus* (Vol. 2). I asked Mac Gregor the other day when or if he intends bringing out the published play, in book form. It's been taken by three Scandinavian countries now— nothing yet from England or America or France. Well, that's it. All the best to you meanwhile, and to your good wife whom I always enjoy meeting.

H E N R Y

/ • /

Patchen: Kenneth Patchen's poetry was first published by ND in 1939 and regularly thereafter; ND would publish his *Collected Poems* in 1968. Both HM and JL wrote essays on Patchen, HM an early tribute, JL a posthumous reminiscence, recalling among other associations that Patchen and his wife Miriam ran the ND office in Norfolk in 1939.

the published play: On January 26 RM replied: "About the publishing of the play, I had misunderstood. I had thought you didn't want it published until it was produced. The nibbles have not been very strong recently, and I was thinking of trying a completely different world with the play. I'm a little disgusted with off-Broadway at the moment anyway. It seems to be a world of fast-buck artists!"

176. CC-2   January 29, 1962

DEAR HENRY,

Thanks so much for your good letter of January 17th, which is chiefly about Kenneth Patchen. Let me assure you that I do have him constantly on my mind. In fact, I keep trying to get him various grants and awards from different foundations or societies, but not, to date, with much success. In fact, with no success. I keep after them all.

I saw a bit of the Patchens when I was out in California last summer and I agree with you that the situation is pretty desperate, and heaven only knows what will happen to them in the end. The last "appeal," with its related benefit readings and performances of various kinds in different parts of the country, which I think took place while you were in Europe, was fairly successful. I believe that something over five thousand dollars was raised from various sources at that time. But I suppose that money will soon be used up and there will be another emergency.

Bob and I have given a great deal of thought to Kenneth's idea for a big collected volume of his poems, and we have come to the conclusion that, while it might be nice for him to have it, it would not make him much money, because people simply are not buying big expensive books of poetry now, and tying up so much capital in it would just prevent us from getting out the smaller paperbacks which we can sell well for him, which will bring him in some royalties. The kind of book he wants would have to sell for $10. and people just aren't laying out that kind of money for poetry these days. But they are buying the little $1.50 paperbacks quite well, and we would plan to try to do one of these about each year for Patchen. As you may know, we recently brought out a new paperback edition of his *Journal of Albion Moonlight.*

I have approached a number of the largest New York publishers on behalf of Patchen with this idea of the collected volume—we would be glad to let any one of the good ones do such a project with all of the royalties going to Patchen—but all of them seem to feel about as we do on the practicality of such a large volume. . . .

That is great news about the play coming up in Berlin. I can't understand why any of the New York off-Broadway producers have not taken it up. I know that Bob has been showing it around to them very thoroughly. I suppose it is just that they lack imagination. But I can assure you that our interest in it is not affected by this temporary lack of success among the producers and we hope definitely to bring it out as a book as soon as we have gotten going on the *Hummingbird.* I believe it should do very well as a little inexpensive paperback.

Do be sure to let us know when you plan to be coming through New York on your way to Europe as we would all love to see you.

As ever,
JAMES LAUGHLIN

177. TLS-2   March 9, 1962
                                 New York

DEAR HENRY,

. . . We have had a note from Jules Feiffer in Los Angeles and are sending him a copy of *Harry* as he requests, and you approve. That would be great if someone out there got interested in doing it. I simply cannot understand what is eating the local producers here not to jump at such a wonderful thing. I have heard, however, that the "off-Broadway" theater is having a rather hard time financially this year and perhaps that makes them cautious. . . .

Bob and I have put *Harry* down on the schedule to be a book for publication late this year, or early 1963. We are eager to do it, and the only reason we have been holding back is that we keep believing that there will be a production at any moment, and, if so, chances are you would want to make changes in rehearsal, and it's always best to have the book agree with the production script.

That certainly was wonderful about the fine court decision on *Tropic of Cancer* in Chicago. There is one judge that has some sense.

With best from us all, as ever,
JL

/ • /

Jules Feiffer: (1929–   ), American playwright and cartoonist. On March 3, HM had written that he had lunch with Pfeiffer, who might be interested in staging *Just Wild About Harry*.

court decision: In January, Elmer Gertz had defended HM and the Grove Press in the Chicago trial of *Tropic of Cancer*. On February 21, Judge Samuel B. Epstein declared the book not obscene. This was not the end of the matter, however, and the Chicago trial was to continue, along with some sixty others, until June 22, 1964, when the U.S. Supreme Court delivered the last word.

178. CC-1   June 4, 1962

DEAR HENRY,

I'm sorry that I was badly tied up the evening you
were in New York and couldn't get over with Bob
to see you, but at least it was good to talk to you on
the telephone, and you sounded "merry and bright"
as you always like to say. I hope you will find all
well there in California, and have fun with the kids.

Not long ago when I was rereading *Harry*—and it
really is a wonderful thing!—I noticed that you had
a line where a rather "pungent" expression is used,
and you had indicated in the stage direction, that it
was to be delivered "in Italian."

Thinking you might like to have the actual Italian
phrase, I did a little discreet research by mail with a
reliable friend in Florence, and am pleased to advise
you of the possible phrases, as follows:

The most usual one for this is probably: *"per quel
che mi fotte, in culo a tua madre."*

However, if you would like something even a little bit stronger, there is: *"per cinque Lire metterei a
buco ritto tua madre."*

This last was supplied to my informant by no less
an authority than the Marchese Torreggiani, who is
seventy years old, and should know by now. He
had, however, the delicacy to turn it over to her in
a "sealed envelope."

I am also told that the effectiveness of the adjura-
tion can be increased if one refers to one's grand-
mother, rather than one's mother. If you desire this
"escalation of intensity," we can simply shift *"tua
madre,"* in either case, to *"tua nonna."*

I am enclosing an extra carbon of this letter so that
you can just write on it which one you would like,

and fire it back to me, and I'll take care of it in the proofs.

> As ever,
> JAMES LAUGHLIN

179. TLS-1   June 22, 1962
                                               New York

DEAR HENRY,

. . . I was so deeply distressed to hear about the death of Jean Wharton. She was an extraordinary woman and it always made me very happy that you had written about her in your book. That will immortalize her as she deserves to be. I had seen her only last summer in California, we had a very happy little visit together, and she seemed quite well, and gave no indication of a serious illness. . . .

> With best wishes,
> JL

/ • /

Jean Wharton: On June 14, HM had written: "Jean Wharton was buried yesterday—died of cancer. Hard to believe this. Such a *wonderful* person—healed others but not herself. So typical. I feel it is a great loss."

180. TLS-2   July 14, 1962
                                               New York

DEAR HENRY:

. . . Mr. Gunther Stuhlmann came in Monday and I spent quite a time with him. Actually I had met him before in a quite different connection. He explained to me that the letters from you to Anaïs Nin have been sort of dumped in his lap. She picked out those she thought she would allow to be published and told him to try to edit the thing into shape. He has not done very much with it, but tells me they fall into three categories: the first group having to do with the writing of *Tropic of Cancer,* etc; second, written on the trip that became *The Air-Conditioned Nightmare;* third, impressions of movies, people, books, ideas, etc. I told him that I thought that in general the exchange would be better if there were some letters from the other side, and he is going to ask Anaïs about this when she comes back from Europe sometime this week. In the meantime the manuscript itself appeared in the office this afternoon and I have only been able to look at it far enough to see that some parts are photocopies of typescripts made from your letters, and others photocopies of the letters themselves, including some that are hand-written. I would think actually that one would not know how valuable this collection is until one can see the manuscript of the Durrell-Miller correspondence and perhaps judge how much duplication there might be. However, I shall be fascinated to get into it myself in any case. . . .

I am delighted you are feeling fine and the plans are going forward to go to Edinburgh August 15th. I fear I haven't a relative I can claim in Scotland. My MacGregor ancestry came to this country in 1680, then got in trouble and had to flee to Canada, or rather his grandson did, when he took the wrong side in the "trouble of '76"—1776, of course. However, I have a special feeling of affinity for Scotland, if only because it is such an attractive country. And Edinburgh I think you will certainly love, one of the most attractive cities physically in the world. Even

the slums have a quite marvellous quality and genuine character, but then don't all slums? And my
Scottish friend, Sara Douglas, who is a niece of
Norman Douglas's, isn't there to look out for you
either, as I know she would enjoy doing. She
in fact has just left for two years in Japan, which is,
of course, where I think you really should be going.
I know there are attractions in Berlin and elsewhere.

Yours,
Bob

/ · /

Gunther Stuhlmann: New York literary agent, who later edited HM's
Letters to Anaïs Nin and five volumes of Nin's diaries. Now editor of
Anaïs: An International Journal.

Edinburgh: HM had been invited to participate in the first Edinburgh
Writers' Conference.

Norman Douglas: (1968–1952), English writer.

181. ALS-1   7/14/62

DEAR HENRY—

Will you be pausing in New York on your way
to Scotland? And old Indian friend of mine, T. V.
Kunhi Krishnan, a journalist from Madras, is eager
to interview you for articles in Indian papers and
magazines. He is attending the International Semi-
nar at Harvard but would come to New York to
meet you. I recommend him. He is outstanding
among young Indians I have known. A no-nonsense
type who would not "sensationalize" in writing

about you, but be serious about philosophical ideas etc. Can I set up a date with him for you?

Best wishes!
JL

182. CC-1

July 27, 1962
[? New York]

DEAR HENRY,

That's great that you might be able to find time to see my Indian journalist friend T. V. Kunhi Krishnan on the 16th of August when you are passing through New York. I have written him up at Harvard, urging him to try to make himself available for most of the day so that he can fit easily into your schedule, which, no doubt, will be crowded.

I thought you might like to have this copy which I made up of the table of contents of the material Tom Moore has assembled for the paperback anthology of your pieces on writing, chosen from various books, and which shows, rather clearly, the various lengths, and the sources from which the excerpts are drawn. I hope we will have a chance to talk about this when you come through because it seems to me that there are some pretty complicated permissions problems on it. No doubt Dr. Hoffman could help a lot in straightening these out, but I thought we should get your slant on the whole matter before we approach him for help.

I think this would make an extremely fascinating book, but I'm not sure that we would get the big public sale on it that some of your other books are having because of the fact that it is not in any way sensational in character. It would be of greatest interest to students and to writers, but probably not to all those who buy the *Tropic* books and such like. So I feel that we probably ought to try to set it up on some sort of pro-rated royalty basis which would be fair to all involved—yourself, Tom Moore and the publishers of the various books.

With best wishes, as ever,
J AMES L AUGHLIN

/ · /

Tom Moore: Co-founder of the Henry Miller Literary Society in Minneapolis and editor of *Henry Miller on Writing* (ND, 1964).

183. ALS-4   Sept. 16th '62
                    chez Hildegard Neff—Bavaria

D EAR B OB—

Got here 2 days ago from Copenhagen. Wonderful spot. Should have come to Bavaria long ago. Tell Jay too, will you? I'm going to explore the region, go to Salzburg, Innsbruck, etc. while here. Hilde is in Zagreb now, making a film of Catherine the Great.

I woke up last night wondering whether any one (music publisher, song writer or heirs) would sue me or us for using his title—"(I'm) Just Wild about Harry." Have you given that a thought ever? I go to Berlin from here, about the 28th or 30th (Sept.) to see what's what about stage production. Renate Gerhardt is handling that for me, you know. She's also going to publish it in book form, and I take it there will be no question of paying N.D. a percentage for foreign rights, as she was *first comer*. O.K.?

Now Mrs. Patti Hardesty writes me again about wanting to produce the play (*Harry*) with some California group. What do you say to that? Can I tell her to go ahead—or should she work through you? Or, should I wait to see how she does with the film of *The Smile?* She doesn't want to *direct* the play—just produce it.

I got a contract from her for the film rights, but it's so damned complicated, so meticulous, scrupulous, and couched in such bewildering legal lingo, I can't make it out. I'm just sitting on it like a chick, to see if it will hatch something. I hate to turn it over to my L.A. lawyers—that will bring on more complications.

And as for the *Cancer* deal, all's clear enough there, *only* by the looks of it the Income [Tax] people would get the lion's share of my earnings—whether I operate as an individual or a corporation. So I'm just standing still there too. I just don't want to work for our bloody government. When you see $100,000.00 it means you can count on getting 6 or 7 thousand. And a headache to boot.

I wonder if you have heard how that bill before the Legislature is doing. It was to put authors in the same category as inventors—in short, to let them pay a flat 25% Capital Gain tax instead of from 50 to 91% as at present. Maybe the Authors' League would know. But don't mention my name if you inquire. I don't want to belong to that outfit.

I'll stop. Seems I'm always giving you work with my questions. Address here, if you want to reach me quicker, is—

Am Muhlberg 2
Percha-bei-Starnberg
(Oberbayern)

West Germany
c/o Cameron—Knef

Cheers! Cha cha!
HENRY

/ • /

whether any one . . . would sue: RM replied: "I don't believe we have to
worry about using just the title *Just Wild About Harry* because of the
song 'I'm Just Wild About Harry.' However, music publishers are the
toughest in the whole world about rights and copyrights. There is a
special publishing house that exists only to collect royalties on 'Happy
Birthday to You!' "

Patti Hardesty: Patricia Hardesty had been in correspondence with HM
and RM, proposing first to do an art film of *The Smile at the Foot of the
Ladder* and subsequently a production of *Just Wild About Harry* with an
art theater group in the San Francisco Bay area. The correspondence
was to continue for years, but nothing ever came of either project.

184. CC-3   October 19, 1962
                                [New York]

DEAR HENRY:

. . . I probably should have made a separate letter
of this, but I want to get it off to you: every year for
the past four, or five, or six years *Poetry* Magazine
in Chicago has had an auction of things contributed
to them by interested friends, for which the Chica-
goans and others pay large sums, all of which goes
to *Poetry* Magazine. In fact by this means they have
managed to pay their deficit. The Joes who buy the
stuff always pay a great deal more than would be
paid in an ordinary auction or through a dealer and
I guess they are able to take it off their income taxes.
J. usually gives them something magnificent, like
some rare first edition by Pound that he bought in
Venice in 1931, when nobody had any money. This
year I think he's giving a small Eliot manuscript that

he bought years ago in Los Angeles. What I have done in the past is usually given a book published by New Directions and a letter from our files from the author that has something to do with the book. J. has taken the line that the letters and so on addressed to me are my property rather than New Directions', which I think most publishing houses would assume, and this is very generous of him. One year I gave a post card from Merton and a limited edition of his *Tower of Babel* abstract play that we had done. Another year something from Tennessee Williams and the copy of the book it was about. Always I ask permission of the author of the letter, although I don't suppose I have to.

Although you are not perhaps a versifying poet— at least I have never seen any verse from you—I think you are a greater poet than most, and I think the editors of *Poetry* Magazine and the people running the auction would think so too. You are in the news, and some millionaire might pay quite a sum for a letter of yours—all a little frightening isn't it?

Anyway, I have been through the folder for *Stand Still Like the Hummingbird* and rejected all the letters that suggest individuals are stinkers and have come up with one that is in your hand (evidently much better than a typescript with corrections), about *Stand Still,* interesting in itself and it takes a swipe at only one person, who is me, and a very gentle swipe at that. In fact it is a swipe about this business of commissions for agents. The date is 6/11/60 and I am enclosing a photocopy, which is what we would leave in our files. It even has something about poetry: "Up Pindar! Up Hölderlin! Up Nerval!" ⟨And⟩ "What is *not* poetry?" by Shapiro. Do you approve?

Best,
ROBERT M. MACGREGOR

185. CC-1   November 13, 1962
                                               [New York]

DEAR HENRY:

Just before we returned the page proofs for *Just Wild About Harry* to the printer and I got up the copyright page, I checked through the proofs to make sure that there did not seem to be any quotations of songs that needed permission of the copyright owners. As you know, song publishers are particularly touchy about these things.

Whether consciously or not, you evidently avoided this problem by having most of your characters merely hum the songs, or if you say they sing them, you don't give the words, or you give only enough of the words to identify them. . . .

Did I ever tell you that in Tennessee Williams' *Period of Adjustment* he quoted three lines of "Happy Birthday to You" which turns out to be the main part of the song? Soon after we published the book, we got a letter from a lawyer-music publisher objecting and asking for a permissions agreement. Our lawyer advised us to reply that we were quoting it under the "fair use" provisions of the copyright law for purposes of atmosphere and color. We never heard from the gentleman again, but we learned that the producers of the play, who can't afford a chance of an injunction and don't anyway have the same freedom that a book publisher has in these matters, had to pay over $1,000. I also learned that this lawyer-music publisher practically exists on the copyright earnings of this one song, which most of us, I think, take for granted is a part of the American folklore heritage!

                                               Best,
                                               ROBERT M. MACGREGOR

/ • /

Tennessee Williams: (1911–1983), ND author best known for his plays. His correspondence with JL is being edited by Peggy Fox.

186. CC-2   March 14, 1963

DEAR HENRY,

. . . I have just reread your *Plexus,* the question having been raised by Dr. Hoffman whether we would publish that here, or Barney, and I wanted to tell you again how much I enjoyed it. It is a "quieter" book than the *Tropics,* of course, but full of wonderful things. I don't believe that a couple of little sexy spots would cause any trouble.

Of course, if Barney is prepared to go ahead with the whole *Rosy Crucifixion* trilogy here, he certainly should. But if you were going to let it be split up here, *Plexus* might well be something that we could do effectively.

I was recently up at Harvard, having a little round-table talk with some of the literary boys there—what an exceedingly bright bunch!—and there was a great deal of interest in you among them, and very intelligent interest, too, I thought.

With best wishes, as ever,
JAMES LAUGHLIN

187. ALS-1   March 17th '63
                                              [Pacific Palisades]

DEAR JAY,

. . . As regards *Plexus* and *Nexus,* I rather think Rosset hopes to get these for publication—nothing

definite yet. Guess he's waiting for the U.S.
Supreme Court decision. I think, don't you, that he
should have these, if he wants them, in view of all
he has done for and with the *Tropics.*

Charles Rembar, the Grove Press lawyer, is now
prepared to appeal to Gov. Rockefeller should the
Brooklyn authorities insist on trying to extradite
me. The Syracuse case comes up in N.Y. State's
highest court week of the 24th. If the verdict is
favorable—and chances are it will be—that will
automatically quash this idiotic Brooklyn business.

I met Joe Levine of Embassy Pictures here twice
recently. (He's the one who financed the *Cancer*
film.) Rather like him—a genuine low-brow, like
another "Brooklyn boy."

Well, again thanks. My best to you and to Ann.

HENRY

/ • /

Plexus and Nexus: The second and third volumes of *The Rosy Crucifixion,* first published in Paris in 1952 and 1959, respectively. Grove Press
brought out the first American editions in 1965.

Cancer film: The plans of producer Joseph E. Levine to make a film of
Tropic of Cancer eventually came to nought.

188. CC-3   March 20, 1963
                                                  [New York]

DEAR HENRY:

Here is the contract for *Just Wild About Harry* in
three copies. It may seem a little absurd to be sign-
ing this contract after publication, but of course we
understand each other and where there is trust, as
here, your word and ours are as good as any written paper. . . .

Two developments here about *Harry:*

1. Edward Padula who is a Broadway producer of musicals *(Bye-Bye Birdie)* seems interested, and says he will come and see me next week with some sort of proposition. Herbert Machiz (see below) says he would want to turn it into a musical and "ruin it." May be special pleading.

2. Herbert Machiz, who directed *The Milk Train Doesn't Stop Here Any More* by Tennessee Williams which closed in New York Saturday night and is now going on tour, called me Friday and we talked again yesterday. I am enclosing a copy of his "experience" which, as you see, is considerable. Between us I'm not crazy about him as a person ⟨or a⟩ director. I am asking Tennessee who is at Key West, exactly what he thinks about the proposal outlined below. I will let you know what he reports. Even with all his drawbacks, however, Machiz does get production of interesting works done.

Last year he did *Milk Train* at the Spoleto Festival in Italy for about four performances with top actors—Hermione Baddeley, Mildred Dunnock, etc. It was as a result of the Spoleto production that Roger L. Stevens produced the play at the Morosco Theatre, opening January 21st.

Herbert Machiz would like to have the right to put on *Just Wild About Harry* at Spoleto this next summer, with an option to do it off-Broadway, or on Broadway if possible, next winter. He argues that the festivals are the only places where interesting "new theatre writers, whether they be T. S. Eliot or Henry Miller," have a chance of making the initial splash that's necessary. The theatre department of the Edinburgh Festival, where Eliot's plays have been several times first shown, is too conservative, he maintains, hence Spoleto is the only other place.

I explained about the Schiller Theatre world premiere, and he explained that that was all very well but he would have to know within two weeks. He went to Puerto Rico yesterday and will be back next Monday. He said by the way he would not object at all to the University of Rochester putting the play on first. In fact it might help him. Dr. Ricono thought that production at Spoleto would help the play all over Europe.

Let me know your initial reaction and I'll rush you all later information. . . .

Best.

As ever,
ROBERT M. MACGREGOR

/ • /

Schiller Theatre world premiere: The proposed production in Berlin had been delayed and was subsequently abandoned when news of the Spoleto production came out.

Dr. Ricono: Connie Ricono, Italian literary agent, had had the play translated and offered it to a theater in Rome.

189. CC-4 *Confidential—please destroy*

June 21, 1963
[New York]

DEAR HENRY:

J and I have been talking and thinking about the volume of your letters to Anaïs Nin, and I have come to the conclusion that the only way to approach the major problem involved is to be frank and open with you about it, knowing that you will understand our point of view, whether you agree with it or not, and with equal frankness and open dealing suggest how we should proceed. Maybe the answer is a simple one.

The volume as presented to us is made up entirely of your letters and of course according to moral as well as legal rights, their publication belongs to you. Unless you have formally and in a legal document assigned these rights to someone else, it would be with you that we would deal, and I hope that this will be the case.

You will remember that Miss Nin's agent took the letters away last year, so that I don't have them to refer to, but I remember that they contain a great deal that is you and are in general quite wonderful. There are a few small problems about the way they are set up, and I can go into them at a later date. We do want to publish them.

The main problem is that neither J nor I feel that we have the strength or courage or inclination to cope with what we foresee if we must deal with her. J seems to have heard stories about her or had direct experiences that have made him very leery. I have heard stories from some of the publishers that indicate unusually demanding, unreasonable, unpredictable behavior. It is true that persons can be direct and straightforward, as well as generous in the extreme with their friends, and be monsters with their publishers (I fear we bring out the worst in people particularly when they have been unsuccessful writers, and especially in comparison to some of their friends and contemporaries). It is quite possible that you cannot believe such stories.

I perhaps wouldn't believe them myself, but I sensed that they were true the only time I ever sat down to talk with her, when many years ago she came here to see me. I can't remember the details, but have a vivid memory of the tension she created, of the combination of coy sweetness ⟨and⟩ twisted thrusts, of a very troubled ego under that enormous charm and seductiveness, ⟨&⟩ a ⟨well⟩ of undirected venom. Possibly she was at her worst, since she was coming to ask for a job. She said she needed money desperately, and since I knew something of her husband it occurred to me that she might have fought with him and the whole visit was a kind of drama she was playing out. If so, it certainly needed a better director, for she had come here to the ND office to ask for a job at The Ford Foundation. She knew that J. Laughlin was in India and that I had almost no direct connection with The Ford Foundation people. I had told her this on the phone but she said she wanted to come anyway. It was certainly all rather strange and even a little fascinating. I remember thinking afterwards that very little of what she said had to do with what she really meant, and one got glimpses of it on the around-the-corner of the words.

In my few conversations with her on the phone about the books, mainly about two or three weeks ago, I got something of this same feeling. The reasons for not wanting to include her letters with yours were also not the real reasons, also I felt. Even they didn't indicate what she wanted them to. When somebody says: "Nobody's interested in me: I was just a little girl who stimulated ⟨him⟩ to write ⟨as he⟩ was attempting to; I was nothing," one wonders. Then instead of going on with arguments she would plunge into something entirely different and her voice would take on a whine and a wheedling—the telephone is shockingly revealing about our voices and our feelings behind them, I sometimes think—and one felt that she was turning on a kind of obvious technique of twisting men around her fingers. This alarmed me more than what she said. In a card that came a day or two later she wrote "I am sure

you will understand that I must wait until my reputation is established before the letters I wrote in my
twenties are of any general interest to the public."
The truth is that this series would benefit enormously by her letters, since the reader often doesn't
know what you are talking about because the things
to which you are replying are not there. However,
these can be put in by good editing jobs with a good
deal of help from you⟨. A⟩nd now Miss Nin says
that her letters disappeared anyway, so that's probably that.

Also in the process she was suddenly, for no
apparent reason connected with our conversation,
saying that we ought to agree to our doing the letters the way she wants them done, because New
Directions has treated her so badly and never published her. She was immediately galvanised into an
emotional state about this and saying in ⟨outraged⟩
tones, "Do you realize that New Directions has
never published anything by me!" I was so taken
aback that I didn't reply what I probably should
have that New Directions has never published many
of the writers whom they admire, but a small publishing company must limit itself and go along the
paths it has chosen and just couldn't publish
everyone.

In another card she tells me "I have waited quite a
while for a decision ever since H.M. expressed the
desire to have them come out." This was after talking about our giving her a decision or her agent. I
think she knows very well that you were the one
who thought they should be delayed until the Durrell correspondence has been published.

In this same card she says, as I understood all
along, "In exchange for past help H.M. wants me to
have the royalties on this book."

Our point is that it would not matter to us who

got the royalties as long as our contract could be
with you. Toward this end it is really profitable that
none of Anaïs's letters are included. We couldn't
publish the books—with Anaïs being close by—
without having some dealings with her, but we
could at least keep these down and have a defence
against a neurotic siege.

By the way about the editing—as I understand it
she told you that she had merely left out things that
were too personal and would be embarrassing to her
and you, also things about people who were alive.
This of course we would approve of wholeheart-
edly, but as the manuscript came to us it had some
other features. The letters aren't dated except for the
days of the week (and except for two or three excep-
tions—letter 45 has the date November 27, 1933 ⟨for
instance⟩.⟩ It seems quite obvious that they have
been arranged actually out of order at times, so that
things that you were commenting on had actually
happened in connection with letters that come later.
Letter No. 1 and the last fragment both contain
rather extravagant ⟨compliments⟩ to Anaïs. This is a
little too obvious! We suspected that the "out of
order" arrangement of some of the other letters may
have been a deliberate one, to gain certain ⟨effects⟩
which however don't seem to come out. In fact they
merely make for confusion.

To be published in a meaningful way the letters
would have to be rearranged in as chronological an
order as possible. Without Miss Nin's letters. ⟨A⟩nd
even if we had them probably, some annotated perhaps quite a lot, and I think that this would have to
be done by someone who is not emotionally
involved or emotionally reacting to facts in the letters or the letters themselves. In other words, I don't
think Miss Nin can do it. In all fairness I think that
the annotating that is indicated in the margins is

probably not hers but written down by her agent, Gunther Stuhlmann who as I recall told me that she just handed this great bundle of papers to him and suggested that he edit them. He may well have been responsible for this arrangement of the first letter and the last fragment. (If he is the one who did, I would think he is not a very good judge of human and literary values.) Actually I don't think he knows enough to do this kind of job. Wickes turned out to be an ideal editor in a way, although the best editing of letters that I have ever seen is in this recent volume published in England and here of the letters of Oscar Wilde, edited by the English publisher Rupert Hart Davies, although I think published by someone else there. Here everything that the reader wants to know or questions is provided, all set down in a matter-of-fact and uncolored way that is both thoughtful and effective.

Well, let's see if we can sort the main problem. Let me repeat that we would respect Anaïs' desire to cut things out. This has already been done in any case, and although I now begin to think that some of her cuts may have to do with extraneous reasons, reasons that are perhaps more connected with her ego and special desires for certain public effects, there is probably very little we can do about that point. However, we would like to have the contract with you—although in it you could have the royalties paid to her—and have you and ⟨us together⟩ choose someone to do the editing from here on, someone who will be expert, judicious, and knowledgeable. It should have an introduction by you, I think.

How about it?

Yours,
ROBERT MACGREGOR

/ · /

Wickes: Lawrence Durrell and Henry Miller: A Private Correspondence,
edited by GW, had recently been published by E. P. Dutton with the
consent of ND.

190. TLS-1　　　　　　　　　　　　　　June 25, 1963
　　　　　　　　　　　　　　　　　　　　[Pacific Palisades]

(More or less confidential)

DEAR BOB:

Your long "confidential" letter of June 21st
digested—oof! Replying in kind.

I understand very well indeed your attitude and
Jay's with regard to A.N. For me, to be frank, it's
a side of her I know little about. She was always
wonderful, generous, forgiving, etc. with me—
until some years back, when the Perlès book came
out. But I forgive her all that. I owe her everything—without her I would never have made it.

Yes, it would be wise to make the contract with
me, and pay her the royalties. And, as you say, it
will need skillful editing. Unless you had some one
in mind, why not George Wickes again? He's due
back this Fall, I believe.

I know the letters were completely out of order
and largely undated; I could help a lot in putting
them in some chronological order as the places indicated would help me. I wonder a bit if it is necessary
to inform the reader, through notes, of what may
not be clear to him. But this is for later.

There are an ungodly lot of letters—cutting them
down wouldn't hurt. There George Wickes has the
right flair.

I don't honestly think that they were arranged either by her or Stuhlmann to influence you.

I think the real reason for not including her letters is that they would reveal too intimate a relationship. These she has selected are supposedly only those relating to my work and travels.

Another thing⟨. . .⟩This year or early next Moore's book on *Writing* comes out, plus another by Wickes, from some University publisher. Maybe there is more . . . so much keeps happening I can't keep track of it all. I mention this so that you don't set too early a date for the publication of these letters.

All her emotional disturbances are due, in my honest opinion, to the very complicated, multiple life she lives. Plus the fact that her Diary, if published, would undoubtedly establish her as the foremost woman writer of our time—and she can't publish it (in toto) until her husband and a few other people die. I have argued with her interminably about this subject, and what to do, but got nowhere. I feel truly sorry for her, knowing all I do. Essentially she is a big soul—but there is a flaw somewhere—and it will eventually be her undoing, I fear.

Your analysis was very keen and astute. I have to laugh though to think that one so tender and frail and shy and delicate as her could cause you such fear and trembling. She wouldn't really hurt a fly. *She's hurt,* that's all. And the hurt is her own doing, regrettably.

All this is very very confidential, Bob. I know you will treat it as such.

However many letters are included, it will make a big book. Were you thinking to bring it out in paperback or hard cover? If the latter, I'm afraid the sales will be minimal and the price prohibitive. And then you'll have her on your neck—for sabotage, maybe.

I hope I have answered all the points you raised. Stay cool, don't be thrown! And good luck. It will be a headache at best—just like this film biz.

HENRY

/ • /

the Perlès book: *My Friend Henry Miller* (1955). HM once told me that Anaïs Nin was furious when she read the original manuscript and tore it up. Evidently she objected to being intimately linked with HM at that time. Perlès subsequently divided her into two characters, the writer Anaïs Nin and a fictitious dancer who fell in love with HM. HM himself was so intimidated by Nin that he crossed out almost all references to her—even the most innocuous—when his correspondence with Durrell was being edited.

film biz: Complications connected with Patricia Hardesty's filmmaking efforts and with litigation between Levine and producers of a film based on *Tropic of Cancer*. On June 19, 1964, HM wrote that the latter had ended in a satisfactory out-of-court settlement.

191. TLS-1

July 8, 1963
[Pacific Palisades]

DEAR BOB:

Anaïs came to see me the other evening, not to discuss the book, but we did anyway, finally. Everything went very smoothly and I don't think you have anything to fear. She said that Gunther Stuhlmann had offered to do the editing of the letters, and agreed that they need to be reduced in volume. I can help about the chronological order.

As for the missing letters of hers, something I had overlooked in our correspondence—that is my fault. Where I put these letters, what happened to them, I haven't the faintest idea about. I think I must have destroyed them in moving from place to place—especially when leaving Paris, for Greece.

Also, I think she is quite sincere as to why hers were not so important; they were usually personal, whereas mine concerned my work and travels.

After she left a disturbing thought arose—about the money problem. If the contract is made with me and royalties credited to me, then disbursed to Anaïs, won't I have to show this money as income on my tax returns? And not only as income but as "gift" to her, which is also taxable. What's your thought on this—to get round it, I mean?

I had a cable from Millard to the effect that seven Italian newspapers were "positive," one against. Suppose he means "favorable." Expect another cable tomorrow. He wants to come visit me again about the first of August, on his way home—is taking the long way round, via the Orient. Has things to tell me, confidentially, about the handling of the play. No doubt he'll open up to you too. I may have a letter in next few days, giving details. . . .

All for now.
HENRY

/ · /

the editing of the letters: HM's *Letters to Anaïs Nin* were eventually published, not by ND but by G. P. Putnam's Sons. On January 29, 1965, RM wrote: "Am delighted that the Anaïs Nin letters are coming ⟨out⟩ and coming out well. I think it is however just as well that we're not doing the book. I will be most interested to see what editorial work has been done to it."

Millard: Harry Millard, American actor who played the title role in *Just Wild About Harry* at the Spoleto Festival. He had visited HM before the festival.

192. CC-3   August 26, 1963
                                               [New York]

DEAR HENRY,

This morning I had a long visit with Harry Millard, and liked him very much⟨. A⟩t least physically, and personally he seems the Harry (of *Just Wild*) to the T.

About an hour before Millard came I talked to Herbert Machiz, told him that I had also written him in Italy, that you were not planning to remove the four letter words and other matters for production in the West End in London, and explained that you had always stood firm on these matters in regard to us and anyone else, so that I did not think you would change your mind. He gave me a blithe reply that that was exactly what he meant and of course you would be "sensible." I got the impression that he just wasn't bothering to listen to what I was saying, and I think this is rather typical of our man. Be that as it may, I probably soon will have to be firm with him, because he seems now to want to come down and talk to me about details with regard to production, and I thought first I would find out the details of his rupture with Tennessee Williams, which may mean that we don't have to be quite so careful with him. When I had lunch with Tennessee last Friday he merely told me that he no longer had any relationship at all with Machiz, and he has a new director for the play which Machiz hoped to revive, *Milk Train,* which Tennessee has completely rewritten and may even call by a different title.

But back to Millard. After listening to him and talking to him at some length and learning more about what went on in Spoleto, I told him that I thought we would indeed be able to allow him to find a producer and a director, but with your approval ⟨and mine⟩ but that I still had to be assured independently for you, that Millard was an actor capable of handling the part. He gave me quite a list of people that he had worked with and theatre people who had hired him for television shows, some of them I know and in about a week I think I will have the picture pretty clear.

I rather suspect that he can act the part, at least if properly directed, because he has the right kind of vitality, and certainly has had a long period of training and acting under very good people.

In the meantime, I gave him the name of Joe Padula, who you will remember was interested in a Broadway production, and also Sidney Bernstein, who I have reason to believe is one of the best off-Broadway producers, and the co-producer of *The Blacks* by Genet, and suggested he could use my name with both.

I also passed on to him what information we had about the Edinburgh production, and I have a sneaking suspicion he is going to fly over there to see it. . . .

> Yours,
> ROBERT MACGREGOR

193. ALS-1   Sept. 23, 1963
                                [Pacific Palisades]

DEAR BOB:

. . . I just heard from composer [Antonio] Bibalo in Norway that the Hamburg Opera are definitely going to produce the opera, but in 1965 instead of '64. Their director Rolf Liebermann went to see Bibalo (in Copenhagen) recently and was even more impressed with the work this time—and with the sets for the opera which Bibalo himself designed. His music publishers, the Hansen Sisters, gave him quite a reception and published more of his other works, and will increase his stipend shortly.

Also, I will soon have a letter drafted by my lawyers here, giving Anaïs the title or copyright (?) to the letters she will select to be published by you. She will then receive the royalties and pay income tax on them; I will pay gift tax only; book will not be valued too highly, on the contrary. You'll see papers soon—this should clear things.

I'm now reading a marvelous document on Céline—témoignages, correspondence, etc. published by *L'Herne,* No. 3 Paris. Some one here ought to do it in translation. He and Cendrars are the two giants of French literature. No one near their stature today. Both neglected. You could clean up on Cendrars, if you had the courage to publish his big books—written during and after occupation.

My best!
HENRY

/ • /

Cendrars: ND published *Selected Writings of Blaise Cendrars* with a preface by HM in 1966.

194. CC-1 February 12, 1964

DEAR HENRY,

That is exciting news that Bob has passed along to me, that your daughter Valentine is getting married. But I daresay it gives you a bit of a twinge, the way they grow up so fast and take off on their own—as I know it will when my own daughter gets married. It seems just yesterday that Val was a little tiny thing playing around near your house in Big Sur, which I remember so well.

I hope you will give her my very best wishes for all happiness, and kindly pass along the enclosed check, a little wedding present which she can surely use for something that will be needed in the new household.

With best wishes, as ever,
JAMES LAUGHLIN

195. ALS-1   March 4th 1964
                                Pacific Palisades

DEAR JAY—

I'm writing on behalf of Val, to thank you for the wedding gift you were so kind as to send her. She was tickled. She went off on a honeymoon immediately after the wedding ceremony and didn't have a chance to open half her gifts. Will be in Europe (she and her husband) from April till September. Lucky kids!

Tony, the boy, is now in a military academy at Carlsbad, California—his own choice. I'll soon be all alone here—looking about now for housekeeper-secretary-chauffeur (all in one!).

The Brooklyn authorities have started up again. Have got a lawyer there and one here to fight extradition. What a farce!

All the best now. Things are humming here.

HENRY

P.S. Hope Renate Gerhardt sent you copy of my play in German. Lovely job, I think. Will be on exhibit at Berlin Pavilion World's Fair.

/ • /

The Brooklyn authorities: Judge Manuel Gomez, presiding over a trial against *Tropic of Cancer,* "was especially keen to see the Brooklyn boy himself in his courtroom" (Robert Ferguson, *Henry Miller: A Life,* p. 350). Three months later the case was rendered moot when the Supreme Court ruled that the book was not obscene.

196. ALS-2

9/19/64
Pacific Palisades

DEAR JAY—

Just got yours of the 19th about "Camera 3." I don't mind their doing it, if Durrell gives his consent. The payment is virtually nil but it's only in rich America, it seems, that there are no funds for aesthetic diversions. . . .

Did you see the September issue of *Playboy*—with Bernie Wolfe and me—interview? I hear now that Steve Allen will broadcast the interview he had with me here at the house some weeks ago in early October. Don't know exact date yet. This may turn out to be *very* interesting. I spent 3 hours with him—I suppose they'll give a half-hour only(?).

Am having quite a big water color show here in Westwood end of this month (Sept 28—five days). Have about 75 paintings in it—quite a few borrowed from "collectors." I made 25 new ones in the last 3 weeks(!)

Still no word about theatre production of *Harry*— but certain it will come off before long. The opera of *The Smile* is definitely scheduled for Hamburg Oper

April or May next year. Miró is doing the decor.
So—things are humming. I ride the bike and swim
in the pool every day. But can't walk much because
of bad hip. Oh well—could be worse.

My best to you!
HENRY

/ • /

"Camera 3": The CBS program proposed a half-hour dramatization of
the Durrell-Miller correspondence. Although HM was willing, Durrell eventually sent a message that "he would not be seen dead on the
stage, and would certainly not allow anyone to impersonate him on
the stage." (RM to HM, Jan. 13, 1965)

Steve Allen: On October 13, JL wrote thanking HM for alerting him
to the program: "I don't know when I have enjoyed anything so much.
. . . Your personality, and your attitude toward life, really came
across. . . . I could sense that he [Steve Allen] really had respect for
you and your work, and wasn't just exploiting you."

Miró: On December 12, HM wrote: "Miró gave up on the decor for
The Smile. Couldn't do it, though he tried. So it seems they may accept
Bibalo's own sketches for the decor. I saw them in Denmark. Might
be better than Miró's!" The opera had its premiere at the Hamburg
Staatsoper on April 6, 1965.

197. CC-1   April 6, 1965

DEAR HENRY,

I thought you would be pleased to hear some
good news that Bob Gales, the sales manager down
at Lippincott, just reported to me today that he had
sold 3500 copies of *Colossus* to the Peace Corps!

Isn't that wonderful? They are to go into kits of
paperbacks for the new Peace Corps trainees, to give
them the feel of foreign lands. Certainly *Colossus* can
do that if any book can. . . .

With best from all here, as ever,
JAMES LAUGHLIN

/ · /

Peace Corps: Although the Peace Corps thought well of *The Colossus of Maroussi,* the U.S. Information Agency banished *Big Sur and the Oranges of Hieronymus Bosch* from its libraries four years later. Reacting to this later development, HM wrote on November 27, 1969, "Why not capitalize on it? Maybe a band around cover of book, reading:

**Pronounced unsuitable for use
by
The U.S.I.A.**

or something like that?"

---

198. ALS-1

Sept. 3rd 1965
Pacific Palisades

DEAR JAY—

Regarding yours of Aug. 24th, anent the request of Editorial Jorge Alvarez—I don't have anything special in this domain (sex) to send him, and frankly, am not much interested. Toujours Sex, Sex, Sex! It's disgusting.

My publisher there, Santiago Rueda, has brought out the *Tropics and* the *Rosy Crucifixion* trilogy, in Spanish. Perhaps Alvarez could get permission from Rueda to publish a fragment from one of these books. . . .

All the best to you and your family. This is my *25th* letter today!

HENRY

/ · /

Jorge Alvarez: Argentine publisher who wanted something from HM for a magazine he was about to launch.

199. ALS-2   2/11/67
                                      Pacific Palisades

DEAR BOB—

. . . I am alone here now. Val got divorced and
is on her own. Tony is living near college in Santa
Monica. Both OK and in fine fettle.

Yes, it was *Eve* who died suddenly & peacefully
in her sleep not long ago. Result of too much booze
and headache pills. *Accidental.*

I'm hoping to get to Japan in late April. May stay
2 months. Maybe bring back Japanese wife.

Can't do much reading—eyes troubling me. Will
have big traveling exhibition of my paintings in
Europe this Fall—a half dozen cities or more, winding up in N.Y. . . .

                          Best to you and Jay always
                                      HENRY

/ • /

Japanese wife: The following September HM married Hiroko Tokuda
("Hoki"), a Japanese singer in Los Angeles he met about the time he
wrote this letter.

200. ALS-2   2/20/67

DEAR HENRY—

I was so very sorry to hear of Eve's death. What a
beautiful woman she was! I remember how she
really bowled me over. Sad that her life took the
turn it did. . . .

I hope your trip to Japan will be great—such a wonderful country.

Very best, as ever,
J

201. CC-1   June 14, 1968

DEAR HENRY:

. . . We have just published a big fat volume of Kenneth Patchen's *Collected Poems,* the work of his lifetime, and I'm sending a copy out to you. I remember so well how you championed him in the early days, one of his first and most effective supporters, and I'm hopeful that you will want to send me a few lines now about him, about his importance and his contribution, which we can use in the promotion for this book.

As you know, we have frequently picked up on jackets of other books lines from what you wrote about him in "Patchen, Man of Anger and Light," but I think it might be good if you could give us, if you will be so kind, something fresh for the *Collected*.

Poor Patchen, I am afraid he is just as badly off as ever, in great pain a lot of the time, since his doctors seem unable to do anything about his back condition, and related ailments. He has really had a grim life.

With best wishes, and many thanks,

JAMES LAUGHLIN

/ • /

"Patchen, Man of Anger and Light": Essay by HM published in 1946.

202. ALS-1   July 1st 1968
                                       Pacific Palisades

DEAR JAY—

Here are a few lines for you about Patchen. Hope it's satisfactory.

HENRY

"From start to finish Kenneth Patchen's work is an event in American literature. And it has been accomplished, this great, living body of work, by one who has known nothing but misfortune, pain and sorrow. His indomitable spirit shines through the magic of his words with unbelievable radiance. Like the saints of old he is one of the strong men of this earth."

HENRY MILLER

203. CC-1   July 15, 1968

DEAR HENRY:

Thank you so much for doing the wonderful statement for Patchen. It was just what we needed—perfect—and it should have very great effect, when we use it in our advertising and circulars, in boosting him and the book, and that all should help his morale, which is at a very low ebb at present, I'm afraid.

Your statement will be used first in an ad in the *New York Times* about the third week in August, and then it will be in a circular which will go to all libraries, and there will be further uses after that in various ways. You have been a wonderful friend to

Patchen over the years, and I'm sure he will be most grateful for this further indication of your support and belief in him.

Very best from all here,

JAMES LAUGHLIN

204. CC-2   April 18, 1969
                                       [New York]

DEAR HENRY:

It was wonderful to get your note and to see your hand so firm. I don't think your handwriting has changed in the twenty years we have been writing each other, and I wish my own were as controlled and young looking. In fact you write, as always, like a very young man.

Royalties are down from the great wave of interest in your work that followed the publication here of the two *Cancer* books. However, I think this kind of thing steadily, year in year out, and you must remember that, in addition there is the monthly checks so that the total is over $4000, is pretty good, considering that there have been no new books. Of course the films will help, and also I'm sure the documentary film by Robert Snyder. I am delighted that it was so well received. . . .

J. Laughlin is down in Kentucky, for a meeting of the three Trustees of the literary trust set up by Merton's Will, but I know he will be delighted to see your letter and to know that you are recovering so well.

Cheers, indeed!

Yours,
ROBERT MACGREGOR

/ • /

Robert Snyder: Documentary filmmaker in Los Angeles who was working on a film biography of HM.

205. ALS-2   4/22/69
                                                Pacific Palisades

DEAR BOB—

. . . Did Gerald write to ask you for leaflets giving titles of all my books, by N.D.—and no other authors? I would like to include these in my fan mail (have big list of names now) to further N.D. sales. I sent out mimeographed post cards about new edition of *To Paint,* because Grossman was too slow and ineffectual, and got excellent results. But shit, I get weary of being publicity agent for my own work.

Anyhow, about publicity⟨. . . . .⟩I often wonder if you could not give notice to public on back inside flaps of your books, regarding certain of my projects or what have you.

For ex: (1) the opera of the *Smile* (given in (3) countries, 3 languages, German, French, Italian).

(2) The *Tropic of Cancer* film—due out end of year.

(3) Bob Snyder's Documentary Film: *The Henry Miller Odyssey.*

Perhaps other things too.* So much is going on. I think we will soon clinch the *Smile* (film) with Robert Bell forking up the dough.

It bugs me somehow to think I earn so little on 13 titles—though 3 or 4 of them now belong to my kids. Jesus, I can earn that much for one article published in *Playboy*!

But enough whining and griping. It's just that sometimes I think publishers are asleep or indifferent or lacking in imagination and ingenuity.

On the other hand it may well be that my day is over—that sales will only jump again 20 years after my death.

I'll survive all right, royalties or no royalties. In fact I may have a resurrection while still in the flesh.

By the way, I admired Merton greatly. He was a real radical, a true anarchist, even if a Christian. (Was St. Francis a Christian—or a great revolutionary spirit killed by the Church?)

Cheerio!
Sholem Aleichem!
HENRY

P.S. My favorite American author is Isaac Bashevis Singer.
★ In Fall or Winter a handsome book based on my talks in documentary film, plus 100 or more photos—by Bradley Smith. Another book by Loujon Press—on my Insomnia Water colors.

/ • /

Gerald: Gerald Robitaille, HM's secretary and factotum at this time.

To Paint: To Paint Is to Love Again (Grossman, 1968) combines the title essay with the text of *Semblance of a Devoted Past* and reproductions of twenty HM watercolors.

Tropic of Cancer film: Directed by Joseph Strick and shot in Paris with HM as a consultant.

Isaac Bashevis Singer: (1904–1991), Polish-born writer who emigrated to New York in 1935 but continued to write stories in Yiddish about Polish Jews. Winner of the Nobel Prize in 1978.

book by Loujon Press: Insomnia or the Devil at Large (1970).

206. CC-2   August 19, 1969
                               [New York]

DEAR HENRY:

. . . George Wickes was here this morning, and left with me the two remaining parts of his manuscript for the *Letters to Emil*. In fact, I have two copies, one of them for you. If you come through New York I'll give them to you personally, otherwise if I know you have gone on to California, we will shoot the package on there. I frankly like what he has done so far, although I think the Introduction could be a little more inspired, and I think he will do it quite differently after everything is finished. An introduction really shouldn't be written until the work is done, and then the editor can see it in retrospect. He told me ⟨he⟩ wanted to get something down to try and ⟨place⟩ the letters, and it is fairly prosaic.

He showed me your letter to him after seeing the first three parts, and of course I think you and he together can decide about where names should be suppressed, for the sake of protecting individuals, and where there is no problem. If necessary we can try to find individuals and get them to sign releases. I think that George plans to show the manuscript to Anaïs Nin when she settles down, and in fact, I offered to send the copy he left with me to her for that purpose. I gather she felt that she was left out of the Durrell correspondence volume, although I guess you have reason to know she can object to what can be published about her. Anyway I guess in that case everyone was being over-careful of her feelings. Possibly it's best to let him handle her and not worry about her feelings at this point.

Anyway I think that the letters read wonderfully. It was a period when you were in a way discovering yourself, and the torrent of language is marvelous, and you watch and listen too ⟨and smell so wonder-fully.⟩ . . .

Yours,
R OBERT M ACGREGOR

/ • /

Letters to Emil: A selection of the letters HM wrote to his longtime friend Emil Schnellock, recording his efforts to become a writer and including passages that were later incorporated into *Tropic of Cancer* and other works.

207. ALS-4   1/14/70
Pacific Palisades

D EAR B OB—

To answer yours (with enclosures) of the 2nd. I am writing with pen owing to stiff neck (arthritis)—forgive me.

I am puzzled myself about Wickes and the *Letters.* Sometimes I think it would be best to drop the whole thing—forget it—and let me pay you what-ever you give Wickes for his work.

The script is a mess now, with all my cuts and marginal observations. My trouble with George is that we see things very differently on almost every-thing. I allowed him to make the "selection" of let-ters because I haven't time to go thru all that material. But, entre nous, I am not sure but what he may have eliminated material I would have included. We always differ on what may be important or *un*important. Worst of all is his refusal to understand that when I cut I am often trying to protect people. And the big letter about June which I cut to ribbons—that was largely to prevent hurting her (she's still alive and corresponds with me) and also to avoid putting explosive material in the hands of the prurient minded, the gossipers, etc.

I don't get his point about writing factual data for each section. There's too much explaining on his part, and he often doesn't grasp the "facts" he wishes to reveal. He *thinks* he knows my life and relationships, but he doesn't. He misinterprets, is too literal, or exaggerates.

If he wants to continue, then let him observe *all* the cuts I made, and send me the *entire* revised script for another going over. When he asks what I consider foolish, trivial, *un*important questions, and I tell him to forget it, let him do so, not argue with me. The Intro. ought to be brief and matter of fact, but there should not be *assumptions* on his part about how, why, when etc. this or that happened. I resent his trying to tell *me* what *I* did or thought—I know better. I don't mind giving him the credit for the work. He talks of no "collaboration"—but my editing and cutting, etc. constitute my part of the collaboration. I hope I make myself clear. I would rather not see him, when he comes—I prefer doing the job by c/s. George is a very nice fellow—I don't hate him. It's just that we see things differently.

In the first paragraph of your letter to Emil's sister (Mrs. Greene) I notice she asked you where the *Letters* were obtained. I am not sure they were *all* given to UCLA by her. A lot of material seemed to be missing. And, *entre nous,* I have always suspected that she withheld or destroyed some of the c/s which she may not have relished or not wished to see published. Nor am I sure, as you write her, that there were always carbon copies of my letters to Emil. Many were written by hand on stationery from cafes. I included in my letters all sorts of interesting things—menus, hand bills, what not. Some of this material I always hoped would be used in the book, illustratively. Has George much of this kind of material? When I saw Emil in Virginia maybe 20 to 25 years ago he had *filled the trunk of his car* with what I sent him from Paris. Only a small part of this treasure was found by the librarian at UCLA when he visited Mrs. Greene. . . .

Both *Cancer* and *Quiet Days in Clichy* film due out March or April. Barney Rosset will distribute *Quiet Days* (a Danish production, in English) in U.S.A. Very sexy, I'm told—which Barney likes, I guess. *Cancer* film due to open at Paris Cinema, N.Y.C. around March 2nd, I believe. I just wrote an article for *Playboy* about my experiences in Paris watching the shooting of the film. (Will be well illustrated with photos from film.) Due out in April—in May issue.

All this so that you can sell a few more of my N.D. books—cash in on the publicity. You lost out during the hectic days of persecution and prosecution of *Cancer* book and the *Rosy Crucifixion*. As her husband tells my secretary sometimes—"Get your ass in gear!"

Enough for today. "The day is sufficient unto itself." Now for some hot towels around my neck and after that *the horse collar*.

Despite all, "am still intact," to quote Rimbaud. Cheers and all the best for 1970!!!

HENRY

P.S. Re reprint of Spanish ed. of *Colossus*. I am told by Spanish readers that publisher cut out anti-American passage(s)—nothing obscene—just didn't want to offend "us" (sic). Could they put same back in again. Ask, please!

/ • /

carbon copies: Most of the letters to Emil Schnellock in the HM Collection at UCLA are typed copies (not carbons) made at an earlier date, possibly as early as 1938, when HM announced that he would publish a book called *Letters to Emil*. The selection may in fact have been his own. What happened to the trunkful of originals remains something of a mystery, though on July 21, 1971, HM wrote that he had learned "through an old sweetheart of Emil Schnellock's . . . that quite a bit of our correspondence, plus water colors and other things were 'accidentally' destroyed by the grand daughter (?) of another of his sweethearts." *Letters to Emil* was finally published by ND in 1989.

Quiet Days in Clichy film: Directed by Danish filmmaker Jens Jorgen Thorsen.

208. ALS-1

May 1st 1970
Pacific Palisades

DEAR JAY—

. . . I often think of Ezra Pound, for some strange reason. He stands out like a tragic loner, but noble and wise. He interests me more now than when he was in his glory.

All the best to you always.

HENRY

209. ALS-3   Jan. 9th 1971
                                      Pacific Palisades

DEAR BOB—

. . . Yes, I know all about the opinions or reactions of some Jews to *Aller Retour*. They are precisely the Jews whose opinions mean nothing to me.
After I read that observation by the young man in
your office I got to thinking about this business of
my "Anti-Semitism." I never was one. I dislike certain types of Jew as I do certain types of other people—German, Irish, French, et alia. Individuals, not
whole peoples! In Europe the charge of Anti-Semitism was never brought against me, to my knowledge. The American Jew is more sensitive on this
score. Always on the defensive. I got to thinking
who my great friends (among Jews) were and are.
What a list! None of them ever dreamed of calling
me a Jew hater. On the contrary, I am often referred
to, by them, as being more of a Jew (in spirit) than
the Jew himself. What time and thought I have
given to the subject! *My* "New Testament," for
example is Erich Gutkind's *The Absolute Collective*.
(Few Jews know of his work or understand it when
they read him.) Just the other day I get a gift copy
from my old friend Carlo Suares (Spanish Jew)—
The Cipher of Genesis—an epoch-making book, in
my opinion. The day before a wonderful letter from
my Israeli brother-in-law, Lilik Schatz, to whom
the American Jew is a caricature. And who is my
favorite American author—the Jew, Isaac Bashevis
Singer, bless his name! My personal physicians—all
Jewish—and regard me as one of the family. My
dear friend Jakob Gimpel, the concert pianist, a
devoted friend. Abe Rattner, another. Ephraim
Doner, painter in Carmel, another. Emil White, Big

Sur, another. My wife June, another—and how I
tried to get her to let us be married by a Rabbi and I
would become a Jew myself! I could go on and on.
In fact, one day, just for the hell of it, I will draw up
a list of the names of my great Jewish friends. It
would be interesting, indeed, to put what they have
to say about my attitude toward the Jews against the
opinions of those who do not know me and brand
me an Anti-Semite. But enuf!

What to do about it, *Aller Retour*? I'd say, let it
wait yet a while. Now that the very existence of the
Jews is at stake why bother to exhume a book which
might rightly or wrongly create a bad impression?

The young man who wrote the note for you has
it all wrong. He means well, but he hasn't thought
it out clearly. "Whether a prejudice against Jews will
mar Miller's reputation⟨. . .⟩" How ridiculous! The
big point, after my death, will be—how to explain
my extraordinary predilection for the Jews! Does he
know, for instance—a small point perhaps—that I
don't celebrate Christian holidays but I do Jewish
ones? I have no prejudice against any people—on the
contrary, I am *for* all peoples of the world, especially
the despised ones. My books and my deeds testify
to that. But I reserve the right to detest individuals
for their behavior.

Cheers!
HENRY

/ • /

Aller Retour: On December 21, 1970, RM had written about "the possible charge of Anti-Semitism" against the book, enclosing the report of
a ND staff member who was "particularly conscious of his Jewishness"
yet urged that the book be published. That new staff member, Peter
Glassgold, eventually became editor-in-chief and along with other
members of the staff decided to publish *Aller Retour New York* despite

JL's misgivings (Griselda Ohannessian letter to GW, Dec. 16, 1994). ND published the book in 1991.

210. ALS-2   March 8th, 1971
                                                 Pacific Palisades

DEAR BOB—

   This explanation of Mishima's suicide by your friend Shimano is most exciting. I wonder if Mr. Shimano would give me permission to quote a few lines from it, especially the last part? Did this text of his appear in some paper, book or magazine—or will it soon? It is, of course, a conjecture on his part, as I read it. He does not say that Mishima told him, or anyone, for that matter, that he expected to be reincarnated. I frankly do not see the connection between his dramatic death and the message of reincarnation to the Japanese people, do you? Particularly if he had not made public this belief. His attack on the Self-Defense Agency would seem needless, in this case.

   Further—two questions⟨. . . .⟩one, do the Zen masters believe in re-incarnation? Two, would not suicide, especially *his* suicide or manner of it, create bad Karma—set him back instead of forward?

   I hate to bother you with these questions. I appreciate very very much your desire to aid me. Mishima is not an easy person to understand, neither in thought nor action. For the moment I feel as if he was full of contradictions—very interesting ones, of course. That's why he intrigues me.

   Just the other night Hoki, who has been reading [Mishima's] *The Sea of Fertility,* was telling me about the theme of reincarnation developed in this work. It fascinated her. It does me, *as story,* but not as proof of anything.

One little after-thought. When Mishima said that he had finished with everything, do you think he meant that he had done *all* that was expected of him in this incarnation? If so, it would seem to me that he was deluding himself. Who can say that he has exhausted his potential? The Buddha (Gautama) lived to a ripe old age. As far as accomplishment was concerned, he might have killed himself at a much earlier age. I simply can't picture the "Masters" committing suicide.

Perhaps your friend can answer these questions. When I hear Alan Watts (on T.V.) explain the real meaning of the wheel of life, the rounds, I get a quite different impression about reincarnation.

Anyway, great thanks, and for Donald Keene's article too. I don't hope to *explain* Mishima, but to reveal the problems in our contemporary life which produced him, his work, his philosophy. And my own reactions—as always.

Cheers!
HENRY

/ • /

Mishima's suicide: The Japanese writer Yukio Mishima (1925–1970) committed ritual suicide on November 25, 1970. On February 16, 1971, RM wrote to HM: "What do you think of Mishima's death? I'm really sorry that you two never met. I'm enclosing a photocopy of a letter I wrote to *The Village Voice* about the matter for what it's worth." RM had known Mishima (a ND author) well, had visited him in Japan, and urged HM to visit him too when HM was contemplating a trip to Japan.

Shimano: Chief monk at the New York Zen Studies Center.

Donald Keene's article: A long essay reflecting on Mishima's life and death, published in the *New York Times Book Review* on January 3, 1971. Donald Keene, a professor of Japanese at Columbia University, was a translator and close friend of Mishima.

211. CC-2   March 23, 1971
                                       [New York]

DEAR HENRY:

I've now been able to talk to Tai-San, who it seems is known as the Rev. Shimano when addressed formally, rather than Mister.

He tells me that I was mistaken, and Soin-roshi, the Zen master, did not have any direct personal connection with Mishima, but is the Abbot of Ryu-takiji-in, an ancient Zen monastery at the town of Mishima. This is on the Tokaido line, the celebrated road from Tokyo to Kyoto. Soin-roshi was long interested in Yukio Mishima's writing, and at this monastery they had a "memorial" every day for Mishima for the 40 days following his death.

The other things I said evidently were correct and suicide in Buddhist terms is not considered an evil act. In fact it would seem that all Buddhas have chosen the time for their death, and the historical Buddha (Sakyamuni) lived to a great age because it was his mission to teach. Evidently, according to Buddhist belief there have been other Buddhas who lived shorter lives in other kalpas, which may be periods of millions and millions and even billions of years. Anyway, the Rev. Shimano says that there have been Zen masters who committed suicide, even some by Seppuku. The Karma created is connected with the reason for the act, and he told me after some thought that he felt that Mishima's death was, because of its altruistic purpose, one that would create a good Karma.

Shimano has just received from Japan the last volume of Mishima's *The Sea of Fertility,* which was evidently published last week in Japan. He thinks that, as a result, he may revise his article about Mishima and the long novel a bit. However, it seems that in Japan quite a few people have said that in his last novel, Mishima rejected the idea of enlightenment and even reincarnation, but Shimano feels from a first, fast reading that this is mistaken and that Mishima purposely left the question slightly obscure (a Zen habit they say). He will send me any revisions that he makes, as he will everyone to whom he gave copies of his little article.

And he says that you may certainly quote any part of it. He believes that he should stand by what he wrote, even if he wants to revise it later.

He says that the theme of *The Sea of Fertility* is the essence of human life, and he is convinced that this makes it one of the greatest novels of all time, because Mishima has comprehended this essence so completely.

Hope all this is of some help,

Yours,
ROBERT MACGREGOR

212. ALS-1   June 21, 1971
                                                  Pacific Palisades

DEAR BOB—

I just got out of hospital yesterday. Operation not what you thought—much more serious, though it has to do with circulation in right leg. Had to implant artificial artery from neck to groin—failed first attempt, had to redo. Hope it will work—can't tell yet.

But I am writing to ask if you received carbon copy of my text on Mishima which Connie sent when I went into hospital. The Japs *(Weekly Post)* accepted & paid for it—$10,000.00—not bad, eh?

I sent a carbon to *Playboy* mag (here in U.S.) as they had expressed a desire to see it—but they have turned it down, saying "they didn't think the subject and the circumstances were well enough known here to devote such attention to it." (sic)

Do you think of any magazines here that might be interested in it? *Harper's, Atlantic, Esquire?* Let me know when you have time, yes? I'm weak as a cat and my little toe is like on fire.

Cheers!
HENRY

/ • /

Connie: Connie Perry, HM's secretary.

213. TLS-1   September 9, 1971
                                           Pacific Palisades

DEAR MR. MACGREGOR,

In mid November Playboy Publishing Co. will bring out a handsome book of mine called *My Life and Times,* and Simon and Schuster will issue a special deluxe edition of same limited to 500 copies. Playboy is mailing a half million announcements of the book. The limited edition is virtually sold out and the trade edition is almost so.

I believe that the launching of this book will create a demand for other Henry Miller titles and would therefore suggest that you make an effort to supply book stores with your publications of my work.

At the present moment none of the leading book-stores in Beverly Hills, California (my neighbor-hood) is carrying any of my books. Something is wrong somewhere.

Respectfully,
HENRY MILLER

214. CC-1   October 14, 1971
                                         [New York]

DEAR HENRY:

I'm enclosing a Xerox of a letter from John Malcolm Brinnin to J. Laughlin, which went the rounds slightly because J. is not in the city, although I believe he is feeling somewhat better.

I am asking Brinnin what he means by "hefty" and when they might want you at Boston University. I'm also telling him that with your hip you're not mad about running around this earth. . . .

By the way, there were people in the office here that took for granted that your letter telling about the publication of the limited edition and trade edition by *Playboy* and addressed to me "Dear Mr. MacGregor" showed affront and coldness on your part. I took for granted that it was a kind of form letter paid for by *Playboy* and probably typed up by *Playboy,* or certainly by someone who didn't know our relationship. Anyway I passed the information on to our distributors, and told them that they should try to get your paperbacks more into the area around Pacific Palisades. They certainly all are on sale around here, and I would suspect around Venice, California and even in downtown Los Angeles.

Perhaps you live in too bourgeois a neighbor-
hood? . . .

All our best from here.

Yours,
RMM

/ · /

John Malcolm Brinnin: American poet, then a professor at Boston University.

215. ALS-2   10/23/71
                                      Pacific Palisades

DEAR BOB—

I'm writing Malcolm Brinnin no go. Never
accept any reading or lecturing jobs. Don't know
who sent you the Playboy letter—not me, certainly.
By the way, the books (which were printed in
Japan) are in a warehouse, tied up because of dock
strike. May not be released till X'mas or later. . . .

I'll have a short piece on Picasso in *Life* any day
now.

All the best!
HENRY

P.S. Didn't know Jay was ill—or is he?

216. ALS-1   May 11th 1972
                                          Pacific Palisades

DEAR BOB—

   . . . I didn't go to the hospital for my operation
after all. Got cold feet at the last minute. But will
have to go through with it sooner or later. Meanwhile I limp along.
   Hope things are going well with you. Give my
best to James Laughlin, please.
   On reaching 80 I find the world ever more horrible—but have no complaints to make as regards my
own personal destiny.

                                          Cheers!
                                          HENRY

217. CC-2   August 11, 1972
                                          [New York]

DEAR HENRY:

   . . . We are delighted that "Reflections on The
Death of Mishima" is being published by Capra
Press in Santa Barbara, and have sent for a copy.
Actually we were feeling that if it were not to be
published in this country, we should do something
about it and include it in the next Annual which is
becoming semi-annual. However, the book is a lot
smaller and can't take anything as long as your piece
easily. Incidentally, do you have any short things
that you have written which would be appropriate
to the new Annual, which is doing somewhat better, I think, in its semi-annual form. . . .
   Our excellent editor, Peter Glassgold, tells me
that he is getting going on the problems of publish-

ing *The Notebook of The Air-Conditioned Nightmare.*
Here is a matter of removing sections that might
offend people, and making it all come out so that it
doesn't look as if a great deal has been removed.
Peter is quite remarkable at this kind of thing, and
he has been held back because he has had to work
over the Thomas Merton *Asian Journal,* which J.
Laughlin has been buried in and editing for over a
year. This is something which I know will interest
you when it comes out sometime next year. J. has
become quite an authority on Buddhist things in the
process, and has been corresponding with learned
Sanskrit scholars and others, and particularly
Tibetan authorities throughout the world.

   I am off early tomorrow morning (Saturday) to
the San Francisco Airport, where we will pick up a
car and a young lady and drive to Tassajara, which
I suspect you knew even before it became the property of the Zen Buddhists, who continue to operate
the resort hotel but mainly have there a mountain
meditation retreat. At least on the map it seems to
be just over the mountains from Big Sur. I will perhaps try to talk to you on the telephone from there
or from San Francisco, where I must retreat after a
week for a convention of the American Educational
Theatre Association, where my Theatre Arts Books
has a display, which also includes some of the New
Directions theatre books, like *Just Wild About Harry.*
I know you hate the telephone, but it would be a
chance to chat without the pressures of transconti-
nental charges. If I do get near Los Angeles, which
seems doubtful, I will call you and try to see you
briefly. It would be great to shake your hand again
and to get your news in person.

                    Yours,
                    Robert M. Macgregor

218. CC-1   9/20/72
                                                   Norfolk

DEAR HENRY—

Just a line of good luck and good cheer, as I heard
from Bob that you were going into the hospital for
an operation on your hip.

I hope it won't be too painful and that you'll get
good results from it. I don't know if it's the "artificial socket" operation, but if it is, I can report that
several friends have had it, with wonderful results in
mobility. In fact, one of them won the Senior Golf
Cup at the club here the other day, only a year after
he had had it.

So I hope and pray it goes as well for you, too.

                                        Very best, as ever,

219. TLS-1   June 14, 1974
                                               Pacific Palisades

DEAR BOB,

I want to write you about my royalties. Each
year, as you probably realize, they remain about the
same—somewhere from five to six thousand
dollars.

You publish more of my books than any other
publisher. (About seventeen or eighteen, if I am not
mistaken.) It's true that royalties on four of them I
have turned over to others. Still there must remain
over a good dozen in my name.

I think that for an author who is as well-known as
I am—my reputation is world wide—what I earn
from the sale of these books is ridiculous.

And so I wonder if I should not look around and see if I can find another publisher to take over some of these titles. I don't mean simply pocket book editions, as with Gleason.

What I would need to know is what you would ask for the purchase of my titles—for the complete rights.

This is a non-sequitur, but I thought you might like to know. The other day M. Peyrefitte, Minister of French Cultural Affairs, wrote to ask if I would accept being made a Chevalier of the Legion of Honor. I already received another honor of this sort from the French.

I wait to hear from you when it suits you.

Cheers!
HENRY

/ • /

Gleason: Robert H. Gleason of Pocket Books had contracted with ND to publish three of HM's books in paperback editions.

220. CC-2   July 3, 1974
                                               [New York]

DEAR HENRY:

The silence at our end is, I fear, entirely my fault, and I guess I don't blame you for becoming shrill and finally, in your June 14th letter, almost unfriendly, although I don't really think you are being fair aside from the situation here. About it, I should explain that I seem to have been crossing my own Tropic of Cancer, without benefit of astrology—or maybe the stars arranged it all. Anyway, about the first week in May, I decided something had to be done with a dry cough that I had developed and a feeling of considerable unreality behind the eyes, and went to my doctor who sent me on for tests to a chest consultant. They found shadows in my left lung, sent me to the Sloan-Kettering/Memorial Hospital for further tests, and about May 20th I underwent surgery, losing part of that lung and some other nodules in the area. As soon as I recovered enough from that, I was having cobalt treatment which didn't give me the usual effects but has knocked me out a bit. Anyway, I should, I guess, have tried to anwer your several letters somehow. About the royalties, I would like to say that I think it is quite remarkable that your royalties with us keep up between $5,000 and $6,000 each year, despite a considerable slump in the book business of the last several years, partially, of course, because of the diversion of funds from education and libraries that your neighbor, Richard Nixon, has effected, ⟨and⟩ a general recession, the endless spiraling of costs, etc. I think that not one of our other major authors has had the same pattern, and almost all have seen their royalties and sales slip considerably since about 1968. Thus I think that the situation with your books is really remarkable. I would be interested in knowing if the same thing has happened to your books at Grove Press, that is, have they kept up to their highest level of sales? I am sure you will remember that the books we have were never the best-sellers by you, and never earned the large sums that were possible because of publicity, bannings, etc. . . .

These books sell steadily year in and year out, and this is not only a tribute to you but also to the first-rate, broad and complete distribution facilities we obtain through the J. B. Lippincott Company, who do our distribution, as you know. I doubt if any other publisher could do as well. It is true that some publisher might take you on, for the prestige, and might in one year boost the sales with a new effort, that is, of all these older titles. However, I think that you would find very quickly that they would do it on a one-shot basis, and soon, when titles drop below a certain point, remainder them and/or let them go out of print. This we have never done with you, as you know. . . .

It is true that you are becoming a world figure, and I am delighted to hear that you are being offered the order of Chevalier of the Legion of Honor by the French government. This is wonderful news and most deserved. It makes me personally happy and proud that these honors are coming to you.

At the same time, however, considering our long friendship, the friendship of New Directions towards you and its willingness to stand by you when you weren't so generally and properly recognized, makes your tone hurt all the more.

Our association has been a firm one, an affectionate one in fact for a long time, and has weathered many a storm. I am sure it can this one too. . . .

Incidentally too, I am delighted to see that Robert Snyder has made a book out of the film on you, and that you have a new book coming out with Doubleday, even though you didn't mention it to me as it developed. Is it possible that your editor is "The Devil at Large" in making you disgruntled?

Yours,
ROBERT M. MACGREGOR

/ • /

Robert Snyder . . . book: This Is Henry, Henry Miller from Brooklyn: Conversations with the Author from The Henry Miller Odyssey by Robert Snyder (Nash Publishing Co., 1974).

new book coming out: Insomnia or the Devil at Large (Doubleday, 1974). Actually this was a trade edition of a text first published in a limited edition by the Loujon Press in 1970.

221. TLS-2   July 9, 1974
                                                         Pacific Palisades

DEAR BOB,

You must be off your rocker to think that I could be, or should be, pleased to earn that absurd sum on all my books. Doesn't it bother you that you yourselves don't earn more? If not, there is something wrong with you.

I am indeed sorry to learn of your illness and your operation. But surely you must have an assistant. Couldn't he or she have let me know your plight and he or she could have answered my questions? You tell me you are *now* assured that Hallmark does not want to republish *The Smile*. But I told you that myself over a month ago, and they probably informed you also. You have always been slow, extremely cautious, and very conservative. When Grove brought ⟨out⟩ the banned books, you failed to cash in with publicity for N.D. books. Gleason of pocket books tells me he had a hell of a time getting you to come to a decision. It took a year when it could have been done in a few months at most. Whenever I tell any one about my meagre earnings chez vous—whether it be a friend, a writer, an editor or a critic—the answer is usually—"What do you expect? New Directions is known to be slow as molasses, etc." No. Doubleday is not "the devil at large." They are merely distributors of Bradley Smith's books. He is the publisher or producer of *Insomnia* as he was for *My Life and Times*. Latter still

doing well—will go into a large sized paperback end
of this year or beginning of next. Probably 100,000
copies printed at once.

That was a poor joke about the devil whispering
in my ear. Nobody has put a bug in my ear. My
friends and my children have been after me for years
to do something about getting another publisher.
Those royalties you send them every year make me
blush.

Now I may decide to get myself an agent here in
L.A. I know several rather well. Perhaps I'll take
one on soon. Obviously I need some one to protect
my interests.

What I hope I am making clear to you—and without animosity, though I am furious, is that it is the
duty of a publisher to promote the interests of his
author. I have held out all these years, thinking each
year that there would be a radical change. The fact
that this inertia does not seem to bother you, the
fact that you take things so complacently makes me
furious. *You* are supposed to be the business man
and I the dreamer, or poet. Instead, the situation is
just the reverse.

To continue⟨.....⟩I can never forget how long it
took you to decide to publish *Siddhartha* and your
reasons for being so reluctant. Today every body
knows ⟨the book⟩—it's like a New Testament. I also
recall my futile efforts to get you to publish the most
interesting fragments (separately) of my books,
something which Kwinter did with alacrity—but
you and your literary agent in London kept quib-
bling about his (Kwinter's) character, can he be
trusted, and so on. You praise the shit out of Lippincott, your distributor, when in truth they are most
inefficient. I get dozens and dozens of letters from
fans saying they don't find your books in the book
stores. I have searched myself here in L.A. Pickwick

is about the only one you can count on—but then they carry just about everything. It's rare to find a book shop that carries all N.D.'s titles. Usually it's one or two.

Yes, I appreciate your helping me out now and then, but I expect a publisher of mine to do that for me. As for the $1,800 I owe you—could that not be considered an advance on *The Nightmare Notebook*? Or is that too much to expect from you?

Those sums you send my children yearly—royalties on my books—are mere chicken feed. What each one receives is about equivalent to one week's salary for a bank clerk. Don't you realize that yourself?

I have said again and again that I regard the publisher, whether friendly or hostile, as the natural enemy of the author, and every day I live to believe it more strongly. We live in different worlds and see life through opposite ends of the telescope. It wouldn't be so bad if the publisher were really a *good* business man and couldn't help but make money for his author as well as for himself. But when he isn't, what the hell *is* he good for?

I could ramble on, get it all off my chest, but I'll save some for my next. Usually it's *you* who write the lengthy letters. I too am loth to break up an association. In my crazy way I am loyal, trusting, credulous. My family thinks of me as naif, and gullible. I prefer to believe and to trust, but your attitude strains even my fatuous credulity.

Believe me, I don't hate you. I know you do your best. Most of us do. But your best ⟨just⟩ isn't good enough, forgive me for saying so.

Enough now!

HENRY

P.S. No, we never received the statements!

P.P.S. In today's paper I read that the street cleaner in S.F. will get $17,500 per year. More than I make from you and Grove Press combined!!!

/ • /

Hallmark: Hallmark Cards Inc. had brought out an edition of *The Smile at the Foot of the Ladder* in 1971.

My Life and Times: Published by the Playboy Press in 1971.

Kwinter: Jeffrey Kwinter, a British businessman who had made his fortune in the clothing business and decided to go into publishing the previous year. RM and Laurence Pollinger had doubts about how serious and how capable he was.

222. ALS-1

11/24/74
[Pacific Palisades]

DEAR JAMES LAUGHLIN—

Your telegram was a bit of a shock—death is always shocking. But I think to myself—how fortunate he was to have died in his sleep! I hope I have such good luck.

You have lost a most loyal and devoted friend. I wonder who will replace him.

Take good care of yourself. I am somewhat incapacitated—the worst is the loss of sight in one eye.

Sincerely,
HENRY

/ • /

death: RM died on November 22, 1974. His last letter to HM is dated November 14.

223. CC-1   December 3, 1974
                                      [New York]

DEAR HENRY MILLER:

I put off writing you for a bit as I wanted to have some definite word about the Notebook schedule. I will very soon as Bert Clarke, who is going to oversee the production, is almost as concerned as I am that it all moves forward and does not get bogged down in the broken deadlines one usually has to anticipate from fine printers. *The Nightmare Notebook* is to me personally very much a matter of the heart—not that I don't hope to use my head, too, but Mr. MacGregor and I spent quite a bit of time going over it, figuring out how best to do it despite the expense. In fact, the very last time I saw him not many days before his death the Notebook was one of the main things we discussed. It was always a pleasure, indeed a privilege, to work with Mr. Mac-Gregor, and now it is a great sadness that he is no longer with us—I am sure you know that. . . .

                    Sincerely yours,
                    GRISELDA OHANNESSIAN

224. CC-2   December 11, 1974
                                      [New York?]

DEAR HENRY:

Thank you so much for your very kind and thoughtful note of condolence about Bob. As you can imagine, his death is a very great blow, even though we had some preparation for it, since he had

the lung cancer operation in the summer, which was
followed by radiation and then chemotherapy, but
nothing that the best doctors in New York—he was
at Memorial Hospital—could do was able to arrest
the disease. The only good thing about it was that
he seems to have had very little pain. It went so rapidly at the end that he was spared that. He had a lot
of discomfort, of course, from the treatments especially, which are pretty brutal themselves, but he
bore it with a gentle stoicism that won the admira-
tion of all. I have never seen anyone meet a hard
fate so courageously and so serenely. He was, as you
probably know, a Buddhist, though not a practicing
one, in the sense that he did not go in for the severe
Zen training. But he had close ties with the Zen
temple here in New York, and they gave him a very
beautiful funeral, which was deeply impressive, the
chanting of the rows of motionless figures along the
walls of the hall, the burning of the ceremonial
incense, and the deep voice of the Roshi who spoke
most beautifully about him, though it was in sym-
bolic terms. You will be interested to know that on
the altar, in front of the Buddha figure, they had not
only Bob's picture, but a little picture of Mishima,
as it was the anniversary of the day of Mishima's
death.

It is a loss that is very hard to bear. Bob was not
only one of my best and oldest friends, but you
know all that he did for New Directions and for the
New Directions office, such solicitude for their wel-
fare. However, he trained up a very fine team,
headed by Fred Martin, who will now be in charge
of the office, and of the operation in general, and
everyone is determined to pull together to keep
things going in the way which Bob would want.

Bob had told me that you had been having your
own health problems recently, but I had not known

about the loss of sight in one of your eyes, which must be very distressing indeed. I do hope that it is only temporary, and that the sight will return. I hope that it is something which can be cured by rest, or perhaps by the kind of exercises which apparently were so successful for Aldous Huxley. I seem to recall that the doctor with whom he worked lived out there somewhere near you, and I wonder if he is still practicing. Surely some of the literary people there in the Los Angeles area would know.

We are all very excited about your *Nightmare Notebook,* which is going to be a magnificent production. The printer-designer who is in charge of the project is one of the very best in New York, and I think that the book has awakened his personal enthusiasm to the point where he will really do something superb. Fred and Griselda are working closely with him on it, and I hope that it won't be too long before we can send you copies, in the spring, perhaps.

I hope that all your family are well and that they have rallied around to look after you and keep you diverted during your convalescence, which I trust will be short.

Very best from us all as ever,
JAMES LAUGHLIN

/ • /

Aldous Huxley: (1894–1963), English writer who lived in Los Angeles. Almost blind from adolescence, he explained in *The Art of Seeing* how exercises restored a considerable portion of his eyesight.

225. ALS-2   6/16/75
                                    Pacific Palisades

DEAR GRISELDA O—

I'm replying immediately to yours of June 13th. Christ, I never thought N.D. would put out a book costing $150.00!! Never, never! Who beside collectors will buy such a book. The list I intended to send you is N.G. for that price. But I have a few collectors in my book and in a day or so I'll send you them. . . .

Thanks a lot for all the info. I'm going on Channel 13 (here) tomorrow with Jakob Gimpel, the pianist. Guess you won't see it in N.Y. No particular subject—open end! I'll try to remember to mention the $150.00 Notebook. Is it made of gold?

                                             H.M.

226. ALS-2   July 4th 1975
                                    Pacific Palisades

DEAR GRISELDA—

I hate to disappoint you but I can't see the Notebook as a $150.00 production! The facsimile work is OK (but I imagine that could have been supervised by a college student). The cover, apparently an imitation of the original, looks dull, dead to me. The tissue paper around it is a joke.

There is no imagination connected with the production. Why didn't you hire a Japanese to design the book? (Have you ever seen their publication of my *To Paint Is to Love Again* or the *Insomnia Book* or

My Life and Times? These are aesthetic and exciting books to look at! . . .

You (N.D.) have never used one of my water colors for a paper cover. Soon I won't have any left. Think what a difference it would have made to have had one of my *crazy* w.c.'s printed on a wrapper!

Well enuf! Forgive me for being so blunt but I can't help it. I expected a near "miracle" from the way you people talked.

All the best to you.

Sincerely,
HENRY MILLER

227. ALS-1   12/17/77
                                      Pacific Palisades

DEAR GRISELDA—

I am trying to recall the *title* of a book by Alain Fournier which I am almost positive was published by N.D. some 15 or 20 years ago. Can you supply it? And is this book still in print?

Haven't heard from you people in quite some time! Are you still in business?

If nobody in the office remembers the above title would you mind asking James Laughlin.

A good holiday season to you all.

Cheers!
HENRY MILLER

/ · /

Alain Fournier: (1886–1914), Henri Alain-Fournier, French writer killed in World War I, author of one novel, published in translation by ND as *The Wanderer* (1946).

228. PCS   1/15/78
                                      [Pacific Palisades]

DEAR J.L.

Many thanks for *The Wanderer*. Still a wonderful
book. Was surprised to see the lengthy Preface by
Havelock Ellis. All forgotten names now. Best to
you for the New Year!

                                      HENRY MILLER

                         / · /

Havelock Ellis: (1859–1939), English psychologist, best known for his
Studies in the Psychology of Sex.

229. PCS   [July 27, 1978]
                                      [Pacific Palisades]

DEAR GRISELDA—

Just discovered that N.Y. Pub. Library at 5th
Ave. & 42nd St. does not have copy of *Nightmare
Notebook*. You could make them order.

                                      H.M.

230. TLS-1   8/23/78
                                      Pacific Palisades

DEAR FRIEND, ⟨JAMES LAUGHLIN⟩

In my attempt to obtain the Nobel Prize for Literature this coming year I hope to enlist your support.

All I ask is for you to write a few succinct lines to:
  Nobel Committee of the Swedish Academy
  Borshuset
  11129 Stockholm
  Sweden
Please note that the Committee urgently requests that the name of the proposed candidate not be publicized.

Sincerely,
HENRY MILLER

231. ALS-1   8/29/79
                                Pacific Palisades

DEAR GRISELDA OHANNESSIAN—

. . . Now the young woman I am deeply in love with—Brenda Venus—is inquiring how to get *film* rights for *Harry*. I told her I thought there was money involved. (I'm too disabled to go searching thru this big house for our contract on *Harry*.) If and when you answer, tell me if you will, whether one pays for permission as well as pays a percentage on profits? I'm still very dumb when it comes to money matters.

By the way, I have several photos of me and Brenda together—rather striking. Would you like one for office or home? Sorry to hear you are troubled. Hope it's not too serious. You always seem jubilant. Indeed you are the only bright spot in N.D. as far as I'm concerned. Good luck! Bien à vous!

HENRY MILLER

/ • /

Brenda Venus: American film actress with whom HM carried on a voluminous erotic correspondence during his last four years. See *Dear, Dear Brenda: The Love Letters of Henry Miller to Brenda Venus* (William Morrow, 1986).

henry miller 444 **ocampo** drive -- **pacific palisades** california 90272

10/14/79

Dear Elsa Albrecht-Carrie' —
Sorry to have ruffled your feelings.
But I hope you are aware that N.D. has
a very poor reputation both among
book buyers and book stores — too slow.
too rigid, too conservative. Glad to know
you are a live wire!

Had letter from Noel Young day or two
ago saying he thought all was OK re
the 3 Lawrence chapters. Maybe you have
been in touch with Evelyn Hinz of Manitoba
— she is putting book together for Capra
Press — it's to be the big thing at
Lawrence Festival in Taos next July.

Don't know yet when my interview
with Barbara Kraft will be broadcast.
It should be nation-wide — on Natl Public Radio

Am still waiting to hear from Delsa
re NAL books. Believe all is well.

Do please send Brenda Venus a
letter as you suggested — no money
involved. Trust you have her address.

And thank you for all your
thoughtful kindnesses.

Forgive hand writing — am
without glasses and half blind!

Henry Miller

P.S. Best to Griselda of course. now ? I mean
who took Bob Mac Gregor's place
— ? is she there, now ?

This is the last letter HM wrote to ND. Two months short of his eighty-eighth birthday and literally half-blind, HM was still writing regularly up to this point, still complaining about ND, and his hand-writing was as firm as ever. He died on June 7, 1980.

Else Albrecht-Carrié: Permissions editor at New Directions. HM was writing for permission to reprint three chapters on D. H. Lawrence originally published in his early ND miscellanies.

Noel Young: Publisher of Capra Press, then in the process of preparing to publish *The World of Lawrence,* written by HM in the 1930s but not previously published in its entirety.

The Zebra Press: A small press that wanted to reissue three HM titles previously published by the New American Library.

BIBLIOGRAPHY:

Writings by Henry Miller Published by New Directions

1936   "Into the Night Life"—*ND 1*
        "Jabberwhorl Cronstadt"—*ND 1*

1937   "Walking Up and Down in China"—*ND 2*

1939   "Three Chapters from *Tropic of Capricorn*"—*ND 4*
        The Cosmological Eye

1941   *The Wisdom of the Heart*

1944   *Sunday After the War*

1945   *The Air-Conditioned Nightmare*
        "A Letter," *Why Abstract?* by Hilaine Hiler, Henry
          Miller & William Saroyan

1946   "A Study of Rimbaud"—*ND 9*
        The Colossus of Maroussi

1947   "Cosmodemonic Rigolade," *Spearhead: 10 Years'
          Experimental Writing in America*
        Remember to Remember

1949   "Rimbaud: Part Two"—*ND 11*

1950   "Two Excerpts from *Plexus*"—*ND 12*

1952   *The Books in My Life*

1956   *The Time of the Assassins: A Study of Rimbaud*

1957   "Obscenity in Literature"—*ND 16*
       Big Sur and the Oranges of Hieronymus Bosch

1958   *The Smile at the Foot of the Ladder*

1959   *The Henry Miller Reader*, ed. Lawrence Durrell

1962   *Stand Still Like the Hummingbird*

1963   *Just Wild About Harry: A Melo-melo in Seven Scenes*

1964   "The Wheel of Destiny"—*A New Directions Reader*
       Henry Miller on Writing, ed. Thomas H. Moore

1975   *The Nightmare Notebook*

1983   "Bonnie and Clyde: A Toccata for Half-Wits"—*ND
       47*

1984   *From Your Capricorn Friend: Henry Miller & the
       Stroker, 1978–1980*, intro. Irving Stettner

1988   *The Durrell–Miller Letters, 1935–80*, ed. Ian S. Mac-
       Niven

1989   *Letters to Emil*, ed. George Wickes

1991   *Into the Heart of Life: Henry Miller at One Hundred*,
       ed. Frederick Turner
       Aller Retour New York, intro. George Wickes

INDEX

Abramson, Ben, 47, 48*n*
Aga Khan, 177
Alain-Fournier, Henri:
  The Wanderer, 269, 270
Albrecht-Carrié, Elsa, 272,
  273*n*
Aldington, Kathryn, 168
Aldington, Richard, 168
Allen, Steve, 232
Alvarez, Jorge, 234
Anaïs: An International Journal,
  208*n*
Anti-Vice League, 70
Atlantic Monthly, xvi, xix, 127,
  252
Auden, W. H., 170*n*

Baddeley, Hermione, 217
Balzac, Honoré de, 86, 117,
  158, 159
Barrows, George, 40*n*
Barzun, Jacques, 169, 170*n*
Beck, Julian, 193
Beckett, Samuel, 195*n*
Bell, Robert, 239
Bergman, Ingmar, xi
Bernstein, Sidney, 229

Bibalo, Antonio, 158*n*, 229–
  230, 233*n*
Birge, Vincent, 189*n*
Black Sun Press, 57*n*
Booster, The, 9, 10*n*,11*n*
Borges, Jorge Luis, 194, 195*n*
Bowles, Paul, 107, 108
  The Sheltering Sky, 109*n*
Boyd, Madeleine, 2, 3*n*
Brady, Millicent Edie:
  "New Cult of Sex and Anar-
  chy, The," 71*n*
Brassaï (Gyula Halasz), 125
Breton, André, 71*n*
Brinnin, John Malcolm, 253,
  254
Brooks, Van Wyck, 138
Buddha, 250, 266
Bye-Bye Birdie, 217

Cairns, Huntington, xv, 9*n*,
  14, 15*n*, 16, 20, 21, 26,
  30, 78, 100, 124, 125,
  141, 161
Cambria Books, 183*n*
"*Camera 3*:", 232, 233*n*

277

Camus, Albert, 71*n*
Capra Press, xxii, 5*n*, 58*n*, 189,
    255, 272, 273*n*
Carrefour Press, 2, 3*n*
Céline, Louis-Ferdinand, 131,
    132*n*, 230
Cendrars, Blaise, xviii, 25,
    26*n*, 80, 158, 159, 160*n*,
    230
  Selected Writings, 230
Cerf, Bennett, 4
Cervantes, Miguel Saavedra
    de, 86
Chagall, Marc, xiv
Chaplin, Charlie, 96, 97*n*, 177
Chesterton, G. K., 186*n*
Chicago Tribune, 6, 7*n*
Circle, 42*n*, 44*n*, 54, 62
Circle Editions, 68*n*
Circle in the Square Theatre,
    187, 188
Clarke, Bert, 265
Colt Press, xiii, 49*n*, 125
Cominos, Nick, 143
Comité de Défense d'Henri
    Miller, 70, 71*n*
Connolly, Cyril, xvi, 2, 3*n*, 38
Cooney, James Peter, 11*n*
Cooper, David, 199*n*
Corrêa, 96, 123
Cossery, Albert, 67
  The House of Certain Death,
    68*n*
  The Lazy Ones, 68*n*
  Men God Forgot, 68*n*
Covici, Pascal, 136
Cowley, Malcolm, 136, 137,
    139, 144, 155, 167
Cowley, Muriel, 155
Crosby, Caresse, 56–57

Delta, 11, 14
Doner, Ephraim, 143, 144*n*,
    246

Dos Passos, John, 76
Dostoevski, Fyodor, 18
Doubleday, 260, 261
Doubleday Doran, xv, 38, 50
Douglas, Norman, 208
Douglas, Sara, 208
Dubliners, 157
Duell, Sloan & Pearce, 24*n*,
    97*n*, 133
Duhamel, Marcel, 55
Dumont-Schauberg, 182
Dunnock, Mildred, 217
Durrell, Lawrence, 9*n*, 10*n*, 23,
    24, 27, 148, 155*n*, 168,
    207, 224*n*, 226*n*, 232,
    233*n*, 241
  The Black Book, 8, 12*n*, 16,
    17*n*
  The Henry Miller Reader (edi-
    tor), 41–42, 136, 137,
    138–143, 144, 145*n*,
    170, 171*n*, 154, 156–
    157, 158, 159, 160, 169,
    172, 191, 192
  Justine, 129
  The Durrell-Miller Letters,
    1935–80, 9*n*, 148*n*

Edinburgh Festival, 217,
    229
Editions du Chêne, 51
Eliot, T. S., 76, 212, 217
  The Waste Land, 25
Ellis, Havelock, 270
  *Studies in the Psychology of
    Sex*, 270*n*
Emerson, Ralph Waldo, 126
E. P. Dutton, 9*n*, 148*n*, 224*n*
Epstein, Samuel B., 204*n*
Ernst, Max, xiv
Ernst, Morris, 17
Esquire, 152, 192, 252
Evans, Keith, 55, 57
Evergreen Review, 170, 171*n*

Faulkner, William, 29, 42
Feiffer, Jules, 203, 204n
Feltrinelli, 182
Ferguson, Robert, 232n
Ferlinghetti, Lawrence, 195–196
  A Coney Island of the Mind, 196n
Fitzgerald, F. Scott:
  The Crack-Up, 108
Fles, Barthold, 2, 6
Foley, Martha, 7
Ford Foundation, xix, 91, 93, 103, 127, 220
Foreman, Clark, 161, 162n
Formentor Prize, 195n, 201
Fox, Peggy, 215n
Fraenkel, Michael, 2, 3n, 4, 96, 168n, 171n
Frere, A. S., 131, 132n
Frost, Robert, 25

Gales, Bob, 233
Gallimard, 54, 67
García Lorca, Federico, 189
  Blood Wedding, 51n
Gelber, Jack:
  The Connection, 193
Genet, Jean:
  The Balcony, 187
  The Blacks, 189, 229
Gerhardt, Renate, 179, 210–211, 232
Gertz, Elmer, 204n
Gide, André, 71
Gillam, Daphne Moschos, 167, 168n
Gimpel, Jakob, 246, 268
Ginsberg, Allen:
  Howl, 141, 143n
Giono, Jean, xviii, 80, 81n
Girodias, Maurice, 51, 52n, 56, 57, 64, 67, 70, 71n, 72, 123, 124n, 164

Glassgold, Peter, 247n, 255–256
Gleason, Robert H., 258, 261
Gomez, Manuel, 232n
Gotham Book Mart, 29, 30n, 33, 35
G. P. Putnam's Sons, 227
Grabhorn, Jane, xiii, 48, 49n
Greenwood Press, 132, 133
Grossman, 239, 240n
Grove Press, 162, 166, 171n, 180, 192, 193, 204n, 259, 261, 264
Guilde du Livre, 123
Gutkind, Erich:
  The Absolute Collective, 197, 246
  Choose Life, 198

Hachette, 100
Haggard, H. Rider, 81n, 85
  She, 80
Halasz, Gyula (Brassaï), 125
Hallmark, 261, 264n
Hamburg Oper, 229, 232
Hansen Sisters, 230
"Happy Birthday" (song), 214
Harcourt Brace, 24n
Hardesty, Patricia, 211, 212n, 226n
Harper's, 70, 71n, 252
Hart Davies, Rupert, 223
Harvard *Advocate,* x
Harvard Library, 125
Heath & Co., 57
Heinemann, William, 131, 132n
Henghes, Henri (Heinz Winterfeld Klussmann), 180, 181n
Henry Miller Odyssey, The (film), 239
Herz, Evelyn, 272

Hesse, Hermann:
  Siddhartha, xviii, 72, 77, 85,
    93, 262
  Steppenwolf, 49
Hiler, Hilaire, 2, 3*n*
Hirohito, 38
Hirsch, Trygve, 170, 171*n*
Hitler, Adolf, 38
Hoffman, Michael, xviii, 64,
    65*n*, 98, 100, 149–150,
    156, 159, 164, 167, 176,
    185, 186, 188, 190, 192,
    215
Holve, Norman, 40*n*
Horizon, xvi, 38
Horn, Clayton W., 141, 143*n*
Hudson Review, 86
Huebsch, Benjamin, 4
Huxley, Aldous, 267

Intercultural Publications, xix,
    103, 107, 127

Jackson, Roger, 31*n*, 62*n*
Jake (mailman), xvii
James, Henry, 126
Janis, Sidney, 147
J. B. Lippincott, 233, 259, 262
Jeffers, Robinson, 25, 42, 43*n*,
    143
John Day Company, 113
Joyce, James:
  Ulysses, 17, 137, 138*n*
"Just Wild about Harry"
    (song), 210

Kahane, Jack, 4, 5*n,* 7, 10, 14,
    16, 17, 20, 25, 26, 51,
    52*n,* 118
Kaplan, H. J., 55*n*
Katsimbalis, George, 24–25,
    26*n,* 27
Keene, Donald, 249
Kemeisha, 99

Kenner, Hugh, 88, 89*n*
*Kenneth Rexroth and James Laugh-
    lin: Selected Letters,* 69*n*
Keyserling, Hermann:
  Travel Diary, 49
Klussmann, Heinz Winterfeld
    (Henri Henghes), 180,
    181*n*
Knef, Hildegard, 178, 182,
    210, 212
Knopf, 4, 16
Knopf, Blanche, 15
Kraft, Barbara, 272
Kreymborg, Alfred, 1
Krishnan, T. V. Kunhi, 208,
    209
Krock, Arthur, 78, 79*n*
Kwinter, Jeffrey, 262, 264*n*

Laughlin, Ann, 146–147, 148,
    151, 152, 153, 154, 176
Laughlin, James, 95, 98, 107–
    108, 119, 136, 149, 174,
    199*n, 201n,* 219, 220,
    253, 254, 255
  The Man in the Wall, 181*n*
  "Perspective of Burma,"
    127, 133
  Pound as Wuz, 181*n*
  "Thomas Merton and His
    Poetry," 199*n*
Lawrence, D. H., x, 4, 5*n,*
    167, 272, 273*n*
  Lady Chatterley's Lover, 161–
    162, 164, 165–166, 174
Ledig-Rowohlt, H. M., 178,
    179–80, 181*n*
Léger, Fernand, xiv, 145, 146–
    147, 150, 152
  Le Cirque, 154
Legman, G. (Gershon), 30,
    31*n*
Leite, George, xiii, 41, 42*n,*
    54, 57, 58, 62, 68*n*

Lepska, Janina Martha, 50,
   51*n*, 58, 59, 66*n*, 90
Levin, Harry:
   The Portable James Joyce (edi-
      tor), 156, 157
Levine, Joseph E., 216, 226*n*
L'Herne, 230
Liebermann, Rolf, 229
Life, 254
Living Theatre, 193
London, Jack, 44
Longanesi, 123
Lorca, Federico García, 51*n*,
   189
Loujon Press, 240, 261*n*
Lowenfels, Walter, 2, 3*n*, 69*n*

MacGregor, Robert M., xix,
   93*n*, 175*n*, 186*n*, 192,
   201, 202*n*, 264, 265–266
Machiz, Herbert, 217, 228
MacNiven, Ian S.:
   *The Durrell-Miller Letters
      1935–1980* (editor), 148
Mann, Ted, 188
Mansfield, June, 49*n*, 247
Martin, Fred, 266, 267
Martin Secker & Warburg,
   132*n*
Matisse, Pierre, 7, 147, 149,
   151, 152, 153, 156
Medici, Lorenzo de', 59
Mencken, H. L., 4, 5*n*
Merton, Thomas, xx, xxiii,
   186, 197–199, 201, 240
   Asian Journal, 256
   Seeds of Contemplation, 108
   Tower of Babel, 213
Mid-Century Book Society,
   169, 170*n*
Millard, Harry, 227, 228–229
Miller, Eve McClure, 122,
   123*n*, 143, 200, 235
Miller, Henry:

*The Air-Conditioned Night-
   mare,* xv, xvi, xxii, 3*n*,
   19, 29, 38, 47, 48*n*, 50,
   52, 62, 66, 123*n*, 136,
   171*n*, 207
Aller Retour New York, x, 1,
   2, 3*n*, 5, 8, 47, 48*n*,
   123, 194, 246–247
"The Angel Is My Water-
   mark," 183*n*
The Angel Is My Watermark,
   40
"Astrological Fricassee," 150
"Automotive Passacaglia,"
   170, 171*n*
"Berthe," 156, 157*n*
*Big Sur and the Oranges of
   Hieronymus Bosch,* xvi,
   72*n*, 105–106, 108, 115,
   116–119, 120*n*, 130,
   131, 144*n*, 234*n*
Black Spring, xiv, x, 2, 3*n*,
   5*n*, 7, 8, 12, 18, 22*n*,
   24, 40*n*, 52, 61, 67, 69*n*,
   71, 99, 118, 183*n*, 196*n*
"A Bodhisattva Artist,"
   123*n*
The Books in My Life, xviii,
   26*n*, 81*n*, 85, 92, 97,
   104, 105, 136, 159
"Christmas Eve at the Villa
   Seurat," 183
The Colossus of Maroussi,
   xiii, 26*n*, 37, 48, 49*n*,
   61, 101–102, 123, 125,
   132, 136, 233, 234*n*,
   244
The Cosmological Eye, xi,
   xii, 5*n*, 9*n*, 22*n*, 32, 36,
   68*n*, 191
Dear, Dear Brenda, 272*n*
A Devil in Paradise, 120*n*
"The Eye of Paris," 125*n*
"Glittering Pie," xi, xii

Hamlet (with Fraenkel), 2,
3*n*, 4, 41, 96, 118, 123,
167, 168*n*, 171*n*

Henery Miller on Writing
(Moore, ed.), 209,
210*n*, 225

The Henry Miller Reader
(Durrell, ed)., 41–42,
136, 137, 138–43, 144,
145*n*, 154, 156–157,
159, 160, 169, 170,
171*n*, 172, 191, 192

"Hiler and His Murals," 3*n*

*Insomnia or the Devil at
Large*, 240*n*, 261, 268

The Intimate Henry Miller,
155*n*

"Into the Night Life," 2, 61

"Jabberwhorl Cronstadt," 1,
2, 3*n*, 68, 69*n*

Just Wild About Harry, xx,
183*n*, 185–186, 187,
188–189, 203–204, 205,
210–11, 212*n*, 214,
216–218, 227*n*, 228,
232, 256, 271

Letters to Anaïs Nin, 208*n*,
227

Letters to Emil, 4, 5*n*, 241,
241–245

"Mademoiselle Claude,"
155*n*

"Mara-Marignan," 78, 79*n*

"Maurizius Forever," 78

"Max," 6

*Max and the White Phago-
cytes*, 5*n*, 8, 9*n*, 12*n*, 14,
15*n*, 20, 22, 27, 125*n*

"*Money*—and how it gets
that way," 7

Murder the Murderer, 47, 48*n*,
50

My Bike and Other Friends,
58*n*, 189*n*

My Life and Times, 252, 261,
264*n*, 267

Nexus, 49*n*, 150, 179*n*, 201,
215, 216*n*

The Nightmare Notebook, 256,
263, 265, 267, 268, 270

Nights of Love and Laughter,
87*n*, 119, 155*n*

"Obscenity and the Law of
Reflection," 68

"The Oranges of the Millen-
nium," 106, 117

"Paradise Lost," 72*n*, 105,
106, 120*n*

"Patchen, Man of Anger
and Light," 236

"Peace and Solitude: a potpourri," 106, 117

Plasma and Magma, 32

Plexus, 49*n*, 83*n*, 100, 101,
102, 104, 123, 215,
216*n*

*The Plight of the Creative Art-
ist in the United States of
America*, xiii, 39*n*

Quiet Days in Clichy, 79*n*,
123, 124, 157*n*

"Reflections on the Death of
Mishima," xx, 251–52,
255

Remember to Remember, xvi,
44*n*, 48*n*, 53, 62, 68,
123, 150*n*, 191

"Reunion in Brooklyn," 35*n*

The Rosy Crucifixion, 49, 52,
62, 73, 74*n*, 78, 79*n*,
81*n*, 83*n*, 215, 216*n*,
234, 244

"Scenario," 4, 5*n*

Semblance of a Devoted Past,
96, 97*n*, 146, 240*n*

Sexus, 49*n*, 79*n*, 99, 104, 171*n*

*The Smile at the Foot of the
Ladder*, 24*n*, 78, 96,

97*n*, 102, 132, 133, 134*n*, 145, 158*n*, 182, 183*n*, 211, 212*n*, 261, 264*n*

The Smile at the Foot of the Ladder (opera), 232, 233*n*, 239

Stand Still Like the Hummingbird, 183*n*, 195*n*, 203, 213

"Stand Still Like the Hummingbird," 181, 192

Sunday After the War, xiv, 35, 39*n*, 52, 89, 191

"This Is My Answer," 105, 106

The Time of the Assassins, xviii, 62*n*, 103, 104, 114, 190, 191

To Paint Is to Love Again, 182, 183*n*, 239, 240*n*, 268

Tropic of Cancer, ix, xiii, xv, xxii, 2, 3*n*, 4, 5*n*, 7*n*, 8, 12, 16, 17*n*, 18–19, 20, 21–22, 24, 28, 29, 35, 41–42, 67, 71*n*, 87, 99, 118, 124, 138, 140, 141, 161, 162–164, 165, 167, 168*n*, 172, 174, 176, 185, 187, 189, 191, 192, 193*n*, 194, 196, 204, 207, 210, 211, 215, 216, 226*n*, 232*n*, 234, 238, 239, 240*n*, 242*n*, 244

Tropic of Capricorn, xi, xxii, 4, 5*n*, 8, 12, 14, 20–21, 22, 23, 25, 27, 29, 35, 67, 71*n*, 81*n*, 87, 99, 118, 155*n*, 161, 162– 164, 165, 168*n*, 172, 174, 176, 185, 187, 191, 192, 210, 215, 216, 234

"Un Etre Etoilique," 8, 9*n*

"Varda: The Master Builder," 44*n*

"The Waters Reglitterized," 78, 79*n*

What Are You Going to Do About Alf?, 3*n*, 5*n*

Why Abstract? (with Hiler & Saroyan), 3*n*

The Wisdom of the Heart, xi–xiii, 33*n*, 89, 125*n*, 136, 179

The World of Lawrence, 5*n*, 273*n*

The World of Sex, 48*n*

Miller, Hiroko Tokuda "Hoki," 235*n*, 248

Miller, Janina Martha Lepska, 50, 51*n*, 58, 59, 66*n*, 90

Miller, June Mansfield, 49*n*, 247

Miller, Tony, 90, 168, 231, 235

Miller, Valentine, 58, 90, 168, 230–231, 235

Milton, John, *Paradise Lost*, 116

Miró, Joan, xiv, 182, 183*n*, 233

Mishima, Yukio, xx, 248–249, 250–251, 266

  The Sea of Fertility, 248, 250–251

Moore, Tom, 209, 210*n*, 225

Moricand, Conrad, 71–72, 114, 115*n*, 116, 118, 120*n*, 121*n*

Murphy, Dennis, 150

Narayan, R. K., 126

Nation, 134

Neiman, Gilbert, 50, 51*n*

Neiman, Margaret, 51*n*, 57

New American Library, 86, 87, 154, 155*n*, 272, 273*n*

New Directions in Prose and Poetry 1 (1936), x

New Directions in Prose and Poetry 3 (1938), 27

New Directions in Prose and Poetry 4 (1939), 22, 27

New Directions in Prose and Poetry 9 (1946), 53

New Directions in Prose and Poetry 10, 109n

New Directions in Prose and Poetry 11 (1949), 62n, 109n

New Directions in Prose and Poetry 12 (1951), 84n, 109n

New Republic, xiii–xiv, 39

New Review, 120n, 155n

New York Society for the Prevention of Vice, 17n

New York Times, 161, 167, 188, 191, 193, 237

New York Times Book Review, 249n

Nin, Anaïs, 8, 9n, 207, 218–223, 224–227, 230, 241
   The House of Incest, 5n
   The Winter of Artifice, 12n

Nixon, Richard, 259

Noonday Review, 181

Obelisk Press, xvii, 5n, 9n, 12n, 15n, 17n, 32, 51, 52n, 79n, 118

Ohannessian, Griselda Jackson, 170, 171n, 248n, 265, 267, 272

Olympia Press, 124n

Once Upon a Sunday (film), 143

O'Neill, Eugene, 76

O'Neill, Hugh, 143, 144n

Padula, Edward, 217, 229

Pantheon, 50, 72

"Paper," 200

Parker, Daniel, 70, 71n

Partisan Review, 77, 86

Patchen, Kenneth, 63, 78, 108, 199–201, 202–203, 236–238
   Collected Poems, 236
   Journal of Albion Moonlight, 203

Patchen, Miriam, 201n

Peace Corps, U.S., 233, 234n

Pearce, Charles A., 24

Pelorson, Roger, 12n

Perlès, Alfred, 2, 3n, 10n, 104, 111, 113, 141, 224
   My Friend Henry Miller, 226n

Perry, Connie, 251–252

Perspectives USA, xix, 91, 92, 121

Peyrefitte, Alain (Minister of French Cultural Affairs), 258

Pfeffer, Max, 65, 66n

Phoenix, 11

Picasso, Pablo, 177

Playboy, 150, 152, 158, 232, 239, 244, 252, 253

Playboy Publishing Co., 252, 264n

Pocket Books, 261

Poetry, 212, 213

Pollinger, Laurence, 167, 168n, 264n

Porter, Bern, xiii, xiv, 39n, 48n, 97n

Pound, Ezra, ix, xxiii, 7, 35, 65, 66n, 212, 245
   Cantos, 177n

Powell, Lawrence Clark, 80, 81n, 148

Powys, John Cowper, 111, 112, 113

Publishers Weekly, 194

Putnam, Samuel, 119, 120n, 155n

Queneau, Raymond, 54–55, 67
  The Skin of Dreams, 55n, 63
Quiet Days in Clichy (film),
    244, 245n
Quintero, Jose, 187

Rabelais, François, 86
Random House, 4, 107
Rattner, Abraham, 122, 123n,
    124, 147, 149–150, 171,
    246
Rau, Santha Rama, 120
Reichel, Hans, 67, 68n
Rexroth, Kenneth, xvi, xxiii,
    68, 69n, 108, 195, 200
Rexroth, Marie, 88
Ricono, Connie, 218
Rimbaud, Arthur, xviii, 42n,
    49, 62, 63, 103, 104,
    114, 190, 191
  Illuminations, 122
  Season in Hell, 41, 42n, 46,
    53
Robitaille, Gerald, 240n
Rockefeller, Nelson, 216
Rosenfeld, Paul, 1
Rosset, Barney, xv, 161, 162,
    164, 165, 167, 168n,
    171n, 172–174, 175n,
    176, 185, 186, 187, 191,
    192, 194, 215–216, 244
Rowohlt, Ernst, 178, 181n
Rowohlt Verlag, 149, 178,
    181n, 182, 183, 184, 190
Rueda, Santiago, 234
Rupa & Co., 128
Russell & Volkening, xii, 39,
    40n, 50
Rykr, Dzenek, 14

Sakyamuni, 250
San Francisco Examiner, 70, 71n
Sargent, Lynda, 42, 43n, 45
Saroyan, William, 3n, 4, 5n

Sartre, Jean-Paul, 71n
Sarwat, Mohamed Ali, 119,
    120n
"Satprem":
  L'Orpailleur, 184
Saunders, Marion, 1, 8
Scarlet, Albertine, 64, 65n
Schatz, Bezazel, 61, 123, 246
Schifferli, 123
Schiller Theatre, 218
Schnellock, Emil, 5n, 101n,
    242n, 243, 244, 245n
Schubert, Franz:
  Ave Maria, 126
Schuster, Lincoln, 4
Seferiades, Giorgos Stylianou,
    25, 26n, 27
Shapiro, Karl, 193, 213
Shimano (Tai-San), 248, 249n,
    250–251
Signet, 35, 118, 120n, 150
Simenon, Georges, 177
Simon, Michel, 177, 178n
Simon and Schuster, 4, 252
Singer, Isaac Bashevis, 240, 246
Slocum, John, xii, 78
Smith, Bradley, 240, 261
Snyder, Robert, 238, 239
  *This Is Henry, Henry Miller
    from Brooklyn,* 260
Soin-roshi, 250
Souckova, Milada, 14
Spearman, Neville, 104
Spoleto Festival, 217, 218, 228
Sri Aurobindo Ashram, 184
Stalin, Josef, 76n
Stanislavsky, Constantin, xix
Stegner, Wallace, 126, 127n
Steinbeck, John, 29
Steloff, Frances, 30n, 97n, 145
Sterling, George, 44
Stevens, Roger L., 217
Story, 7n
Strick, Joseph, 240n

Stuhlmann, Gunther, 206–207, 208*n*, 223, 225, 226
Suares, Carlo, 246
Subway in the Sky (film), 178
Sumner, John S., 17
Suzuki, Daisetz T., 197, 198

Tai-San (Shimano), 250–251
Theatre Arts Books, xix, xxi, 184, 256
Theatre of Nations, 193
Thomas, Dylan:
   The Collected Poems of Dylan Thomas, 108
   Under Milk Wood, 188, 189*n*
Thorsen, Jens Jorgen, 245*n*
Three Strange Loves (film), xi
Time, 20
Tokuda, Hiroko, 235*n*, 248
Tolstoy, Leo:
   War and Peace, 118
Torreggiani, Marchese, 205
Trilling, Lionel, 169, 170*n*
Tropic of Cancer (film), 240*n*, 244
Twain, Mark, 42

Varda, Jean, 44, 55, 57, 58, 68
Venus, Brenda, 271, 272
Viking Press, 4, 136*n*, 139, 144, 156
Village Voice, 194, 249
Villa Seurat Series, 11, 12*n*
Volontés, 11, 12*n*

Warburg, Fredric J., 131, 132*n*
Watts, Alan, 131, 249

Weekly Post (Tokyo), 252
Weidler, Miss, 151
West, Nathanael, 63
Weybright, Victor, 86, 87*n*, 90, 99
Wharton, Jean, xvii, 69, 112, 206
White, Emil, 57, 58*n*, 246
Whitman, Walt, 42
Wickes, George, 223, 224, 241–244
   Lawrence Durrell and Henry Miller: A Private Correspondence, (editor), 148*n*, 224*n*
Wilde, Oscar, 223
William Heinemann, 131, 132*n*
Williams, Tennessee, 215*n*
   The Milk Train Doesn't Stop Here Any More, 217, 228
   Period of Adjustment, 214
   A Streetcar Named Desire, 108
Williams, William Carlos, xxiii, 2, 3*n*, 107, 108, 193
Wittenberg, Phillip, 163, 166
Wolfe, Bernie, 232
Wolff, Kurt, 72
Woolsey, John M., 137, 138*n*

Young, Noel, 272, 273*n*

Zaccagnini, Dante T., 111, 113*n*
Zebra Press, 272, 273*n*